W9-ASP-560

IMAGINING INDIANS in the SOUTHWEST

SMITHSONIAN
INSTITUTION
PRESS
WASHINGTON
AND LONDON

IMAGINING INDIANS in the SOUTHWEST

Persistent Visions of a Primitive Past

LEAH DILWORTH

Grateful acknowledgment is made for permission to reprint excerpts from Nora Naranjo-Morse's *Mud Woman: Poems from the Clay* (Tucson: University of Arizona Press), © 1992

Copy Editor: Karin Kaufman
Production Editor: Duke Johns
Designer: Linda McKnight

Library of Congress Cataloging-in-Publication Data
Dilworth, Leah.
Imagining Indians in the Southwest : persistent visions of a primitive past / Leah Dilworth.
p. cm.
Includes bibliographical references and index.
ISBN 1-56098-641-7 (alk. paper)
1. Indians of North America—Southwest, New—Pictorial works. 2. Indians of North America in literature. 3. Indians of North America—Southwest, New—Public opinion. 4. Public opinion—United States. 5. Indians of North Ameria—Southwest, New—Industries. 6. Fred Harvey (Firm)—History. 7. Tourist trade—Southwest, New—History. I. Title.
E78.S7D525 1996
979'.00497—dc20 95-26790

British Library Cataloguing-in-Publication Data is available

Manufactured in the United States of America
03 02 01 00 99 98 97 96 5 4 3 2 1

∞ The paper used in this publication meets the minimum requirements of the American National Standard for Information Sciences—Permanence of Paper for Printed Library Materials ANSI Z39.48-1984.

On the cover: "Taos Indian-Detour" by Behn, from 1930 Fred Harvey pamphlet, "Indian Detours: Most Distinctive Motor Cruise Service in the World." Courtesy The Heard Museum, Phoenix, Arizona.

To the memory of Coke Bryant Dilworth

CONTENTS

ILLUSTRATIONS

ACKNOWLEDGMENTS

Many people and institutions have contributed to this book's development and completion. Many, many thanks are in order.

This book grew out of my dissertation for the Ph.D. in American Studies at Yale University. Bryan Wolf, Howard Lamar, and Alan Trachtenberg, who were my dissertation committee, offered consistently helpful and encouraging comments and suggestions. My other teachers at Yale, especially Jean-Christophe Agnew, Richard Brodhead, Abbott Cummings, Ann Fabian, Jim Fisher, Robert Herbert, R. W. B. Lewis, Jules Prown, and Candace Waid, were always intellectually challenging and inspiring. New Haven friends and fellow graduate students provided a community of support during the dissertation years. Special thanks go to Scott Casper, Phil Deloria, Amy Green, Alex Nemerov, Chris Shannon, and Martha Viehmann for their interest and help. I am grateful to Yale University for providing financial support in the form of a four-year Yale University Fellowship and a John F. Enders Fellowship to do research in the Southwest. Thanks also to the Mrs. Giles Whiting Foundation for fellowship support in 1991–92.

The Smithsonian Institution has served in many ways as intellectual home for this project. In 1990 the Smithsonian granted me a ten-week Graduate Student Fellowship, which turned out to be crucial to the book's development. During that time and since, many scholars at the Smithsonian have generously shared their knowledge and advice. I am extremely grateful to Richard Ahlborn, Joallyn Archambault, Andrew Connors, Lois M. Fink, Rayna Green, Martin Kalfatovic, Pat Lynagh, Emelia Seubert, Wendy Shay, Bill Truettner, Elizabeth Weatherford, and Pam Wintle. I owe a special debt of gratitude to Cathy Creek, James Harwood, Jim Glenn, Paula Fleming, and Vyrtis Thomas of the National Anthropological Archives for their patience and help in researching photographs. At the Smithsonian Institution Press everyone was consistently enthusiastic and supportive of this project. Thanks to Mark Hirsch, my wonderful acquisitions editor, for providing just the right balance of cogent criticism and kind encouragement; to Karin Kaufman for her sensitive and effective copy editing; and to Duke Johns, Hilary Reeves, and Linda McKnight for their first-rate work in production, marketing, and design.

This project owes its present shape also to many scholars, librarians, and archivists in the Southwest. Thanks to Kathleen Howard and Mario Klimiades at the Heard Museum Library in Phoenix. Louis Hieb at the University of Arizona Library Special Collections offered helpful advice and located some exceptional archival materials for me, and Theresa Salazar obtained reproducible materials for this book. Thanks also to Riva Dean, reference librarian at the Arizona Historical Society in Tucson, and Stephanie Bucholz at Northland Publishing. I owe special thanks to Barbara A. Babcock at the University of Arizona, who has given me inspiration, help, and criticism all along the way.

In New Mexico, John Grassham, the photo archivist at the Museum of Albuquerque, Joe Traugott at the Jonson Gallery in Albuquerque, and Chris Wilson offered suggestions and advice. At the University of New Mexico, Marta Weigle and Sylvia Rodríguez understood the scope and aims of this project and were extremely helpful. Thanks are also due B. Michael Miller at the University of New Mexico's Library Center for Southwest Research. The days I spent at the Museum of New Mexico in Santa Fe were especially fruitful; I thank Arthur Olivas, Orlando Romero, and Richard Rudisill for spending hours of their valuable time with me. I am also very grateful to Mrs. Mary Jean Cook of Santa Fe for sharing her knowledge of the Hopi Snake dance. At the Laboratory of Anthropology archivist Willow Powers was extremely helpful, as was librarian Laura J. Holt.

In California the Braun Research Library at the Southwest Museum proved a rich resource. Thanks to reference librarian Richard Buchen and photo archivist Craig Klyver for their help.

Along the way, scholars at other institutions have given me invaluable comments and suggestions. I offer sincere thanks to Kenneth Dauber, John Faragher, Don Fowler, Richard Handler, Curtis M. Hinsley, Melanie Herzog, Lea S. McChesney, Victor Masayesva Jr., Molly Mullin, Martha Sandweiss, Peggy Shaffer, Robert St. George, Sally Stein, and Timothy Troy. Many thanks also to Judy Metro, Janet Francendese, and anonymous readers at Yale University Press, Temple University Press, and the Smithsonian Institution Press.

I would like to acknowledge permissions from the following: from the Heard Museum and the University of Arizona Press, to reproduce material from *The Great Southwest of the Fred Harvey Company and the Santa Fe Railway* (1996); from the University of Arizona Press, to reproduce portions of Nora Naranjo-Morse's *Mud Woman: Poems from the Clay* (1992). For permission to cite their as-yet-unpublished papers, I thank Melanie Herzog, Curtis M. Hinsley, Thomas W. Kavanagh, and David L. Moore.

Early versions of Chapters 2, 3, and 4 were papers presented at the annual meetings of the American Studies Association in 1994, 1990, and 1992, respectively. Thanks to the association and to fellow panel members for the opportunity to develop my ideas and for feedback. The paper on Mary Austin and *The American Rhythm* appeared in the British journal *Democratic Vistas* (autumn 1993).

My colleagues at Long Island University, Brooklyn Campus, have been unfailingly encouraging and helpful. Special thanks go to Patrick Horrigan, Christine Kessler, Seymour Kleinberg, and Annette Zilversmit. Thanks to the Trustees of Long Island University and the Long Island University Faculty Federation Release Time Awards Committee for one of the most precious gifts: time to do research and to write. I am also very grateful to my students at LIU and at Trinity College in Hartford, Connecticut, who, through their interest and curiosity, have kept alive my enthusiasm for this project.

I thank my friends in New York and elsewhere for their steady interest and support. I am extremely grateful to Brian Cohen, Eileen

Colón, Wynne Evans, Jill and David Fenichell, John Kaehny, Brad Klein, Karyl Krug, Jeanne Lawrence, Moira McCarty, Marvette Pérez, Maggie Poxon, Susan Rosalsky, Ken Rose, Margaret Savage, David Steinberg, Patty Sutliff, Delphine Taylor, and Mike Trost. To my companion, Andy Staub, I owe the deepest thanks.

Finally, I thank my family for their love and encouragement.

INTRODUCTION

It is a land of quaint, swart faces, of Oriental dress and unspelled speech; a land where distance is lost, and the eye is a liar; a land of ineffable lights and sudden shadows; of polytheism and superstition, where the rattlesnake is a demigod, and the cigarette a means of grace, and where Christians mangle and crucify themselves—the heart of Africa beating against the ribs of the Rockies.

CHARLES LUMMIS, *The Land of Poco Tiempo* (1893)

The uniqueness of the Pueblo contribution lies in its being, sole among peoples of the earth, a society in which there is no partition between cultural and economic interests. Here is the only organized group in which group-mindedness runs higher than the individual reach. This is the only society in the world in which culture exists as an expression of the whole, unaffected by schisms of class and caste, incapable of being rated in terms of power or property.

MARY AUSTIN, *The Land of Journey's Ending* (1924)

Art, culture and history, like good food, are synonymous with the Land of Enchantment. The arts are historically interwoven with lifestyle, dating back to the first inhabitants of New Mexico, and there is an exceptional force propelling the creative impulse here, tied to heritage and inspiration.

1990 New Mexico Vacation Guide

The American Southwest is not simply a place. It is a region of the imagination, a "land"—of "poco tiempo," "journey's ending," and "enchantment"—on which Americans have long focused their fantasies of renewal and authenticity. Characterized by its desert landscape and "tricultural" history, the Southwest—usually meaning Arizona and New Mexico—has been for the last one hundred years variously perceived as a kind of American Orient, a place conducive to utopian communality, and the source of a "lifestyle."[1]

The Native American inhabitants of the Southwest have always been central to these imaginings. To visitors over the last century the Pueblos, Navajos, and Apaches seemed to be exotic, primitive people who lived self-sufficiently in a harsh but beautiful desert landscape. The Pueblos were especially appealing; they practiced picturesque religious ceremonials, made beautiful objects, and suggested to many non-Indian Americans life as it was lived in a simple, Edenic past.

American scientists, artists, and writers had been visiting the Southwest since the early nineteenth century, but in the 1880s interest in the region increased. The arrival of the railroads, which connected the region to the rest of the country, and ethnographers' interest in the native peoples of Arizona and New Mexico corresponded with the increased awareness. Anglo artists began arriving and painting Indian subjects; writers soon followed. In the mid-1890s railroads, such as the Atchison, Topeka and Santa Fe, began to promote tourism in the area. All of these groups made it their business to represent Indian cultures to people outside the region. Representations of Native Americans by ethnographers, writers, artists, photographers, and tourist entrepreneurs circulated throughout the nation in ethnological monographs and the popular press, in the markets for Indian-crafted objects, and in regional and national galleries and museums.

This study concentrates on the period from the 1880s to the 1920s, focusing on four case studies that move, more or less, chronologically: representations of the Hopi Snake dance, publications of the Fred Harvey Company, representations of Indian artisans, and Mary Austin's (1923) book *The American Rhythm.* Through close readings of a variety of published texts, including articles in periodicals, tourist literature, photographs, paintings, fiction, and ethnographic materials, I will show how Indians of the Southwest were mythologized within the contexts of ethnography, tourism, reformist strategies such as the arts and crafts movement, and modernist art and poetry. The iconography of these representations (both written and visual) presented images of Indians as ruins, ritualists, and artisans; that is, Native Americans were represented as people doomed to vanish or as living relics of the past, as performers of colorful ceremonies, and as makers of pots, baskets, blankets, and jewelry. These images were more about their makers than about Native Americans and imagined a primitive that was a locus for idealized versions of history, spirituality, and unalienated labor.

The case studies I have chosen demonstrate a shift in these imaginings of Indians. Between the 1880s, when American ethnographers first became interested in the Southwest, and the 1920s, when many modernist artists and writers were incorporating into their work primitivist idioms drawn from Native American cultures, southwestern Indians evolved in the non-Indian American imagination from a "vanishing race" into the ideal American artist, and the objects they made, understood initially as ethnographic curiosities or data, came to be considered art. This project attempts to understand the cultural circumstances that made this transformation possible and will show that cultural primitivism, as practiced in the Southwest by non-Indians at the turn of the century, has had lasting social and cultural implications.

The primitivist practices established in the first decades of this century are still operating and still serving similar cultural functions. To a great degree, Native Americans of the Southwest continue in the nation's imagination as artisans (or artists), as living relics of the past, and as performers of spiritually authentic rituals. Look in any issue of *Native Peoples* magazine: virtually all the ads are for Native American art and crafts. The New Mexico Board of Tourism continues to market the state as "America's Land of Enchantment," and its promotional materials feature images of costumed Pueblo dancers, "olla maidens," and artisans. New Age seekers continue to appropriate Native American spiritual beliefs and practices in an attempt to achieve spiritual and cultural authenticity. The list of (admittedly interesting and multitudinous) shapes and forms of cultural appropriation and exploitation goes on, but I am more interested in why this kind of primitivism is such a potent mythologizing strategy. Rather than condemning these practices as patently inauthentic and exposing the untruth of the ideology by demonstrating the "truth" about Native Americans, I want to look closely at primitivism to see how it works, to understand why it is successful. I am also interested in conceptual and representational strategies that offer alternatives to primitivism. To that end, the epilogue considers works by two Native American artists working in the Southwest today, the potter and poet Nora Naranjo-Morse and the video and filmmaker Victor Masayesva Jr. Their works speak directly to the history of representations of Indians and suggest alternative ways of understanding and representing cultural differences.

THE USES OF THE PRIMITIVE

The primitive is a concept that has existed, in Western cultures at least, since ancient times. It depends on a comparison between some standard of "civilization" and "others" thought to be somehow simpler and has traditionally functioned as a kind field on which "we" write fantasies about "them." These fantasies can portray others as good (noble savages) or bad (just plain savages). The primitive is usually imagined as existing in the past, although in its utopian mode it can exist in the future.[2]

Primitivism, a belief in the superiority of seemingly simpler ways of life, is as old as the notion of the primitive. As Michael Bell has written, "Primitivism is always by definition the paradoxical product of civilization itself. Primitivism, then, is born of the interplay between the civilized self and the desire to reject or transform it" (1972, 80). Primitivism is a reactionary response. In the face of industrialization, it values the preindustrial. In the face of irony and alienated individualism, it values sincerity and communality. These yearned-for values are thought to dwell in the primitive other. Primitivism is also a self-reflexive practice. For its practitioners, primitivism is a source of authority, a gesture that demonstrates the essential nature or the primacy of their notions, because the primitive is imagined at a state somehow previous to modernity and therefore more real, more authentic. The sense of modern life as being fragmented and, therefore, alienating has plagued Europeans and Americans for hundreds of years but especially since the end of the nineteenth century. Primitivism seems to offer a cure for what ails modernity, because it imagines that differentiation is a later, inauthentic development, that things were more whole, more harmonious at some time "before."[3]

At the turn of the twentieth century, evocations of southwestern Indians proliferated and served many primitivist uses. In the middle-class literature of strenuosity and the simple life, these Indians were held up as examples to overcivilized urban white folk. Collector and photographer George Wharton James, in his book *What the White Race May Learn from the Indian* (1908), called "upon the white race to incorporate into its civilization the good things of the Indian civilization; to forsake the injurious things of its pseudo-civilization, artificial, and over-refined life, and to return to the simple, healthful, and natural life which the Indians largely lived before and after they came under the dominion of the Spanish padres" (11–12). This sort of rhetoric was very much in line with the writings of other strenuous primitivists, such as Theodore Roosevelt, and spoke to national concerns about materialism, urbanization, labor, and gender roles (Higham 1965; Roosevelt 1900).

Primitivism played a major part in defining the Southwest as a distinct cultural region. In its association with its Native American inhabitants, the Southwest became known as a place of the unique, the handmade, the rural, and the authentic, as opposed to the modern metropolis, which was characterized as a place of mass-produced objects and culture, the urban, and the spurious. In the tourist literature as well as the early ethnography of the region, the Southwest was often compared to the biblical Middle East or ancient Greece. Americans were told that they need not journey to distant lands when ancient ruins, magnificent landscapes, and exotic peoples existed within their nation's own borders (McLuhan 1985, 43; Lummis [1893] 1952, 3–12). This regionalist (and nationalist) rhetoric was often similar to the discourse of orientalism. Barbara Babcock has written that "the Southwest *is* America's Orient," and Marta Weigle has called the development of the region's cultural distinctiveness "Southwesternism" (Babcock 1990, 406; Weigle 1990, 535–36). Both scholars identify conceptions of the primitive as crucial to constructing and maintaining the Southwest as an other to the nation.

In the representation of the Southwest as a regional other, Indians became a kind of folk. The Pueblos, and to some extent the Navajos, attained this status. Unlike the Plains Indians, who were usually represented as savage (though sometimes noble) warriors, the Pueblos were a "semicivilized," self-sufficient, settled, and agricultural people who lived in houses and produced attractive handicrafts. They were not like the urban poor; they seemed to be ethnic others who were happy to remain outside modernity.[4]

The representation of southwestern Indians as "orientalized," primitive folk was part of the rhetoric of empire building and colonialism. Manifest Destiny rested in part on the assumption that the native inhabitants of the North American continent were not capable of using the land appropriately or of governing themselves. Therefore, it remained the burden of American civilization to take command of these primitives in the name of progress. (The same reasoning justified the nation's imperialist expansion into the Philippines.) But even as Indians were seen as obstacles to progress, the forces of empire recognized the use of primitive energies to drive civilization. Thus figures such as Theodore Roosevelt, an avid imperialist, made strenuous primitivism, which often invoked the figure of the Indian, into a kind of progressivist religion.

Artists, anthropologists, promoters of tourism, and writers followed in the wake of the political conquest of Native Americans and established an essentially colonial relationship with them. Those who made representations of Indians used Native American cultures as a kind of raw material that they turned into art, scientific data, or dollars, and those who produced texts explained the new territories and their inhabitants to the nation and how they would be "imaginatively reconfigured as part of the national identity" (Hinsley 1994, 3). In 1916 *El Palacio,* a periodical publication of the School of American Archaeology in Santa Fe, presented a series of articles about local artists. The first article, about the painter Walter Ufer, summarized the progress of civilization in the Southwest:

> The Southwest has been conquered at various intervals by diverse peoples. There are those who came with the trappings of war and

> again those who held aloft the cross. There came finally commercialism and with it the modern industries. Each had their day and their function and each conquest was more far-reaching than that which preceded it.
>
> Within the past few years there has appeared the advance guard of a new conquering host which is doing more than merely occupying the land, a host that is taking hold of the imagination of men and creating in them a new and nobler spirit. These invaders are the men of science, literature and of art. They are in reality rediscovering the Southwest, its potentialities, its beauties. ("Walter Ufer" 1916, 75)

Thus the history of conquest is simply part of the evolution of civilization: from military might, to religion, to commerce, to science, literature, and art. All the invaders made the region productive, but the last "host"—scientists, artists, and writers—discovered and would develop the region's cultural riches.

THE POLITICS OF REPRESENTATION

In my analysis of the strategies deployed to represent Indians, I invoke several critical metaphors. The first is collecting. In addition to actual collections of Native American material culture made by ethnographers, museums, dealers, tourists, and private collectors, I examine collecting as a representational strategy implicit in the process of writing, painting, photographing, and sightseeing. Another helpful metaphor is the spectacle, in the Debordian sense of a social relationship among people mediated by commodified images (Debord 1983, 4). Once collected (or represented), southwestern Indian life circulated as a spectacle for middle-class consumption in museum displays, books, magazines, and galleries, and as tourist attractions. This spectacle—in which what did not appear was as significant as what did—was a discourse in which meaning and power relationships were continually constructed and negotiated. Another strategy, "playing Indian," involved a kind of appropriation of Indian identity.[5] One of the effects of the collecting and spectacularization of Indian life was the proliferation of Indian signifiers. In the primitivist Bohemian life-styles of people such as Mabel Dodge Luhan or the assumption of an Indian narrative voice in the poetry of Mary Austin, the Indian was a set of attributes that non-Indians could appropriate to assume, temporarily, an Indian identity.

These representational strategies all work, that is, serve the interests of primitivism, because they are ultimately self-reflexive. This is not intrinsically a bad thing, but the effect of these strategies on the represented was to create textualized or objectified Indians that disappeared as human subjects; such strategies induced a relationship between representer and represented based on consumption and appropriation rather than on communication between subjects. Of course, Native Americans have persisted, in reality, as subjects, and part of my task has been to find a way to reveal Native American "subalterns" in these representations as having a "constitutive rather than a reflective role in colonial and domestic imperial discourse and subjectivity" (Chrisman and Williams 1994, 16). In showing how Native Americans have participated in this discourse as agents, I read their utterances not as "authentic" or unmediated, but, like all the other utterances under consideration, including this book, as part of a larger discourse about the formations of cultural authority and identity.

In regard to my own cultural authority, I am, of course, implicated in the web of representations. Even though I have tried to ensure that my representation of Native Americans is informed by my own critique of primitivism, there is no way for me to rise above a discourse that has a history of exploiting information about Native Americans. The idea of region, again, provides a way to talk about my own cultural situation and the situation of this book. As I was working on this project, whenever I described it to anyone, I was always asked if I would get to go to the Southwest—as if it were a special perk of the project, which I had craftily devised as a way of spending time in Santa Fe. I did, in fact, spend a very productive two weeks visiting archives and libraries in New Mexico and Arizona, but most of my research over the course of three years was in libraries on the East Coast, at Yale, the New York Public Library, and, especially, the Smithsonian Institution. This book is very much the product of metropolitan institutions. But I see these institutions in a relationship with the Southwest that is not simply a recapitulation of the metropolis and periphery; both region and metropolis bear the burden of the history of conquest and colonialism, and consequently, both are sites where cultural identities and political relationships continue to be constituted. Thus, in the National Anthropological Archives (NAA) of the Smithsonian Institution, a repository established in the wake of the U.S. conquest of Native American populations, I sat next to Native Americans who were researching their own history. And while I was in Santa Fe, controversy brewed concerning a Native American jewelry maker who had been barred from selling his wares in front of the Palace of the Governors because it was revealed that his wife, who was not Native American, had assisted him in making the jewelry. These sites, the NAA and the porch of the Palace of the Governors, do not work as discrete, pristine sources of metropolitan authority and regional authenticity. Rather, they are more like Michael J. Riley's description of a "borderland," "a contested semiotic construction negotiated and bounded by relationships of power," or Mary Louise Pratt's "contact zone," a social space "where disparate cultures meet, clash, and grapple with each other, often in highly asymmetrical relations of domination and subordination—like colonialism, slavery, or their aftermaths as they are lived out across the globe today" (Riley 1993, 223; Pratt 1992, 4). I see this book as such a contact zone, where readers may examine the structures of and their responses to these textual encounters with Native Americans and others.

In making my arguments about primitivism, I have avoided claiming either metropolitan or regional authority, but I have tried to show the ways meanings have been made by way of boundaries constructed, crossed, and negotiated. Having rejected the fetishization of authenticity upon which primitivism is based, I have accepted the idea that mediation and negotiation are real: in making meaning, they are what we have to work with. I have not given up on the idea of truth, but I accept that it is almost never simple, that it may be possible to achieve in many ways, and, furthermore, that it might not always be available.

THE PLAYERS IN CONTEXT

Most of the texts under consideration in this study were made by non-Indian ethnographers, writers, artists, and photographers; a few were made by Native Americans. All of the texts circulated in national and regional literary, art, and tourist markets, through institutions such as museums and galleries, artists' societies and colonies, magazines, and railroads. Because one of my aims is to show the connections among these individuals and institutions, some background information is in order. And so is a caveat: the following history of the Native Americans and Anglos who figure in this study is in no way comprehensive. The Native American part of that history is particularly difficult to relate. I have tried to show Native Americans' agency in negotiations with different political and cultural powers, but the end result can only be a sketch of significant events and individuals that shaped and have continued to shape Indian-white relations.

In 1848, when the United States "annexed" the Arizona and New Mexico Territories as a result of the war with Mexico and the signing of the Treaty of Guadalupe Hidalgo, the most populous Native American groups living in the region were the Pueblos, Navajos, and Apaches. The eastern Pueblos lived in villages along the Rio Grande in New Mexico and spoke the languages Keres, Piro, Tiwa, Towa, Tewa, and Tano. Farther to the west were the Zuni Pueblo—just to the east of the New Mexico border with Arizona—and the Hopi villages, located on three mesas in northern Arizona. Whereas the Rio Grande Pueblos had been heavily missionized by the Spanish, the Zunis and the Hopis, being more remotely located, had less contact with Spanish rule. In the Pueblo Revolt of 1680 the eastern and western Pueblos united and kicked out the Spanish, who returned in 1692 and gradually reestablished rule over the Rio Grande Pueblos. During the eighteenth century the Hopis and the Zunis continued to resist missionization and other Spanish cultural and political influences.

In the land between the Rio Grande Pueblos and the Hopis and Zunis lived the Athapaskan-speaking Navajos. They were partially nomadic, practiced some agriculture, and frequently raided the pueblos on either side of them for livestock and food. They were not a unified "tribe" but lived in many small communities of from ten to forty families (Spicer 1962, 214–15). The Apaches, also Athapaskan speaking, lived in northeastern New Mexico and in southwestern New Mexico and southeastern Arizona and Sonora. The western

Apaches were culturally more similar to the Navajos than were the more northern, Plains-influenced Apache groups; they were organized into bands, and they farmed but also relied on raiding into Sonora and Chihuahua to supplement their food supply. The Spanish had identified and named five groups of western Apaches: Mimbreños, Chiricahuas, Pinaleños, Coyoteros (later distinguished by ethnographers as White Mountain and Cibecue bands), and Tontos (244). Neither the Navajos nor the Apaches had been missionized to the extent the Pueblos had been, and they did not participate in the Pueblo Revolt of 1680.

Each group's experience of the United States' conquest was different. In 1846 General Stephen Kearny occupied Santa Fe, encountering little resistance, and in 1847 the New Mexico territorial legislature allowed the Pueblo villages (including Zuni) to retain their rights to the land they had held under Spanish and Mexican rule (Spicer 1962, 170). Settled on these land grants and regarded as peaceful by the U.S. government, the Pueblos were receptive to the government's irrigation and other agricultural reforms. Nevertheless, conflict between the Pueblos and Anglo-Americans over grazing, farming, and water rights began after the conquest and continues to this day. Neither the Hopis nor the Zunis had "felt the touch of Mexican political authority," but they were not ignorant of the Europeans in the region; throughout the first half of the nineteenth century, they had maintained relationships with European and American trappers and traders (197). It wasn't until the early 1880s that the United States began exerting more authority over the Hopis and Zunis. In 1882 the government established a Hopi reservation of 3,863 square miles within the Navajo Reservation (202).

Because the Hopis, Zunis, and Rio Grande Pueblos were regarded as peaceful, settled agriculturalists, they did not suffer the American military persecution that the Navajos and Apaches did. The Navajos continued to raid the Hopis and Pueblos until they were "subdued" by Colonel Kit Carson and the U.S. Army in 1863. The army marched the Navajos to Fort Sumner (Bosque Redondo) on the Little Pecos River in eastern New Mexico, where they were confined for four years. In 1868 a number of Navajo leaders, including Barboncito of Canyon de Chelly, Manuelito of Tohatchi, and Ganado Mucho of the Klagetoh area, signed a treaty and agreed to move to a reservation, which occupied part of the northeastern corner of Arizona and extended into the northwestern portion of New Mexico. There they began to live by means of farming and herding sheep and goats. But the next ten years were difficult; crops failed, and they remained dependent on government rations. In 1876 railroad surveys took good land from the southern part of the reservation. In 1878 and 1880 the reservation was expanded to the west and north, around the Hopi land. The Navajo population continued to grow, and by 1880 about twelve thousand people lived on the reservation (Spicer 1962, 220–22).

After the Mexican-American War, Apache leaders felt that because the Americans were also enemies of the Mexicans, they should encourage Apache raids into Mexico. But the Treaty of Guadalupe Hidalgo required the Apaches to make treaties with the Americans that would deny them the right to do this. Through the 1850s, "Apaches were apparently ready to grant permission for Anglos to pass through their territory, but they were not ready to accept prohibition of raids into Mexico nor unregulated settlement in their territory by incoming Anglos" (Spicer 1962, 246–47). Some Apaches allowed Anglos to ranch and mine on their land for fees, but in 1861 these arrangements were upset by the Civil War. The Union captured New Mexico and launched a war of extermination on Apaches in order to maintain the routes for the Overland Mail. The war years were marked by much violent conflict between Anglo settlers, the army, and Apaches. After the war, U.S. policy toward the Apaches was unfocused and disorganized, and its implementation corrupt. Although some Apache groups seemed interested in peaceful relations with the United States and settling down to farming, others did not. In 1871 the government established reservations for Apaches in southwestern New Mexico and central Arizona, and General George Crook was sent to move them into these reservations. Many Apaches came, but many did not. By 1878, after years of confused government policy and corruption and Apache resistance, about five thousand of the western Apaches had been settled at San Carlos on the Gila River in Arizona (252). As Anglos encroached on the reservation to mine deposits of copper, silver, and gold, and to farm, the Apaches became restless and discouraged. In 1882 the Chiricahua leader Geronimo and his followers fled the reservation and joined the Mimbreño leader Victorio in Mexico. Over the next four years the U.S. Army sporadically tracked down and fought Geronimo and other "hostile" Apaches. In 1886 Geronimo surrendered to General Nelson A. Miles. Consequently, Geronimo and other Apaches were sent by train to prison in Florida. In 1894 they and their families were moved to Fort Sill, Oklahoma, where Geronimo died in 1909 (Prucha 1984, 652).

As Native Americans were moved onto reservations throughout the West, lawmakers and reformers tried to figure out how to bring them into American society culturally and economically. From the 1880s to the 1920s, the federal government's policy toward Native Americans was one of assimilation (as opposed to extermination or isolation on reservations), which meant the eradication of Indian cultural forms. Although by the end of the nineteenth century there was a clear tension between those who believed that assimilation was the way and those (including Anglos and Native Americans) who thought Native Americans should be allowed to preserve their cultural practices, the government continued to try to "civilize" or "Americanize" the nation's Native American population through various forms of land allotment and reeducation.[6]

Created to end collective ownership of tribal lands and break up tribal governments, the Dawes General Allotment Act of 1887 called for tribal land to be divided into small, privately owned farms. In the Southwest, the law did not apply to the Pueblos, whose rights to their land grants remained, but the legislation had mixed receptions elsewhere. On the Hopi reservation, for example, although some people accepted their allotments, others pulled up surveyors' stakes. In the mid-1890s the United States ended efforts to continue the severalty program, but by then, through land allotment and railway rights-of-way, Indian people had lost half the land they held before allotment (Hoxie 1977, 127).

For assimilationists such as Richard Pratt, who founded the Carlisle Indian School at Carlisle, Pennsylvania, Indian education meant learning English, "practical industrial training," and Christianity. The U.S. government set up day schools on reservations and boarding schools in other locations. Boys learned agricultural and common trades, and girls learned the domestic tasks of white households (Prucha 1984, 689; Hoxie 1977, 488). Catholic and Protestant missionaries were contracted to run these schools, and they discouraged Native American spiritual practices and beliefs. On all the reservations in the Southwest, Native Americans responded in divided ways to these schools and missionaries; some accepted the new ways, others resisted. When total assimilation seemed doomed to failure, government policies gradually changed and began to treat Indian people as culturally backward and dependent elements within American society. They became increasingly peripheralized, their legal, economic, and social status fixed on the fringe of white society (Hoxie 1977, 612).

Meanwhile, cash economies developed on all the southwestern reservations. In the 1890s the Apaches on the San Carlos Reservation were, more or less, peacefully settled and increasingly productive agriculturally, but there was much conflict with Anglos over water rights. More and more Apaches worked for wages in mines, on Anglo ranches on leased reservation land, and for the railroads. During the 1920s white ranchers' leases were discontinued, and the government tried to develop cattle industry among the Apaches. Like the Apaches, many among the Navajos and Pueblos worked for the railroads in the 1880s and at jobs in towns such as Albuquerque and Santa Fe. Among the Pueblos and the Navajos, the government tried to develop markets for crafts such as silver work, basketry, pottery, and blankets.

In 1912 Arizona and New Mexico became states. Still, some western states found ways to limit native voting rights, and Native Americans did not become U.S. citizens until 1924. Even then their civil rights remained under question and suffered serious limitations and infringements. The federal policy of assimilation began to change in the early 1930s, largely due to the activism of Native Americans and southwestern artists and literati such as John Sloan, Mary Austin, and John Collier.[7] In the early 1920s Austin and others lobbied against the Bursum bill, which would have dispossessed Pueblos of land and water rights, and formed organizations to promote Indian welfare and civil rights and to preserve their religious practices and arts and crafts (Gibson 1983, 259). In 1933 Collier was appointed commissioner of Indian Affairs and oversaw the reversal of many of the anti-Indian policies that had prevailed for so long. The Indian Reorganization Act of 1934 "precluded the alienation of a tribe's land or shares in a tribal corporation other than to the tribe itself, authorized the Secretary of the Interior to restore certain Indian lands and to purchase other lands for Indian use, and established a revolving credit fund from which the Secretary of the Interior could make loans to tribal corporations." It also allowed tribes to form their own constitutional tribal governments and thus encouraged politics based on democracy rather than theocracy (Rushforth and Upham 1992, 154).

American ethnographic interest in Native Americans of the Southwest had existed since the military expeditions to and surveys of the region in the early nineteenth century, but it intensified in the wake of the American conquest of the region. It was not until 1879, when the Bureau of Ethnology (later the Bureau of American Ethnology, or BAE) was established as part of the Smithsonian Institution, that the native populations came under systematic scrutiny as the government tried to figure out what to do about the "Indian problem." The 1880s and 1890s were a boom time for American ethnology, and the Southwest was a major area of interest. Expeditions were financed by the government as well as private individuals. For example, the Bureau of Ethnology sponsored Frank Hamilton Cushing's expedition to Zuni in 1879. After 1886 Cushing was sponsored by Bostonian Mary Hemenway, and when Cushing left, Jesse Walter Fewkes headed the expedition. Then, in the mid-1890s, Fewkes began working for the BAE doing fieldwork among the Hopis and other Pueblos. Other private patrons of southwestern expeditions at the turn of the century were the department store owner John Wanamaker and the collector George Heye. In the 1880s and 1890s ethnographers who worked in the Southwest included John G. Bourke, Walter Hough, George Dorsey, Herman F. C. Ten Kate, Alexander Stephen, Frederick W. Hodge, Matilda Coxe Stevenson, James Stevenson, Adolph Bandelier, and H. R. Voth. Anthropologists continued to be interested in the Southwest in the twentieth century. In the 1920s and 1930s Ruth Benedict and Ruth Bunzel, both students of Franz Boas, worked among the Pueblos.

Ethnographic interest in the Southwest initially concentrated on the Zunis, Hopis, and, to some extent, the other Pueblo groups. The Zunis and Hopis were appealing because they appeared less influenced by European cultures than other groups and did not put up hostile resistance to U.S. military conquest of the region. The Navajos and Apaches did not come under ethnographic scrutiny until much later. (Exceptions are Washington Matthews's work among the Navajos in the 1890s and Bourke's 1892 book, *The Medicine Men of the Apache.*) The Navajos, relative newcomers to the region who lived a nomadic existence and had a habit of raiding other groups for livestock, did not exemplify the purely primitive traits that interested most ethnographers. And the Apaches, who successfully resisted being put on reservations until 1884, seemed too hostile and savage to warrant study.

The explicit ethnographic mission to salvage information about the primitive life of Zunis and Hopis before they "disappeared" had the effect of making the last two decades of the nineteenth century a kind of "ethnographic present"—the moment when these cultures were last perceived to be culturally intact, before the transforming influence of civilization. Another result of the salvage approach was that ethnographers tended to ignore changes going on in Native American societies; because they were looking for Indians as they existed before European contact, they omitted from their accounts evidence of change and outside influence. Some of these early ethnologists were the first and last to have access to many rituals (many Native American groups have since limited outsiders' access to religious practices); as a result, their works have stood for the last one hundred years as the most thorough—and the most invasive—descriptions of these rituals.[8]

As ethnographers' interest in the native peoples of the Southwest grew, the railroad arrived. In 1880 the Atchison, Topeka and Santa Fe Railroad (ATSF) reached Santa Fe. By 1885 it had made the Pueblos accessible by rail from both coasts. Before the mid-1890s, tourism was not a major concern of the ATSF. It and other railroads in the Southwest, such as the Denver and Rio Grande, the Great Northern, the Northern Pacific, and the Southern Pacific, concentrated on colonizing the region, and their promotional literature was aimed at potential settlers and business people. The ATSF initially published pamphlets promoting the Southwest to "home-seekers" and, slightly later, in the mid-1890s, to those in search of good health. Pamphlets like the 1887 *New Mexico: Some Practical and Authentic Information about Its Resources* provided information about mean annual rainfall, public schools, mines, business opportunities, and horticulture. *The Land of Sunshine* (1892), by C. A. Higgins, and

Health Resorts of New Mexico (1897) featured long tables showing the range of temperatures and rainfall and promoted the idea that invalids of limited means might earn a living through light farming and beekeeping. There is little or no information about Indians in any of these books.

But with the reorganization of the ATSF in 1895, the railroad's desire for more passengers and ticket sales led to the promotion of tourism. In 1895 the ATSF formed an advertising office whose head, William H. Simpson, began to hire ethnographers, artists, photographers, and writers to publicize the attractions of the region. Among these attractions, Simpson and other ATSF officials astutely realized, were the region's aboriginal inhabitants, and information about and representations of Indians began making regular appearances in ATSF promotional material.

In shifting the emphasis from colonization to tourism, the Santa Fe, working in conjunction with the Fred Harvey Company, began to present the region in a way that organized it as a collection of attractions, which people visited for a while and then left. In its tourist publications, the rhetoric of colonization began to recede and the rhetoric of sightseeing began to take over. Because the practice of sightseeing is the governing experience of tourism (MacCannell 1976, 13), organizing the region into various tourist attractions meant presenting discrete aspects of it as sights. Guidebooks began to include information on how to find and appreciate the pueblos, and representations of Indian life in the Southwest began to appear in all of the railway's promotional literature.

Using Indian imagery in this way was nothing new; representations of Indians circulated nationally in dime novels, museums and expositions, Wild West shows, paintings, illustrations, lithography, photography and sculpture, and advertising, as well as on sheet music (Berkhofer 1988, 535–38; Green 1988a, 592–606). But the ATSF, of all the railroads in the region, was the most aggressive in using images of Indians. In the 1890s it hired artists Thomas Moran, Henry Farney, Fernand H. Lungren, and Maynard Dixon to paint the region's attractions (Bryant 1978, 438; Armitage 1948, 118). The paintings hung in offices, stations, and hotels, and reproductions of them graced the ATSF promotional literature and the famous ATSF calendars, which were widely distributed and always featured paintings of

Indians. After 1900 the frequency of Simpson's purchases increased and he began what would eventually become the Santa Fe Railway Collection. Some of the artists who worked for the Santa Fe after 1900 were Louis Akin, who toured Arizona for the ATSF painting pictures of Hopis in 1903, and William R. Leigh, the "Sagebrush Rembrandt," who accepted transportation for his first visit to the West in 1906 (Bryant 1978, 442). Many of these artists produced landscapes, but others, such as Lungren and Akin, painted Indian subjects. The ATSF advertising department under Simpson continued until the Depression to buy paintings from Taos artists such as E. Irving Couse (a particular favorite), Joseph Henry Sharp, and Ernest Blumenschein. Often the artists were paid with railroad tickets and Fred Harvey meals and accommodations in lieu of cash, and Simpson also suggested subjects or alterations in composition (Bryant 1978, 447). The Santa Fe and the artists had a symbiotic relationship: the artists benefited from the publicity machine of the railroad, and the railroad acquired a corporate image based on romantic images of Indians ("Santa Fe Collects" 1926, 932). The Fred Harvey Company, which ran the hotel and dining concessions along the Santa Fe route, followed a similar course of using Indian and, to some extent, Hispanic imagery in its displays and promotional material.

Many of the ATSF artists were associated with the burgeoning artist colony at Taos. Painters such as Joseph Henry Sharp, the artist "discoverer" of Taos, Ernest L. Blumenschein, Bert Geer Phillips, and Oscar E. Berninghaus began visiting the area in the mid-1890s. Most of these men came under the auspices of magazines or railroads, but some came on their own, drawn by the region's picturesque qualities. By 1914 eight of these "first-generation" artists (Sharp, Berninghaus, Blumenschein, Phillips, Couse, W. Herbert Dunton, Victor Higgins, and Walter Ufer) had formed the Taos Society of Artists to promote their work nationally and internationally. Later artists associated with Taos were Emil Bisttram, Maurice Sterne, Andrew Dasburg, and Georgia O'Keeffe. As in Taos, a colony of artists developed in Santa Fe. The Santa Fe art colony was larger and more diverse than the Taos scene and included artists who worked in more modernist idioms and who depicted Hispanic in addition to Indian subjects. During and after World War I painters such as William P. Henderson, Sheldon Parsons, Marsden Hartley, Robert Henri, Gerald Cassidy, and John Sloan were either residents or regular visitors. After 1920 artists such as B. J. O. Nordfeldt and Randall Davey arrived.[9]

At Santa Fe there was an institutional conflation of art and anthropology. This development was embodied in the person of Dr. Edgar Hewett, who founded the School of American Archaeology in Santa Fe in 1909. It was reorganized as the School of American Research in 1917, the same year the Museum of Fine Arts opened. Hewett was an untiring promoter of southwestern art, anthropology, archaeology, and tourism and was instrumental in organizing the New Mexico displays at the 1915 Panama-California Exposition in San Diego as well as the revival of the Santa Fe Fiesta in 1919 and the Southwest Indian Fair in 1922 (Frost 1980, 57–58; Stocking 1982).

Northern New Mexico also appealed to writers. In the 1890s several writers published works that exhibited an appreciation of the region's landscape and Native Americans. Archaeologist Adolph Bandelier's *Delight Makers,* a fictionalized account of ancient Pueblo life, appeared in 1890; Charles Lummis's *Land of Poco Tiempo* (1893) presented sketches of life in New Mexico; and Edna Dean Proctor's *Song of the Ancient People* (1892) was a long poem about the prehistoric inhabitants of the region. Writers came to New Mexico slightly later than the artists, and there was no acknowledged writers' colony until the 1920s. These writers published their work nationally and established local presses and magazines. Alice Corbin Henderson, who had been editor of *Poetry* magazine in Chicago, came to Santa Fe in 1916 to recover from tuberculosis. She was accompanied by her husband, the painter William Penhallow Henderson. The poet Witter Bynner also came through her connection in 1921. Other literary colonists who visited Santa Fe and wrote about the Southwest were Ina Sizer Cassidy (wife of painter Gerald Cassidy), Frank Applegate, Ruth Laughlin Barker, Willard "Spud" Johnson, and the anthropologist Oliver La Farge, author of the novel *Laughing Boy* (1929). Mary Austin settled permanently in Santa Fe in 1924, but she had been a frequent visitor since 1918. Willa Cather visited in summer months after 1915 and finished *Death Comes for the Archbishop* while staying in Austin's house in 1926. In Taos, Mabel Dodge Luhan, who first came in 1916, attracted writers such as D. H. Lawrence and Robinson Jeffers to her home. Lawrence in turn induced Frieda Lawrence, Dorothy Brett, and Aldous Huxley to come to Taos (Gibson 1983, 179–98; Weigle and Fiore 1982).

All of these writers and artists came from outside New Mexico, and they appreciated the region for its differences. Artists, writers, ethnographers, and tourist entrepreneurs had vested interests in preserving Indian cultures, as picturesque subject matter, tourist attractions, collectible data, and sources of souvenirs and art objects. Their imaginings of Indians were instrumental in the formation of cultural identities for the nation and region, for urban middle-class Americans, and for Native Americans.

CHAPTER 1

REPRESENTING THE HOPI SNAKE DANCE

From 1880 to 1920, the Hopi Snake and Antelope ceremony, popularly known as the Snake dance, was far and away the most widely depicted Southwest Native American ritual. Usually performed in August to ensure abundant rainfall for the corn crops, it was only one ritual in the round of ceremonies that Hopis enacted throughout the year, but because it involved the handling of live snakes, it was the ceremony most often described by non-Indian observers.

Ethnographers began publishing accounts of the Snake dance in both the popular press and museum monographs in the 1880s. By the early 1890s it had become a national ritual for newspapers and magazines to report on the "Weird Arizona Snake Dance" or "Hideous Rites" in their August issues.[1] Photographs, drawings, and paintings of the Snake dance appeared in the press, on postcards, and as stereographs. The ceremony also became a major tourist attraction; thousands of people, including many celebrities and luminaries, descended on the Hopi mesas every year, and detailed accounts of the ritual appeared in travel narratives, guidebooks, and railroad promotional pamphlets.

The focus of all this attention was actually the final day of a nine-day ceremony. The public dance, in which the participants handled snakes, took place at the end of the last day, which began with a foot race and proceeded through various rites performed by the men of the Snake and Antelope societies. Crowds (including Hopis and outsiders) gathered early in anticipation of the climax of the ceremony, a processional dance in which Snake priests carried live snakes, many of them rattlesnakes, in their mouths. The ceremony ended with the snakes being let go and the participants' ingestion of an emetic.[2]

Accounts of the Snake dance began to reach a mass audience just as the Apaches of New Mexico and Arizona had been "subdued" by the U.S. Army and the region was joined by railroad to the rest of the nation. Concomitantly, the "Indian problem" shifted from the matter of conquest to the question of how to incorporate the region's Native Americans socially and culturally into the nation. The Snake dance—the event itself as well as the burgeoning representations of it—became a spectacle that defined and displayed the cultural differences between the "primitive" Hopis and "civilized" Americans.

The early ethnographic accounts of the Snake dance are especially interesting in this regard, because the people who produced them were concerned with describing and codifying the nature of the "primitive." They addressed in particular the problem of ethnic differences, and because ethnology was a relatively new science, their efforts reveal how they struggled with ways of defining and representing those differences. Popular accounts and representations of the Snake dance portrayed it as an exotic, orientalized tourist attraction. At the same time, literary (and other) observers of the ceremony, which seemed so troublingly primitive, tried to understand its (and the Hopis') cultural significance to the nation.

Caught in the flurry of ethnographic, artistic, literary, and touristic interest in the Snake dance, Hopis quickly discovered that the proliferation of representations was just as threatening to their cultural practices as government schools, land allotment, and missionaries. By the early 1920s they had forbidden sketching and taking photographs of the ceremony, and eventually they closed it to outsiders altogether.

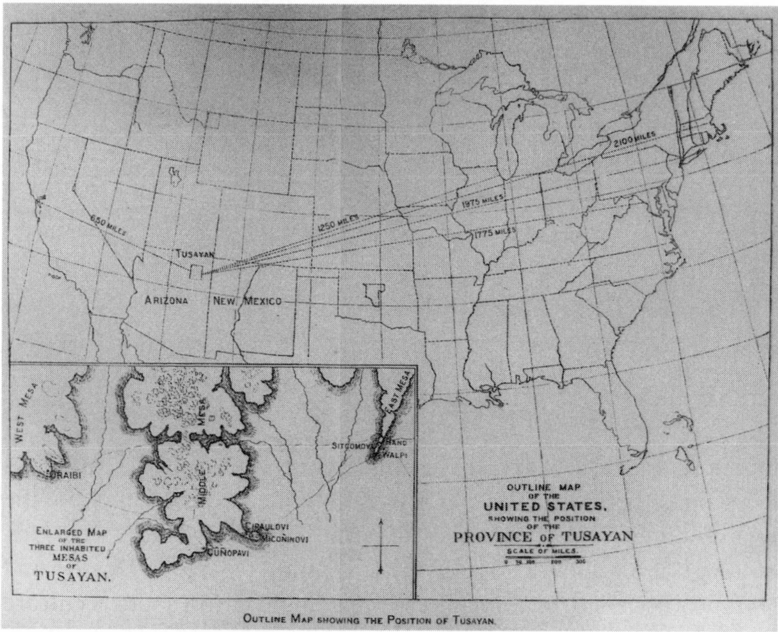

Figure 1. "Outline Map Showing the Position of Tusayan." At the end of the nineteenth century, Hopi people lived in six pueblos on three mesas in northern Arizona. (A seventh village, Hano, was inhabited mainly by Tewa speakers.) This map configures the Hopi area as a region, *defined by its distance from the nation's urban metropolises. (Reprinted from Fewkes, "Snake Ceremonials at Walpi")*

In writing this analysis of representations of the Snake and Antelope ceremony, my aim is not to recapitulate the modes of representation that have proved so oppressive to Hopi people. Rather, I want to investigate and defuse the power these images and texts exert over readers, viewers, and the subjects depicted. The decision to include some visual representations of the ceremony is based on the desire to have my argument clearly understood and on the belief that removing them from view will only further mystify these imaginings of the primitive. I hope that this analysis is useful to Hopi as well as non-Hopi people. If "fascination" or "offense," "enchantment" or "shock" is what these images elicit, I ask readers to examine those responses. What is it that fascinates or offends? What are the mechanisms of those responses? Furthermore, I invite readers to think about their own role in the continuing "spectacle" of Native American life in the Southwest and how they might disrupt it and its politics. To these ends, I have only reproduced images of the public parts of the ceremony, images that are crucial to my discussion and that give readers a sense of the scope, content, and context of the spectacle of which these representations were a part. I have not included any images or passages of text that depict ritual activities inside kivas.

TEXTUALIZING THE SNAKE DANCE

In the last two decades of the nineteenth century, ethnographers working on both federally and privately funded expeditions were the first observers to systematically describe the Snake dance. Men such as John Gregory Bourke, Jesse Walter Fewkes, George A. Dorsey, and H. R. Voth were determined to salvage information about a culture that many Americans believed would disappear through the "progress" of civilization. Many of these men were influenced by the writings of anthropologist Lewis Henry Morgan, who developed a theory of cultural evolution. He argued that all cultures represented different stages of social development along a progressive, evolutionary scale: from savage to barbaric to civilized, with European society being the standard of civilization. In Hopi culture American ethnographers believed they were seeing previous stages in the evolution of their own culture, the difference between the two being a degree of civilization.[3]

These ethnographers believed anthropology was a science that could be an agent of social reform; by observing civilization at earlier stages of its evolution they could understand the nature of progress and use this knowledge to further the nation's progress. They also felt their studies would provide answers to the "Indian problem," which, after the Civil War, seemed soluble by either "civilization or extermination" (Hinsley 1981, 146, 149–51; Porter 1986, 80–81). The Hopis seemed good candidates for civilization. They were "peaceful," lived in houses, practiced agriculture, and crafted objects of beauty and utility. However, the process of civilizing the Hopis apparently would involve the "loss" of their culture. As they became more civilized, more like white Americans, they would give up their Hopi ways. Ethnographers, therefore, went to the Hopi mesas to salvage what they could of Hopi culture before it disappeared, and they believed their data would help show how the Hopis could be incorporated into the nation.

Ethnographers "saved" the Snake dance, in part, by rendering it as a text. To make their texts, ethnographers, the writers of culture, used the tools of literacy and image making: paper, pens, pencils, paints, cameras, and phonographs. They published their findings in books and journals, in which Hopi culture appeared as bits of data, artifacts, ruins—collected for study and display (Fabian 1983, 120). But in this textualization, the *presence* of the Hopis was lost. Hopis did not exist as subjects but as objects of exchange or as signifiers available for moral and allegorical interpretation (Clifford 1986, 113). By positing a disappearing Indian, the ethnographic representations of the Snake dance seemed to serve the interests of Indian assimilation through "civilization." But by disseminating increasingly detailed information about the ritual, more and more non-Indians began to value and support the preservation of Hopi culture. In the end, ethnography failed to provide an easy solution to the Indian problem.

One of the earliest ethnographic observers of the Snake dance was John G. Bourke, a "soldier-scientist" who participated in the campaigns against the Apaches and the war against the Sioux and Cheyenne in 1876–77. During 1880–81 he received a year's leave from the army to collect ethnographic information about Native Americans of the Plains and the Southwest, and he saw the Snake dance at Walpi in August 1881. His book about what he observed in the Southwest, *The Snake-Dance of the Moquis of Arizona* (1884), brought Bourke national attention and established his reputation as an ethnographer.[4]

The Snake-Dance of the Moquis of Arizona was intended for "popular perusal" and was as much travel narrative as scientific observation ([1884] 1984, xx). Bourke related his journey through the Southwest and his encounters with the Pueblos of the Rio Grande; it is an account full of local color and travel anecdotes, but the centerpiece of the book is the last day of the Snake and Antelope ceremonies. The book's full title promised to describe "the revolting religious rite, The Snake-Dance; to which is added a Brief Dissertation upon Serpent-Worship in General." In the hours before the public dance, Bourke was allowed into a kiva to observe the participants preparing the snakes. His account displays a combination of revulsion and cool detachment: "The air [in the kiva] was heavy with a stench like that of a rotten cesspool: only a stern sense of responsibility kept me at my post" (138). Bourke believed he was the first white man to "carefully note this strange heathen rite during the moment of its celebration," and his "responsibility" was to record it as thoroughly and accurately as he could (1). He took notes continually, asked questions, and lifted lids on covered ceremonial bowls (138).

At the public dance he was a careful and thorough observer, noting the presence of about 750 visitors, only half a dozen of whom were Anglos. In addition to describing the activities of all the participants, he was moved to write that the Snake dance had the "lurid tinge of a nightmare":

> The spectacle was an astonishing one, and one felt at once bewildered and horrified at this long column of weird figures, naked in all excepting the snake-painted cotton kilts and red buckskin moccasins; bodies a dark greenish-brown, relieved only by the broad white armlets and the bright yellowish-gray of the fox skins dangling behind them; long elfin locks brushed straight back from the head, tufted with scarlet parrot or woodpecker feathers; faces painted black, as with a mask of charcoal, from brow to upper lip, where the ghastly white of kaolin began, and continued down over chin and neck; the crowning point being the deadly reptiles borne in mouth and hand, which imparted to the drama the lurid tinge of a nightmare. (162–63)

Concluding his description of the Snake dance, Bourke made clear the Hopis' presence as pagan primitives within the American nation:

> This was the Snake-Dance of the Moquis, a tribe of people living within our own boundaries, less than seventy miles from the Atlantic and Pacific Railroad in the year of our Lord 1881. And in this same year, as a clipping from the Omaha *Nebraska Herald* states, the women of the United States subscribed for the diffusion of the Gospel in *foreign* lands, the munificent sum of six hundred thousand dollars. (169–70)

Bourke's call to missionary action was about to be answered by Christian reformers committed to the spiritual salvation and "Americanization" of Indians. Reform groups organized in the early 1880s thought the government's policy of maintaining reservations as separate, alien entities was an impediment to this process. They argued that Indians should be civilized via land allotment, education, and evangelism. Organizations such as the powerful Indian Rights Association, founded in Philadelphia in 1882, began lobbying the government to establish schools, in which Indian people would learn English and manual skills, and to allot reservation lands in severalty so that they might learn to be self-sufficient farmers and ranchers (Prucha 1984, 611–13). Reformers and policy makers assumed that in the process of assimilation, Native Americans would give up their religion and take up Christianity (Hoxie 1984, 41–81).

The theory of cultural evolution, as it turned out, dovetailed nicely with the notion of assimilation; it made the process of civilization seem inevitable and natural. Forced assimilation merely accelerated a "natural" process. When Bourke observed the Snake dance at Walpi in 1881, assimilation as a policy was not in place, but Bourke's work was overshadowed by the idea that the Hopi way of life was doomed to disappear. Bourke, a member of the conquering army and a believer in cultural evolution, assumed that the Hopis were destined to give up their ways and accept the blessings of civilization. As a work of salvage ethnography, Bourke's account of the Snake dance is accurate in that it presents a detailed description of the procedures of the ceremony, but it also demonstrates that the Hopis were different to a degree that was intolerable to the idea of the modern nation and the ideology of progress.

Ten years after Bourke's account of the Snake dance appeared, the ethnologist Jesse Walter Fewkes published "The Snake Ceremonials at Walpi" (1894) under the auspices of the Hemenway Southwest Expedition. Fewkes had begun his career as a natural scientist working under Alexander Agassiz at the Museum of Comparative Zoology at Harvard. When he was not reappointed to this post, he accepted the offer of Mary Hemenway's son to take over their Southwest Expedition from Frank Hamilton Cushing, whose performance the Hemenways did not like. One of Cushing's failings in the Hemenways' view was that he did not produce enough publishable material. As Cushing's replacement, Fewkes set about making up for this shortcoming, publishing prolifically on Zuni and Hopi subjects.[5]

Compared to Bourke's, the expedition Fewkes oversaw was highly organized, with many observers working together to collect data, including photographs and phonographic recordings of ceremonial songs. And unlike Bourke's account, Fewkes's was less a travelogue for popular consumption and more a scientific report for other ethnologists.[6] In "The Snake Ceremonials at Walpi," Fewkes took the objective and taxonomic approach of the natural scientist, cataloguing details in dispassionate, precise language. Even so, his writing occasionally echoes Bourke's evocation of Gothic horror. After witnessing some of the men handling the snakes, Fewkes commented:

> The sight haunted me for weeks afterwards, and I can never forget this wildest of all the aboriginal rites of this strange people, which showed no element of our present civilization. It was a performance which might have been expected in the heart of Africa rather than in the American Union, and certainly one could not realize that he was in the United States at the end of the nineteenth century. ([1894] 1977, 85)

Like Bourke, Fewkes asserted that the Snake dance was out of place in the modern Union. Comparing the dance to something more African than American was already a standard trope in the popular literature about the ritual (e.g., Lummis [1893] 1952, 3). The Snake dance seemed to be a cultural and geographic anomaly, and by asserting its anomalousness in this way, Fewkes suggested that it should disappear so that the correct geographic and cultural order—that is, the "natural" order—could prevail.

The passage's allusion to slavery and Reconstruction is also apt; the Indian problem in the 1890s presented a dilemma similar to that concerning incorporation of freedmen after the Civil War. By the time Fewkes began publishing, the Indian Commission's policy of assimilation, in which Indians would be reconstructed as white people, was under way. The efforts of Christian reformers had paid off: the Allotment Act was passed in 1887. It provided for, among other things, allotment of reservation lands in severalty and stipulated that each person receiving an allotment would become a citizen of the

United States. Remaining lands would be purchased by the government and then sold. Also, each year the Indian Commission received more money to establish day and boarding schools for Indian students; to ensure that this education would be Christian, the government contracted with Protestant and Catholic missionaries to run the reservation schools (Prucha 1984, 689).

But the policy of assimilation was not a success; from the beginning (and even before) it was clear that Indian people would not simply give up their cultural practices and adopt "American" ones. The Hopi experience provides a good example of how much conflict surrounded this policy. When allotment surveyors came to the Hopi mesas in 1891, although some Hopis were willing to accept their allotments, a group of Oraibi men pulled up all the surveyors' stakes around Third Mesa. This act stalled the allotment process but also resulted in the arrival of federal troops and the arrest of several Hopi men. Many whites were also opposed to allotment at Hopi, and a group of them, as well as more than a hundred Hopi men, signed a petition against it in 1894. Allotment was discontinued on the Hopi reservation later that year (Whiteley 1988, 78–81).[7]

The education portion of the assimilation policy was also not well received by Hopis. In 1887 a boarding school opened at Keam's Canyon, but many Hopis refused to send their children. A day school opened near Oraibi in 1893 and encountered the same problem. These acts of resistance against government control were complicated by ongoing factionalism within the Hopi communities. At Oraibi, "Hostile" and "Friendly" factions were so named according to their general attitude toward government policies, but the factions also expressed older fissures within Oraibi society. In 1906, as a result of more than twenty years of disputes among Hopi leaders, the Hostiles were forced to leave Oraibi and resettle at Hotevilla. Their departure happened just a few days after the Snake dance, which had been delayed until September that year because of the internal strife.[8]

Even though ethnographers were working at Hopi amidst these political and social conflicts, this information was, for the most part, absent from Fewkes's and other ethnographic accounts. These accounts were not histories; their purpose was to distill a cultural essence. These scientists were interested in the essential Hopi, because, in addition to understanding the Hopis, they were interested in formulating theories about humanity as a whole. If Hopis were survivors of an earlier stage of cultural evolution, they must share some characteristics with other, similarly "primitive" peoples. For example, early ethnographic accounts tried to relate the Hopi Snake dance to other forms of "serpent worship." In an 1886 article about the Snake dance at Mishongnovi, the Smithsonian ethnographer Cosmos Mindeleff tried to connect the dance to serpent worship in ancient Mexico, snakes mentioned in the Bible, and snake rituals in India and China. And Bourke quoted at length from other authorities' meditations on serpent worship around the world and through history, but he stopped short of making an explicit connection between Hindu snake handling and the Hopi ritual (209–25).

Similarly, the Snake and Antelope ceremony Fewkes described in "The Snake Ceremonials at Walpi" was not a record of one particular performance but a conflation of observations he made at the ceremonies in 1891 and 1893. This combined account, then, was presented as the essential Snake dance. Like Bourke, Fewkes was interested in recording data about the ceremony before it disappeared, but he was more explicit about the Snake dance's being a "curious survival" of cultural evolution ([1894] 1977, 9). His main purpose in observing the dance was to determine which of five Hopi villages had the most primitive variant, which to Fewkes meant the one "more nearly like the ancestral performance" or the "oldest variants of the ceremonies" ([1900] 1986, 986). By 1898 he had seen all five variants and concluded that the most primitive was in Oraibi, the most isolated of the villages and, therefore, the least affected by outside influences. Fewkes's search demanded that he elide from his accounts the local politics of the Hopis themselves and their dealings with the world beyond their mesas. This had the effect of dehistoricizing Hopi culture, of isolating it in an imagined past, not in the present, which was full of conflict and "contaminating" influences.

Fewkes's accounts of the Hopis represented what would come to be known as the "ethnographic present," an imagined time when ethnicity last existed in a "pure" form, which in the case of North American Indians was the moment just before the Columbian "discovery" (Lyman 1982, 50). Fewkes's reference to the "heart of Africa" is an echo of this ethnographic present, imagining the ethnographer as explorer and discoverer, a kind of Livingstone of the Southwest.

Allusions to the Columbian discovery were common in the literature about the Indians of the Southwest.[9] With their settled, agricultural, and artisanal way of life, the Hopis and other Pueblo groups seemed to recall the ancient civilizations of Mesoamerica at the time of European contact. Their supposed similarities to these civilizations and their success in resisting European influence may also explain why they, and not the Navajos or the Apaches, attracted so much ethnographic attention. Because Apache and Navajo cultures had been more violently disrupted by European contact and were thus perceived as less purely "primitive," they did not fit the discovery scenario.

Ethnographic renderings of the Snake dance simultaneously recapitulated the "discovery" and the "loss" of the primitive, not only in the content of the narratives but also in their very textuality. As James Clifford has argued, the process of textualization suggested a fall from a prelapsarian, authentic oral or physical act to the word and picture. Performances of the Snake dance were authentic but transitory; writing endured. And precisely because of writing's endurance, the ethnographer became a "custodian of an essence, unimpeachable witness to an authenticity" (Clifford 1986, 113). Thus the ethnographer's authority was established not only by his ability to "discover" the true or essential primitive but also by his literacy.

"The Snake Ceremonials at Walpi," in which Fewkes included a version of the "Legend of Tí-yo, the Snake Hero" (106–19), contains a good example of how textualization ensured ethnographic authority. The legend was recorded by Alexander M. Stephen, who heard it from Wiki, a member of the Antelope society.[10] This version of the Snake legend is worth noting, because it was widely referred to and quoted in many subsequent representations of the Snake dance. It appears as a written translation of Wiki's words and so is a representation of the Indian's narrative voice. Following it is Fewkes's "Interpretation of the Myth," in which he notes that there are many variations of the story and that using it to determine the meaning of the Snake dance required interpretation:

> We see, as it were, only the crudest outlines, and only partial explanations of the ritual, and it is probably impossible for us to arrive at the true explanation from a study of the story alone. There are

> many evidences of later invention, of incorporation, and of individual explanations. I am not sanguine that the true explanation of the Snake Dance can be obtained from the Indians themselves, and if my want of faith is well grounded, this fact is without doubt of greatest importance. ([1894] 1977, 119)

As in his search for the most primitive variant of the performed Snake dance, Fewkes was interested in finding the essential meaning of the ritual. He logically sought a Hopi explanation but then rejected its "truth." Fewkes's lack of faith in the Hopis' ability to explain the meaning of the Snake dance and his faith in his own ability to do so point to how textualization helped create and enforce the unequal relationship between ethnographer and subject. Wiki is gone, as is the moment and context of his narrative, but the text remains. As a text, Wiki's version of the Snake legend is available for an interpretation—in fact, requires interpretation—that will reveal its true meaning. The scientist, not the Hopi, has the ability to "read" Hopi culture.

The illustrations that accompanied Bourke's *Snake-Dance of the Mokis of Arizona* illuminate another aspect of the process of textualization: how it "purified" the ethnographic information by erasing its native subjects. These illustrations were made by Alexander F. Harmer, a sergeant in the U.S. Army and "a student of the Philadelphia Academy of Fine Arts" (Bourke [1884] 1984, xix–xx). Apparently, Harmer's illustrations were made after the fact, based on Bourke's sketches and on the objects Bourke collected.[11] The illustration of the Snake dance in Figure 2 was meant to be understood with the help of Bourke's text, which explains in detail the number of participants and the order in which they appeared. The image is organized spatially to emphasize the number and categories of dancers and the repetition of their posture and movements. This view of the procession shows a relatively accurate, or informationally dense, view of the ceremony, complete with crowds of observers and the ubiquitous pueblo dogs. The groups are rigidly ordered for ease of classification; each figure is secure in its place and easily identifiable when referred to in the text.

Figures 3 and 4 further disassemble the first view. Figure 3 reproduces the first Snake priest to the left of the rock outcropping in Figure 2, and Figure 4 is almost literally a deconstruction of the

Figure 2. Snake Dance of the Moquis: Pueblo of Hualpi, Arizona, August 12th, 1881, *by Alexander F. Harmer. (Reprinted from Bourke,* Snake-Dance of the Moquis, *plate 2)*

Snake priest. These last two drawings decontextualize the dancer and make a taxonomy of the ceremony's paraphernalia. The whole is categorized and broken down to its smallest parts, as if to say the ritual is understandable as the sum of its parts, that what may seem mysterious in its entirety, once subjected to collection and categorization, is entirely understandable.

At the same time, the Snake priest has completely disappeared, and all that remains is his costume, turning him into a kind of paper doll and reducing the ceremony to the sort of ethnographic evidence one might find in a museum. And this, in fact, was what Bourke believed would be the fate of the Snake dance; eventually, only the bits and pieces of the costume would survive. By means of these three illustrations, Bourke "preserved" the material culture and the context of the dance by relegating its relics to the museum and the book. The ethnographies of Bourke and Fewkes are like pastoral elegies in that they evoke the figure of the Indian as a ruin, "an always-disappearing structure that invites imaginative reconstruction."[12] By "vanishing"

Figure 3. Dancer Holding Snake in Mouth, *by Alexander F. Harmer. (Reprinted from Bourke,* Snake-Dance of the Moquis, *plate 14)*

the Indian subject, these texts leave a set of "Indian" signifiers available for "imaginative reconstruction" by the reader. The gradual erasure of Hopis in the three Harmer illustrations also suggests that this imaginative reconstruction might involve a kind of substitution, in which the reader substitutes him- or herself for the Indian. Figure 3 is reminiscent of a mid-nineteenth-century fashion plate; the infor-

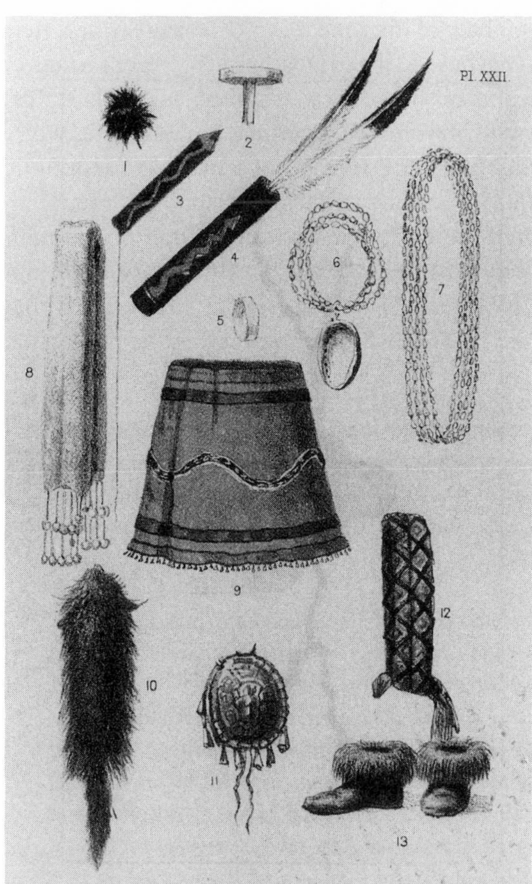

Figure 4. Illustration depicting parts of the Snake dancer's costume, by Alexander F. Harmer. (Reprinted from Bourke, Snake-Dance of the Moquis, *plate 22)*

mation presented is embodied in the costume, not the Indian "model," and suggests that the costume is something the reader might acquire or even wear. Indeed, one might see the items in Figure 4 in a museum case, but the manner in which the items are depicted is also reminiscent of the way goods were displayed in mail-order catalogues and department-store windows. Thus the vanished Indian in these representations could serve a reflexive purpose; the space left by the vanished subject could serve as a mirror, and the residual relics could become available and appropriable.

Like other ethnographers of his time, Bourke was creating a new form of representation; in these early ethnographic representations of the Snake dance, the seams of the narrative showed, as did rhetorical experiments and borrowings from other genres. For example, while the drawings in Bourke's account are rigorous in their taxonomic organization, they employ or allude to various visual grammars, including, as we have seen, the representational grammar of commercial displays. Bourke's writing, too, is peppered not only with moments of Gothic frisson but also with picturesque descriptions that recall travel writing. Just before he begins to describe the procession illustrated in Figure 2, he sets the stage in a more dramatic way:

> Fill every nook and cranny of this mass of buildings with a congregation of Moqui women, maids and matrons, dressed in their graceful garb of dark-blue cloth with lemon stitching; tie up the little girl's hair in big Chinese Puffs at the sides; throw in a liberal allowance of children, naked and half-naked; give color and tone by using blankets of scarlet and blue and black, girdles of red and green, and necklaces of silver and coral, abalone, and chalchihuitl.
>
> For variety's sake add a half-dozen tall, lithe, square-shouldered Navajoes, and as many keen, dyspeptic-looking Americans, one of these a lady; localise the scene by the introduction of ladders, earthenware chimneys, piles of cedar-fuel and sheep manure, scores of mangy pups, and other scores of old squaws carrying on their backs little babies or great ollas of water, and with a hazy atmosphere and partially-clouded sky as accessories, you have a faithful picture of the square in the Pueblo of Hualpi, Arizona, as it appeared on this eventful 12th day of August 1881. ([1884] 1984, 156)

Bourke, in employing the language of the picturesque traveler as defined in the eighteenth century by William Gilpin, illustrates the aesthetic appeal of the ritual's setting. His concern with color, shading, and composition turns the empirical catalogue into a "picture." It became formulaic to describe observers of the Snake dance in this way. Writers almost always mentioned the variety and colorfulness of the observers—Hopi, Navajo, and Anglo—demonstrating that these groups could, as observers of the spectacle, share common ground.

Cosmos Mindeleff's 1886 account of the Snake dance contains another example of representational experimentation. His article in the journal *Science* was illustrated with several line drawings, in-

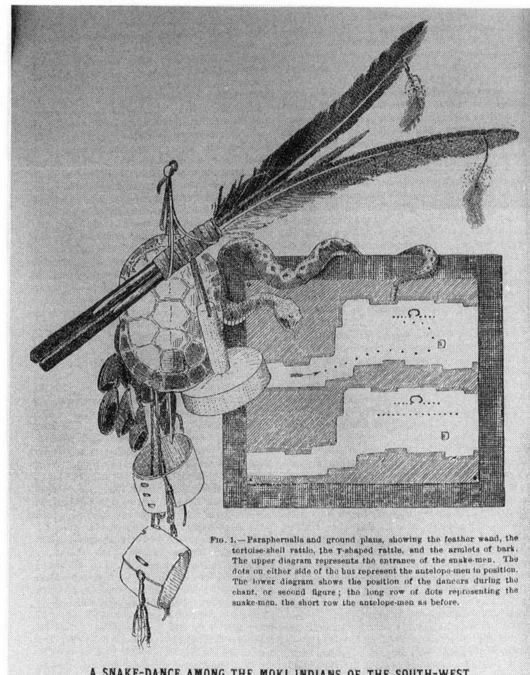

Figure 5. Illustration accompanying Mindeleff's "Indian Snake Dance."

cluding Figure 5. This image, whose maker is not credited, combines ground plans for the dance at Mishongnovi with drawings of parts of a Snake dancer's costume and a live snake. The diagrams of the dance appear as a drawing tacked onto a board around which a snake coils. The "paraphernalia" are shown tied together with cord hanging from a nail or tack driven into an invisible wall. It is an artful arrangement, combining the picturesque and scientific, like something one might find in a museum or a man's library. The drawing presents both the artifacts collected at the Snake dance and diagrams showing the context for the objects' deployment. The image reveals something about the problems of representation; the collected data is reassembled, re-presented using the vocabulary of still-life painting. These disparate objects are forced together into an arrangement whose representational conceit calls attention to itself: the diagrams of the dance are presented as three-dimensional, but the "live" snake is a two-dimensional drawing, as is the tack from which the paraphernalia hang.

The representation of the snake is especially interesting. It is part of the dance paraphernalia, but the dancers are absent, or rather are represented by dots in the diagram. In this regard, the image is very much like Harmer's illustration of the Snake dancer's costume in Bourke's text. The snake is "alive," serving almost as a stand-in for the dancer. The absence of human beings suggests a scientific purity about the information presented. Like writing, the objects will endure, but not the Indian. The imaginary ethnographic present is represented better by the objects than by the human being, whose presence suggests history. This image is purified of that presence.

Fewkes's "Snake Ceremonials at Walpi" employs a great variety of graphic media; the written account is accompanied by numerous drawings, charts, diagrams, photographs, and paintings that seem to record every detail of the ceremony. Drawings of disembodied arms and legs illustrate body-paint markings; a diagram renders a bird's-eye view of the inside of a kiva; there is a photograph of the Snake priest, Kopeli; several color plates depict sand paintings; and two drawings by Julian Scott show *A Group of Snake Dancers* and *Chief of the Antelope Priests.* Some of the drawings are based on Fewkes's notebooks in which he recorded data in the field. Fewkes also arranged for artists Julian Scott, F. H. Lungren, and W. K. Fales to be initiated into the Antelope clan and admitted into the kiva to witness part of the Walpi ceremony in 1893 (Fewkes [1894] 1977, 5). But it seems that only Scott's images were included in the published account, and he painted the color plates.[13]

The graphic representations in Fewkes's account function like a series of architectural renderings, presenting the context of the ceremony as well as separate details. For example, in one drawing a snake kilt is shown stretched out flat, in another, as it is worn. One of the sand paintings is shown in context in a diagram of the kiva and is enlarged as a color plate on another page. And Kopeli appears alone in a photograph as well as in the bird's-eye view of the kiva interior. These various representations were meant to render a complete and understandable account of the Snake dance. As in the Mindeleff illustration, the proliferation of media and points of view is assumed to reproduce reality more accurately.

Fewkes's account also rendered the world of the ceremony in miniature. The experience of reading his book is like holding the data, which is miniaturized and framed by the text, in one's hand. This feeling is intensified by a life-sized rendering of a portion of the hand of one of the participants. As Susan Stewart has written, "The miniature, linked to nostalgic versions of childhood and history, presents a diminutive, and thereby manipulatable, version of experience, a version which is domesticated and protected from contamination" (1984, 69). As the reader "operates" the book by reading and juxtaposing the diagrams, drawings, and photographs, a total, pristine, other world emerges. The reader *apprehends* the data as virtually "at hand," as a collection of significant objects. The book becomes a kind of "social space," a "talisman to the body and emblem of the self; . . . microcosm and macrocosm; . . . commodity and knowledge, . . . fact and fiction" (Stewart 1984, 41).

In addition to drawings and paintings, one of the most powerful tools of representation the ethnographers used in recording the Snake dance was photography, which was considered the most transparent medium for apprehending and representing ethnographic information.[14] From the beginning of ethnographic interest in the Southwest, photography had been an important method of collecting information. John K. Hillers and William H. Jackson photographed the Hopis in the 1870s as part of the government surveys of the region, and by the 1890s photographers were participating in every ethnographic expedition to the Southwest. Photographs began to appear in published accounts of the Snake dance in the 1890s with the invention of halftone reproduction. Many of the early ethnographic photographs were portraits of individuals or groups of Indians; the glass plates and tripods of the 1870s and 1880s prohibited more "candid" images.[15] There were also many commercial photographers working in the region, George Wharton James, Ben Wittick, and Adam Clark Vroman being among the most active (Hooper 1989, 14–15). They all photographed the Snake dance, and many of their photographs found their way into ethnographic accounts.

In 1902 the Field Columbian Museum published "The Mishongnovi Ceremonies of the Snake and Antelope Fraternities" under the auspices of the Stanley McCormick Hopi Expedition and written by ethnologists George A. Dorsey and H. R. Voth. Voth, who began as a

Mennonite missionary to the Hopis, later published many ethnographic accounts of their culture (Eggan 1971). This publication contains a very detailed description of all nine days of the Snake and Antelope ceremony, the four days following it, and a retelling of the Snake legend. It is profusely illustrated with photographs by the commercial photographers George Wharton James and Sumner W. Matteson, Field Museum photographer Charles H. Carpenter, and Voth himself. All four had access to kivas and, apparently, the cooperation of some Hopis. Many of the photographs were made inside the kivas and show members of the Snake and Antelope societies engaged in various activities in the days prior to the public ceremony. The completeness and detail of this account seem to be a result of the unprecedented openness of some of the participants and the changes in photographic technology, such as roll film and flash light, which enabled the photographers to make images in low light with relatively short exposures.

One of the most impressive things about these photographs is their intrusive nature. They fascinate because they seem candid, but they also pry. One in particular stands out. Captioned "Snake priests asleep on the roof of the Snake kiva (a flashlight picture in the open air at three o'clock in the morning)," it was taken between the fifth and sixth day of the ceremony and has a distinctly voyeuristic quality to it. It reminds one of Jacob Riis's flashlight photographs of the urban poor in *How the Other Half Lives* (1890) and demonstrates the similar aims and methods of Fewkes's work and Riis's urban ethnography. Like Riis's, these photographs expose what was hidden, but they also make clear the power of the photographic gaze to objectify its subject.

Another photograph from this expedition, Figure 6, was not reproduced in the museum's publication. Taken by Sumner Matteson, it shows Charles Carpenter photographing a member of the Snake society while Dorsey takes notes (Longo 1980, 19). A large-format camera on a tripod is aimed at a Hopi man seated in a chair placed against a wall. The imbalance of power is clear: the complicated, overbearing apparatus of ethnographic collection and representation and the Hopi man alone, representative of something "Hopi." One can imagine the contrast between this photograph and the image Carpenter is making—the one suitable for publication. Carpenter's

Figure 6. Charles Carpenter photographing a member of the Snake clan as George Dorsey takes notes at Mishongnovi. Photographed by Sumner Matteson (1902). (Courtesy of the Milwaukee Public Museum)

portrait will appear "natural," but the text will not reveal that its production required substantial staging and manipulation.

It would be tempting to claim that the hegemony of ethnographers over Hopis was complete and unrelenting, but that would be oversimplifying the situation. The relationship between ethnographers and Hopis was complex and locked in a process of continual negotiation. Within the ethnographies of the Snake dance there are moments when this process of negotiation surfaces. For example, Bourke included in his *Snake-Dance of the Moquis* a remarkable account of a conversation he had in November of 1881 at Zuni with Nanahe, a Hopi man who had observed Bourke at the Snake dance at Walpi. Frank Cushing was their interpreter. When he met Bourke, Nanahe said:

> We saw you writing down everything as you sat in the Estufa, and we knew that you had all that man could learn from his eyes. We

> didn't like to have you down there. No other man has ever shown so little regard for what we thought, but we knew that you had come there under orders, and that you were only doing what you thought you ought to do to learn all about our ceremonies. So we concluded to let you stay. ([1884] 1984, 182)

Cushing had apparently prepared the Hopis for Bourke's arrival, and his influence had something to do with their decision to let Bourke into the kiva. But Nanahe makes it clear that they were extremely reluctant to do so. Bourke wasn't the last ethnographer allowed to record ceremonial activities inside kivas, however, and most ethnographers did not include in their accounts of the Snake dance any record of how intrusive their presence was.

According to Bourke, although initially Nanahe refused to tell him anything about the secret societies, he eventually agreed to explain some of the rituals he witnessed. But he prefaced his remarks thus:

> A secret order is for the benefit of the whole world, that it may call the whole world its children, and that the whole world may call it father, and not for the exclusive benefits of the few men who belong to it. But its privileges are the property of its members, and should be preserved with jealous vigilance; since, if they became known to the whole world, they would cease to be secrets, and the order would be destroyed, and its benefit to the world would pass away. (183–84)

Nahane clearly explained why the members of the Snake and Antelope societies would not want Bourke or anyone else to witness their activities. The knowledge these societies held was of benefit to the world.[16]

Ethnographers made it their business to "discover" and then publicize Hopi ritual knowledge. Consequently, the men who recorded their rituals (particularly the Snake dance) most thoroughly—Voth, Stephen, and Fewkes—were and still are not well regarded among Hopis. In *Sun Chief: The Autobiography of a Hopi Indian* (1942), Don Talayesva, who was born at Oraibi in 1890, remembered Voth in connection with a year of drought:

> The land was very dry, the crops suffered, and even the Snake dance failed to bring much rain. We tried to discover the reason for our

> plight, and remembered the Rev. Voth who had stolen so many of our ceremonial secrets and had even carried off sacred images and altars to equip a museum and become a rich man. When he had worked here in my boyhood, the Hopi were afraid of him and dared not lay their hands on him or any other missionary, lest they be jailed by the Whites. During the ceremonies this wicked man would force his way into the kiva and write down everything that he saw. He wore shoes with solid heels, and when the Hopi tried to put him out of the kiva he would kick them. (Talayesva 1942, 252)[17]

In this account one gets some sense of the position Hopis were in as they tried to negotiate with ethnographers determined to "save" Hopi culture.

As ethnographers were creating narratives about Hopis, so Hopis were creating narratives about ethnographers. In 1980 Edmund Nequatewa published a story he said Hopis have for decades told about why Fewkes abruptly interrupted his research at Walpi in the fall of 1898. The official explanation, published in the Bureau of American Ethnology's (BAE) annual report for that year, states that an outbreak of smallpox both interrupted the Hopis' ceremonial cycle and endangered Fewkes. According to Nequatewa, Hopis have quite a different story: at the end of a day of note taking in a kiva, Fewkes was asked to leave because the fearsome earth god, Masauwu, was about to appear. Fewkes retired to his house and locked the door. While he was writing his notes, Masauwu appeared in the room with him. At first Fewkes told the being to go away, because he was busy, but when he realized who it was, he became afraid:

> Then the being talked and talked to him, and finally the Doctor "gave up to him" and said he would become a Hopi and be like them and believe in Masauwu, and Masauwu cast his spell on him and they both became like little children and all night long they played around together and Masauwu gave the Doctor no rest.
>
> And it was not long after that Dr. Fewkes went away but it was not on account of the smallpox as you now know. (37)

Two aspects of this story are striking. First, just as Fewkes reinterpreted the explanations of the Snake dance offered by Hopis, this story reinterprets the official explanation for Fewkes's departure. Second, the story imagines Fewkes's coming under the spell of Masauwu, demonstrating that the greater power lies with the deity, not the ethnographer. The result is not only that Fewkes "becomes a Hopi" but also, and perhaps more important, that he stops his note taking. Masauwu's appearance brings to an end the Fewkesian inscription of Hopi culture.

THE SNAKE DANCE IN ETHNOGRAPHIC EXHIBITS

The "textualization" of Native American cultures falls within the metaphor of collecting scientific data. But at a more literal level, ethnologists were deeply involved in collecting the material culture of the groups they studied. The collections they made were another form of representation, and the process of collecting and displaying ethnographic artifacts was another means by which Native Americans were rendered culturally useful. The irony was that the ethnographers traded manufactured goods for native goods, thereby dismantling the very cultures they sought to preserve (Parezo 1986, 3; Coombes 1991, 199).

Like other ethnographic representations, the process of collecting caused Indians to "vanish" and made relics of their cultures. These relics were in turn preserved in museums, which were like Noah's arks of salvaged cultures (Stewart 1984, 152). In the museum each object stood for the whole, and the collection of fragments stood for the totality of the Indian's world in microcosm. The aim of ethnographic collecting was completeness, like Audubon's *Birds of North America* or Catlin's Indian Gallery, but at the same time each object was overburdened with meaning, because the scientist-collectors assumed that one could know an entire culture from its smallest artifact. Furthermore, the process of collecting reinforced the *availability* of Indian cultures; collecting appeared as a simple process: Indians simply gave up their belongings (Todorov 1984, 39). As in the ideology of Manifest Destiny, which claimed in part that Indians were not fit to possess the vast land of the continent, the ideology of collecting insisted that Indians were not fit "keepers" of their culture. They did not know the value of their cultural property—which was sure to increase as it became (inevitably) scarcer; and even if they did value it as the ethnographers did, they weren't equipped to preserve it.

Assembled back east in the American Museum of Natural History in New York, the National Museum of the Smithsonian Institution, or the Peabody Museum at Harvard, Native American artifacts and other documentation were displayed alongside natural science specimens. The "presence" of Indians in museums of natural history was possible and even inevitable given anthropological understanding of the primitive. Indian objects were moved into the pure, innocent realm of nature, into a lost natural past—this loss of nature being demonstrated by the presence of natural specimens in the museum. Donna Haraway has called the American Museum of Natural History in New York City "a monumental reproduction of the Garden of Eden." Situated on the edge of Central Park, whose purpose was to "heal the over-wrought or decadent city dweller with a prophylactic dose of nature," the museum offered a similar healing experience by taking the visitor back to a prelapsarian time when the relationship between humans and nature was uncomplicated and "pure" (20). The American Indian was the icon of this state of being.

In the last quarter of the nineteenth century, as more and more museums of natural history were established, with at least part of their missions being to educate the public, and as ethnographic collections grew, museum ethnologists were faced with the problem of how to display ethnographic artifacts. In the 1870s and 1880s in American museums and expositions such artifacts were arranged on shelves in glass-enclosed cases or were displayed on the occasional wax manikin. But after the World's Columbian Exposition in Chicago, a new display technique came into use: the "life group." The practice of using individual life-sized models of native peoples to display material culture was in practice by the mid-1870s, but at the Chicago exposition ethnologists designed displays that grouped manikins inside glass cases. Each arrangement depicted a number of individuals engaged in a particular activity, the aim being to show more contextual information and action. Ethnographers from the United States National Museum made several groups especially for the Chicago exposition, including "Zuni Ritual of Creation" and "Zuni Bread-makers," as well as potters, a belt maker, weavers, Sioux women dressing hides, and a Jivaro Indian. The figures were based on photographs by Hillers, Jackson, and others; on actual Native Americans, such as the Zuni men who accompanied Cushing to Washington in 1882; and on the ethnologists themselves. In 1895 Boas posed for the Kwakiutl Hamatsa dance, and Cushing posed for several Zuni and Plains figures (Hinsley 1983, 59; Truettner 1985, 67). After the Chicago exposition these figures appeared in exhibits at the National Museum and had long and varied "lives." For example, some 1893 Zuni manikins were recycled later as Navajo weavers, and the Zuni bread makers of 1893 appeared as a "Hopi Household" in about 1910. Sometime between 1910 and 1920, a life group of the Snake dance appeared in the National Museum.[18]

The life group was one way to solve the problem of how to represent collected ethnographic information about a ceremony (or other primitive activity). But how could ethnographers reconstitute an event such as the Snake dance, which existed in a certain time and place and was performed by living people in another time*less* place? In the first few decades of the twentieth century the makers of life groups answered this question by striving for greater realism: the displays became increasingly illusionistic, employing theatrical techniques such as realistically painted backdrops and elaborate lighting, and the manikins went from being "pieces of sculpture to 'pictures from life'" (Hinsley 1981, 108). At the peak of this trend Clark Wissler wrote in praise of the Hopi life group at the American Museum of Natural History in 1915:

> Thus, in the group as a whole, we get a veritable snapshot of Hopi life, precisely what one might see in a glance through a village. It was not designed to force into the composition many phases of life not usually seen in juxtaposition, but to present one of the commonest scenes of prosaic life. It was not our aim to instruct the visitor in details, such as how cloth is made, how houses are built, the whole life history of a clay pot from the grinding of the clay to the firing, and the like—all subjects far better treated in the exhibition cases of the hall—but to give a concrete idea of Hopi life in its native setting. In a way, the production is a human habitat group, analogous to bird and mammal habitat groups. (344)

Wissler's evocation of the "snapshot" as the ideal aim of the life group and his comparison of life groups to "bird and mammal habitat groups" suggest that in the life group photographic representation and taxidermy came together. In bringing the photograph to life, or into three dimensions, the life group aimed to capture something lost. The ultimate referent of the life group was the life of Indians, but manikins stood in for living Indians, and one cannot help but compare the manikins to the taxidermied animals that inhabit the same museums. The Indian collected, like the collected bird or mammal, is, metaphorically, the Indian hunted and killed, and Indians' presence in the museum is a kind of taxidermic preservation.

The aesthetic of realism that governed design of the life groups and nature dioramas provided the means to make real a profoundly idealistic wish for a primal, pure past in which humans and animals lived together in an orderly, Edenic world. In spite of its grotesque overtones, the Snake dance seemed to typify this wish, because it showed humans and animals in an intimate relationship. However, the aesthetic of the life groups rendered invisible the massive capital and the violence of collecting that created the "world" of the natural history museum. As textual representations caused Native Americans to "vanish," so life groups erased living Indians and replaced them with manikins, which were themselves interchangeable. And as the renderings of individual Snake dancers in Bourke's account suggested fashion plates or department-store windows, so life groups invited the viewer to "try on" various Indian identities.

Another approach to the problem of representing Indians to the public in ethnographic displays was, of course, to present actual Native Americans, and this strategy was employed on a grand scale at world's fairs. In the United States the first world's fair to present exhibits of living Native Americans was the 1893 Columbian Exposition in Chicago. Among those on display, the Indians of the Southwest were widely represented, especially the Pueblo groups. A group of Navajos lived on the grounds next to the Anthropological Building and made and sold jewelry and blankets, and some Pueblos lived on the Midway Plaisance in a plaster representation of their home (Trennert 1987, 136).[19]

At Chicago, the ethnographic exhibits in the Anthropological Building were overseen by Frederic Ward Putnam, director and curator of the Peabody Museum at Harvard and head of the Department of Ethnology and Archaeology for the fair. Putnam had the help of, among others, Franz Boas. In the Government Building, Otis T. Mason of the United States National Museum and William H. Holmes, who was working for the Smithsonian, organized and presented exhibits about primitive peoples of the world. The Chicago exposition established a cultural geography for American Indians. On one hand the anthropological and government exhibits showed the Indians' role in the evolution of humans from savage to civilized. The ethnographic displays in the Anthropological Building and in the Government Building and the living Native Americans on display nearby depicted what was "vanishing." On the other hand, there was the exotic appeal of the Midway. There, American Indians and other primitive peoples were presented as entertaining but not threatening. All of these displays depicted versions of the past; the future of Native Americans was not represented.

The 1904 Louisiana Purchase Exposition in St. Louis was planned to rival the Chicago exposition and included, among other things, more elaborate and bigger Indian exhibits, which were assembled under the direction of William J. McGee of the Smithsonian. The Department of Anthropology's exhibits were designed to show "the evolution of industrial art, and the expansion of those mental and moral forces which obtain in modern civilization" (*History* 1905, 43) and were presented in several sections in the Anthropology Building, which contained the Archeology Section, History Section, and Laboratories of Anthropometry and Psychometry. A large "Congress of the Races" surrounded the Anthropology Building and presented primitive people from around the world, including representatives from North American groups, "Patagonian Giants," and "African Pygmies." These groups lived in reconstructions of their native dwellings and were arranged in evolutionary order. The largest anthropological exhibit was the Philippine exhibit, which covered forty-seven acres and represented the United States' newest colonial subjects (Hoxie 1977, 290). Among the Native Americans present almost half were from the Southwest and California, including Navajos, Apaches, Pueblos, Hopis, Papagos, Pimas and Maricopas, and Cocopahs (Trennert 1987, 146–47).

The Bureau of Indian Affairs building (the "Indian Building") overlooked the Congress of Races and housed a model Indian school, which showed the process of assimilation in progress as Native

Figure 7. Geronimo at the Louisiana Purchase Exposition in St. Louis, 1904. (National Anthropological Archives, Smithsonian Institution)

American students learned to become useful citizens. In the Indian Building, Geronimo, who was still a prisoner of war, sat in a booth, between a Pueblo potter and women grinding corn, and sold bows and arrows as well as photographs and autographs (Drinnon 1980, 340) (Fig. 7). This tableau was a reminder, no doubt, of the military conquest of the Apaches and other "hostile" Indians, but it also represents the twin strains of primitivism associated with Native Americans. The women grinding corn and making ceramic vessels fit the stereotype of Southwest Indians as artisans, as peaceful, industrious people who work with their hands. In contrast, Geronimo was presented not only as a relic of a savage past (witness the bows and arrows) but also as a celebrity (selling autographs and photos of himself). Both strains of primitive stereotyping, the noble (but doomed) savage and the industrious artisan, represented a past that vanished or was vanquished. Juxtaposed with the model school, which depicted the future, Geronimo and the Pueblo women represented what was passing away. But Geronimo and the Pueblo women weren't simply going to disappear; they would persist as mythologies about the primitive, and these mythologies would continue to define the cultural roles Indian people could play in American culture.

On the mile-long Pike, the Midway Plaisance of the St. Louis exposition, one could see what was by now the standard encyclopedic accumulation of exotic attractions, the world in microcosm. Visitors to the Pike could see a spectacle of the Boer War staged twice a day, an "Irish Village," the Tyrolean Alps, streets of Cairo, Constantinople, Jerusalem, and Seville, an "Esquimau Village," and a Cliff Dwellers exhibit (*History* 1905, 717).[20] Visitors to the Cliff Dwellers exhibit passed through a gateway made to look like rocky cliffs, into an outdoor area that contained what was purported to be a replica of Taos Pueblo. Inside this structure was a theater called the "Snake Kiva," where visitors could see reenactments of a "Pueblo Snake Dance" (Trennert 1987, 149). *The Complete Portfolio of Photographs of the World's Fair,* a souvenir book of the exposition, reproduced a photograph of a group of Snake dancers (Fig. 8). The caption claimed that "there were many famous dances given by the Pueblo Indians of the Pike which visitors to the exposition saw for the first, and probably for the last time in their lives. Some were graceful, some were fantastic and some were horrible. None combined all these features in a greater degree than the Snake Dance, which the trio above are about to execute" (n.p.). This passage is haunted by the specter of the vanishing Indian as well as the Gothic thrill of the Snake dance. The appeal of the Snake dance came not only from seeing men handle snakes but also from the notion that the dance was about to disappear. Its presence on the Pike seems to indicate that it was not considered a legitimate part of the Indian's future and that it was best relegated to the realm of entertainment.

One mission of ethnographic displays was to educate the public about cultural difference and national identity. The standard against which "others" were understood was late nineteenth-century American civilization. Industrial expositions and natural history museums, as encyclopedic representations of the world, showed where Native Americans fit in and displayed the superiority of civilization and the inferiority of the primitive. These spectacles of otherness si-

Figure 8. Pueblo Snake Dance. *(Reprinted from* Complete Portfolio of Photographs of the World's Fair, St. Louis, 1904*)*

multaneously created and demonstrated difference and then accrued power by incorporating it. Judith Williamson notes that "to have something 'different' captive in our midst reassures us of the liberality of our own system and provides a way of re-presenting real difference in tamed form" (1986, 116). That Indians were represented in the high as well as low culture areas of the fairs is testimony to this process, and the exhibits of Indian people also call to mind John Berger's meditations on looking at animals in zoos: "Everywhere animals disappear. In zoos they constitute the living monument to their own disappearance." Zoos, like museums and fairs, are "sites of enforced marginalisation" that operate through enforced visibility (Berger 1980, 24). The museum was the proper place for Indians; in the "real" world, according to government policy, they were supposed to be vanishing through assimilation. But Indian people were not in fact simply assimilating or vanishing. They resisted and persisted.

These representations of the primitive assumed a "civilized" viewer, but at least one observer of the Chicago exposition tried to suggest what a "primitive" viewer might think about the displays. In "Types and People at the Fair," a kind of ethnography of visitors to the fair, J. A. Mitchell imagined an Indian looking back:

> If the native Indian were of a reflective turn of mind, all this might awaken unpleasant thoughts. Judging from outside appearance, however, he has no thoughts whatever. He stalks solemnly about the grounds with a face as impassive as his wooden counterparts on Sixth Avenue. And yet *he* is the American. He is the only one among us who had ancestors to be discovered. He is the aboriginal; the first occupant and owner; the only one here with an hereditary right to the country we are celebrating. (186)

Mitchell's attitude toward the Indian's mental capabilities is clearly condescending, but the passage suggests the tenuousness of the ideological conceits at the heart of the vast display. From the Indian's point of view, history since Columbus might be imagined very differently from the fair's presentation of it. And, however awkwardly or spuriously, Mitchell asks readers to imagine an Indian as an observer, not an exhibit, which suggests that Native Americans persisted as *subjects* capable, at least, of watching the spectacle.

Another example from a later Chicago exposition also illustrates how ethnographic representations might be received by Native Americans. In *Sun Chief,* Don Talayesva recalled that in 1939 a University of Chicago anthropologist, Fred Eggan, showed him a copy of a 1901 account of the Soyal ceremony written by George A. Dorsey and H. R. Voth. Talayesva remembered that Dr. Eggan said,

> You remember that in 1933 some Hopis from here were at the World's Fair in Chicago, went to the Field Museum, and saw what they thought was a statue of you dressed in a ceremonial costume used in the Soyal. You know that when they returned they claimed that you had sold the secrets and ceremonial equipment and made much trouble for you. Now I will let you see this book.

Talayesva continued:

> When he opened it, I was surprised to see pictures of secret altars, how the members of the Soyal dressed and what they did. This evil man Voth had written out all the secrets, not only of the Soyal but

> of other ceremonies. I saw the names and pictures of the Soyal officers, those old timers, and recognized every one of them. Now at the time I was only a little boy and had not been initiated into the Wowochim. Fred also showed me altars of the Snake and the Antelope ceremonies. These things were of greater value to the Hopi than anything else in the world and the Whites had gotten them away from us. I felt very badly. But I did not blame the Whites for buying them as much as I blamed the old Hopis, the head Soyal Priest, Shokhungyoma, and Chief Lolulomai. There was even a picture of my great-uncle, Talasquaptewa, who acted as Star Priest. If those chiefs had not permitted Voth to take the pictures and watch the ceremonies, they would never have been published. Fred urged me not to feel badly about it. When he closed the book, I asked how much it would cost. The only good thing about it was the fact that it was clear proof that I was not the one who had sold the secrets. I wanted it, for if any Hopi ever charged me again with selling secrets all I would need to defend myself was this book. Fred left about nine-thirty, and I went to bed. But I was so worried that I never slept until one-thirty in the morning. With all our ceremonial secrets out, it is no wonder that our gods are offended and fail to send us enough snow and rain, and that sickness, droughts, and other misfortunes come upon us. (344)

The Hopis who saw the manikin of the Soyal ceremony participant did not "read" it as other tourists might have, or as the makers of the exhibit intended it to be read. The exchange of cultural information broke down; the Hopi visitors did not see the manikin as a generic Hopi but as a portrait of Don Talayesva and then assumed that his "presence" in the museum indicated his complicity in the selling of information and ceremonial equipment. This encounter shows how, for the Hopi visitors, the realism of the display failed to purify it of its human presence; rather, what they saw was precisely a human, an individual, Don Talayesva. Furthermore, their interpretation reinserted the historical narrative into the museum display, which was supposed to move the Indian into a realm that was timeless and to erase the actual history of the ethnographic encounter.

The Hopis' encounter with "Don" in the museum is mirrored by Talayesva's encounter with the published ethnography by Dorsey and Voth. He saw individuals also; Talayesva did not read it as an ethnography but as a kind of family album, a different sort of historical record. And the book was both the source and vindication of Talayesva's problem. He suggested another exchange: he would buy the book from Eggan to use as proof that it was not he who gave the information to the ethnologists.

It is not clear from *Sun Chief* whether Talayesva was able to buy the book, but the incident illustrates the confusion that could result when representations of "others" were seen by "others." The codes used in the construction of the ethnographic display were reinterpreted and new meaning was made. The products of colonialism inevitably returned to the site of their origin as commodities sold to the "natives." The products of ethnography—museum displays and monographs—were not produced with the intention of becoming useful to Native Americans, but they did return, in unexpected ways with unforseen consequences.

THE SNAKE DANCE AS A TOURIST ATTRACTION

As the Indians of the Southwest were being presented to the nation at the Chicago and St. Louis expositions, the railroads in the Southwest were encouraging tourists to visit the region. In its tourist literature, the Atchison, Topeka and Santa Fe Railway (ATSF), whose routes came closest to the Hopi mesas, promoted the Snake dance as one of the major attractions of the region. Publicists for the railroad, like the organizers of the fairs and expositions, promised that the spectacle would be educational as well as entertaining.

In 1900 the Santa Fe Railway published a pamphlet called *The Moki Snake Dance, a popular account of that unparalleled dramatic pagan ceremony of the Pueblo Indians of Tusayan, Arizona, with incidental mention of their life and customs,* by Walter Hough, a Smithsonian anthropologist. And in 1903 the railway published *Indians of the Southwest,* by George A. Dorsey, at the time curator of anthropology at the Field Columbian Museum. Both accounts note the region's appeal to overcivilized urbanites. Tourists could "mount a sturdy bronco, and forget for a time the cares and conventionalities of civilized life in a simple, wholesome and joyous existence in the sunlit air of the desert" (Hough 1900, 54). And both works stressed the Indian cultures as the region's main attractions. Hough's account of the Snake dance is a step-by-step description of the final day's events written with the tourist in mind. He describes costumes in the dance to help the visitor identify the various participants, and he quotes Fewkes's Snake legend. Throughout the book he characterizes Hopis using highly romanticized terms: peaceful, childlike, welcoming to tourists. Writing that the "Mokis are so like children that a smile lurks just behind a sorrow," Hough reassures tourists that even though Hopis perform the lurid Snake dance, they are not dangerous, and reminds readers that Indians are living examples of the childhood of man. The pamphlet ends with the warning that if readers wanted to see these charming primitives, they had better hurry: "Fortunate is the person, who before it is too late, sees under so favorable aspect their charming life in the old new world" (51).

Although both Hough's and Dorsey's accounts were sincere efforts to provide accurate information about the Indian cultures they described, they emphasized certain aspects of the cultures that would appeal to tourists, specifically the rituals Indians performed, the objects they crafted, and their peaceful nature. Dorsey's *Indians of the Southwest* is a considerably longer work and is essentially a guidebook, divided into chapters on each culture group, including a day-by-day account of the Snake dance. Dorsey plays tour guide and uses the conceit of journeying through the region, stopping periodically to discuss what he encounters there. In noting the distinguishing characteristics of different groups of Indians, his account is rather like a field guide to birds. He lends scientific validity to the touristic desire to see Indians: "If we may better understand civilized man of to-day by a knowledge of man in more primitive conditions, then surely the Southwest forms a field, not only to scientific students but to all who have a broad interest in mankind, second to that presented by no other region in the world" (5).

Dorsey's involvement in tourism may have come out of a commitment to education, but he was also committed to the Santa Fe Railway. In his book's preface he explains that his host on his 1899 junket was C. A. Higgins, the assistant general passenger agent of the Santa Fe, and in 1901 Dorsey made a trip with another Santa Fe official (5). His account includes plenty of information about how to reach the Indian sights from the Santa Fe lines. Thus, Dorsey, like other ethnographers and anthropologists, worked within a compli-

Figure 9. Photographic montage showing Snake Dance of the Moquis *(August 17, 1889) and* "Ng-Nue-si," Moqui Indian Girl, *by Ben Wittick. Because the public part of the Snake and Antelope ceremony at Walpi was held in the late afternoon and was in the shade, photographs were hard to get, but Wittick managed to take some successful photographs of the 1889 performance. The photograph is paired with another of the Southwest's picturesque attractions, a "Hopi maiden." (National Anthropological Archives, Smithsonian Institution)*

cated institutional matrix that included not only private and public museums and universities but also corporations with vested interests in the region and the people they studied.

Dorsey's and Hough's guidebooks were illustrated with dozens of photographs by commercial photographers, including Ben Wittick, Adam Clark Vroman, and George Wharton James. Although these photographers' works also appeared in ethnographic accounts, the guidebook photos emphasized the formally picturesque aspects of the Indians—the elements of contrast, composition, and rhythm. In addition to the photographs of Hopi men with snakes in their mouths, many photographs depicted Hopi women and men posed with pots, baskets, or blankets. There were also many pictures of

Figure 10. Cover of The Moki Snake Dance, *by Walter Hough.*

children, family groups, and "Hopi maidens" with their distinctive hairdos. Although the texts described the presence of visitors at the Snake dance, no tourists are visible in the photographs. The widespread use of these photographs by ethnologists and tourism entrepreneurs would ensure their circulation until well into the 1930s. Ben Wittick was a particularly astute marketer and promoter of his own work and produced some of the earliest photographs of the Snake dance at Walpi (figure 9).[21]

Although most of the photographs and paintings the Santa Fe Railway used in their publications depicted Hopis and other Pueblo Indians as peaceful and sedentary, a picturesque attraction to tourists and artists, the perceived grotesque appeal of the Snake dance was irresistible. The cover of Hough's pamphlet (Fig. 10) featured a drawing of a Snake dancer, based on a painting by Henry H. Cross called *Moki Indian Snake Priest Training the Rattlesnake to Dance* (1898). This rendering of a Snake "priest" is interestingly inaccurate; his costume looks vaguely Aztec, and the snake is doing the dance, not he. The action has been transformed into a kind of oriental snake charming. As the Cliff Dwellers and Pueblo Indians existed side by side with the Streets of Cairo and Constantinople on the exposition midways, so Cross, who once painted circus wagons for P. T. Barnum, depicted the Hopi as an oriental curiosity (Harmsen 1978, 56). The Santa Fe, in its promotion of the Snake dance as a tourist attraction, borrowed this sideshow strategy by giving Hough's text a veneer of oriental exoticism.

The popular writings about and images of the Indians of the Southwest, and about the Snake dance in particular, were full of allusions to the Orient. In his book of travel sketches about the Southwest, *Some Strange Corners of Our Country* (1891), Charles Lummis referred to the Great American Desert as the "American Sahara" and alluded to "Arabian Simoons" and caravans in his descriptions of the region and its inhabitants (28–33). This orientalist rhetoric characterized tourist literature well into the 1920s. The writer Erna Fergusson reminded tourists in 1928, "Motorists crossing the southwestern states are nearer to the primitive than anywhere else on the continent. They are crossing a land in which a foreign people, with foreign speech and foreign ways, offer them spectacles which can be equaled in a very few Oriental lands" (Thomas 1978, 191; see also Pomeroy 1957, 39). Noting the long history of orientalism in the literature about the Southwest, Barbara Babcock has declared that the region is America's Orient and points to the "olla maiden" as its main icon (Babcock 1990, 406). The figure of the olla maiden, or water carrier (Fig. 11), evokes the biblical Orient, and I read it as the feminine pendant to the more masculine (and dangerously libidinal in its Edenic allusions) Snake dance. Together these icons present a dichotomous image of southwestern Indians as exotic others, good and bad, tamed and wild.

Allusions to the Orient in representations of the Snake dance may also have suggested a parallel between European empires and the American empire. As Europe had colonized the Orient, so had the United States colonized the Indian Southwest. Given its role in

Figure 11. Postcard depicting an "olla maiden" (Detroit: Fred Harvey, c. 1900–1910). The caption on the back of the postcard reads: "The Costume of most of the Pueblo Indians is in a degree picturesque. Although the men of the Pueblos have almost entirely given up the old native costume, the women still cling to the black native made dresses which have been worn for hundreds of years while on their feet they wear a moccasin of buckskin which terminates in a long broad strip which is wound many times about the lower leg." (Special Collections, The University of Arizona Library)

the conquest of the American West, it seems fitting that the railroad would invoke this allusion. Furthermore, the tourist literature often struck a nationalist chord: Americans did not need to travel to Europe or Asia to find the exotic or the ancient; the aboriginal cultures of the Southwest were "our" antiquity. Charles Lummis, in his lifelong boosterism of the Southwest, claimed to have originated the phrase "See America First" to encourage Americans to explore the wonders of their Southwest. He chiefly exhorted them to forego Europe in favor of the ruins, antiquities, and curiosities of America's ancient civilizations (1925, 3–12). As in European orientalism, the

Indian other was reconstructed in a way that distanced it in time but incorporated it as part of the ancient history and tradition of the American nation (Said 1979, 3).

One of the Santa Fe Railway's favorite artists was E. Irving Couse, who first visited the Southwest in 1902. In all, he made paintings for twenty-two of the famous Santa Fe calendars (Bryant 1978, 449). His 1904 painting, *Moki Snake Dance* (Fig. 12), is based on his seeing the dance at Walpi in 1903. This painting occupies a position somewhere between the exoticism of the cover of Hough's *Moki Snake Dance* and the ethnographic representations. Like Harmer's drawing for Bourke (Fig. 2), Couse's painting depicts the moment in the dance when the priests circle the dance plaza carrying the snakes in their mouths. The costumes are detailed and accurate, but Couse's painting lacks the rigid organization of the anthropological drawing. It is realistic in the sense of being an illusionistic rendering, but the ritual is highly romanticized and somewhat sensationalized in the way the painting pushes the viewer into the action. And yet the dance is not presented as threatening or grotesque. There is a serenity and intimacy to the scene; rather than feeling repelled, the viewer is encouraged to contemplate the various activities depicted. There are relatively few observers, and they appear to be Hopis, not outsiders. With the omission of Anglo observers, the viewer has a sense of primal discovery, similar to the ethnographer's point of view. The Couse painting tries to reconcile the tension between the good and the bad Indian, between the merely less evolved primitive and the irredeemable savage. There is a stately, dreamlike quality to the painting, an excessive calmness that completely tames the snakes and Indians and evokes not only the tradition of orientalism in nineteenth-century European painting but also a kind of painterly pastoralism. These Indians resemble not savages so much as European peasants in paintings by Courbet.

The Santa Fe purchased this painting in 1904, and although it was not featured on a calendar, the Fred Harvey Company reproduced it as a postcard after 1907, and it appeared in a profusely illustrated Harvey souvenir book by John F. Huckel, *First Families of the Southwest* ([1913] 1934, n.p.). This volume inserted the painting opposite a description of the Snake dance, titled "The Indian Who Understands Rattlesnakes." Huckel, a company executive, pointed out

Figure 12. Moki Snake Dance, *by E. Irving Couse (1904); oil on canvas; 36 × 48 in. (Photograph by James O. Milmoe; courtesy of The Anschutz Collection)*

that the Indians' holding snakes between their teeth "naturally suggests a state of barbarism close to the lowest degradation. And yet the Hopi . . . have been among the most peaceful of the American tribes, thrifty and industrious and of unusually high moral standards." Huckel speculated that the snake handlers were not bitten because they "understand rattlesnakes. Perhaps the reckless confidence of the Indian makes the snake think more of flight than fight" (n.p.). To the Western observer, the ceremony's salient characteristic was the handling of snakes. Indeed, in all the accounts of the Snake dance, ethnographic, artistic, and touristic, the moments of greatest importance involved handling the snakes, and the first question all recorders of the ceremony tried to answer was, Why were the dancers not bitten? Or if they were bitten, why did they not die? For the most part observers suggested two answers: the snakes had been defanged or their venom milked, or the emetic the participants drank after the dance was an antidote to the snakes' poison. Huckel's explanation that the dancers were protected because they "understood" rattlesnakes is particularly revealing. To the Anglo observer, that the Hopi men apparently had an amiable, or at least not inimical, relationship with reptiles suggested that Hopis were somehow like snakes. Furthermore, Huckel implies that non-Indians could "understand" Hopis as Hopis understand rattlesnakes—thus taming and containing the anomalous primitive within the national culture. However, because in Western, Christian tradition snakes signify dark, forbidden powers, snake handling clearly indicates a dangerous difference between Indians and Anglos.

CULTURAL INCORPORATION OF THE SNAKE DANCE

Government policy in the 1880s tried to enforce the idea that through Indian education, land allotment, and citizenship, Indians could be transformed into something resembling middle-class whites. As primitives, as representatives of the childhood of the race, they could "grow up" into civilized humans. But by the turn of the century this view was changing; Native Americans began to seem more like other "problem" minorities; they weren't disappearing. Rather than assimilating into the American melting pot, Native Americans seemed to be one more static group in a complex society (Hoxie 1977, 612). The Snake dance was emblematic of the dilemma of how to incorporate cultural difference.

In a nation whose founding ideology was based on the freedom of religious practice, the Snake dance tested the limits of that freedom. Hopis seemed eminently assimilable in all their habits of life except their religion. In the Snake dance the otherwise childlike and peaceful Hopis became spiritually problematic and uncanny. In 1900 the Religious Crimes Code made it illegal to participate in ceremonials deemed "offensive" to Christian standards. The code was withdrawn in 1923, but in the intervening years, although the Snake dance was not forbidden, it was not encouraged. It was not outlawed in part because it was such a big tourist attraction; the railroads promoted it and tourists demanded it (Crane 1925, 245). Even within the federal bureaucracy there were those who defended the Snake dance on the grounds that it was a religious practice. In 1893 Thomas Donaldson's *Extra Census Bulletin* on the Hopis recommended that they should basically be let alone because they were among the few self-sufficient Native American groups: "They differ from the whites in the mere matter of creed, but they practice religion. Let them continue to be self-reliant, peaceful citizens" (45).

One person who struggled with the cultural significance of the Snake dance was that most strenuous of tourists, Theodore Roosevelt. In 1913 he witnessed the ritual at Walpi and wrote an account of it for the magazine *Outlook.* As a "former great chief at Washington," he was admitted into a kiva to witness the rituals that preceded the public procession. His account echoed Fewkes and Bourke:

> I have never seen a wilder or, in its way, more impressive spectacle than that of these chanting, swaying, red-skinned medicine-men, their lithe bodies naked, unconcernedly handling the death that glides and strikes while they held their mystic worship in the gray twilight of the kiva. The ritual and the soul-needs it met, and the symbolism and the dark savagery, were all relics of an ages-vanished past, survivals of an elder world. (1913a, 372)

Roosevelt was clearly both strongly attracted to and repelled by what he saw. His overheated prose captures the excited emotions evoked by humans handling snakes and shows a frank admiration for the bravery of the Hopi men. There is also an element of "playing Indian" here in referring to himself as a "great chief" and to the snakes as "the death that glides and strikes." But he mitigates the sensational by reminding the reader that the ritual is merely a "survival" of an earlier stage of civilization and thus doomed to disappear.

Like Bourke and Fewkes, Roosevelt believed that Native Americans would inevitably be assimilated into Anglo-American society, but he was uncertain about the degree of that assimilation. Hopis were "different," and one can see Roosevelt wrestling with the terms of difference in his account. The social cohesion that the Snake dance exhibited held Hopis together on a local level; it did not bind Hopis to the nation but declared their difference as a group from the rest of the nation. As he wrote of the younger generation, whom he believed were moving away from traditional ways, Roosevelt tried to imagine the future of the Hopi people:

> As their type becomes dominant the snake dance and antelope dance will disappear, the Hopi religious myths will become memories, and the Hopis will live in villages on the mesa tops, or scattered out on the plains, as their several inclinations point, just as if they were so many white men. It is to be hoped that the art, the music, the poetry of their elders will be preserved during the change coming over the younger generation. (370)

Roosevelt solved the problem of the Snake dance by saying it would simply disappear as Hopis gradually gave up their religious beliefs. Here we see shades of the vanishing Indian. But at the same time Roosevelt suggested that some characteristics of Hopi "difference" should survive: "the art, the music, the poetry." He argued that Indian incorporation should be shaped "to preserve and develop the very real element of native culture possessed by these Indians" that "may in the end become an important contribution to American cultural life" (367). Under the rubric of salvage ethnology, Indian cultures were worth preserving, but the sites of preservation would be the academy and the museum. Roosevelt is suggesting something a bit different, that artifacts should be preserved but also that Indians should continue some of their cultural practices. This was a new tension in the Indian problem: Native Americans were expected to live like white men, that is, to support themselves in a capitalist economy, but they might also preserve certain aspects of their way of life that Anglos found appealing: these included the things that seemed to Anglos most like the Western categories of art, music, and poetry. The problem with this strategy was that it overlooked the meaning to Hopis of their rituals. Furthermore, it secularized the spiritual aspects of the Snake dance, incorporating it within the sphere of Culture, a secular and peripheral realm. It was analogous to relegating the Snake dance to the midway or the museum, where what was different about Indians became harmless entertainment. To Roosevelt, the Snake dance did not qualify as art, music, or poetry and so was not worth preserving.

In contrast, the accounts of several recorders, ethnographers as well as boosters of regional culture such as George Wharton James and Charles Lummis, redeemed the value of the Snake dance precisely because it was a religious ritual. They countered the idea of the dance as a frightening, weird, pagan ritual with accounts of it as a profoundly religious ceremony. A good example of this redemptive Snake dance literature is the writer Hamlin Garland's 1896 account of the ceremony in *Harper's Weekly.* Garland, like Lummis, was a friend of Roosevelt's; they, along with Charles Bird Grinnell, Frederic Remington, Owen Wister, and Francis Leupp, were members of Roosevelt's "cowboy cabinet." Garland was not from the Southwest, but he was an important theorist of regional literature. Fewkes admired Garland's account of the Snake dance and praised it for its accuracy (Fewkes [1897] 1986, 312). In fact, Fewkes was excavating nearby when Garland visited Walpi to see the dance, and Garland quoted Fewkes's descriptions of the activities in the kivas from his BAE reports. Also, Garland's article was illustrated with paintings made by Fernand Lungren, one of the artists Fewkes had initiated into the Antelope society in 1893. Even though Lungren's illustrations made the Snake dance seem grotesque, Garland's account of the Hopis emphasized the picturesque exoticism of the place and the event and is reminiscent of Bourke's and Fewkes's evocations of life in the Hopi villages. Garland stayed several days at Hano before the ceremony and made these observations:

> I looked out of the window upon the little plaza. Behold a strange America! In the center of the plaza was a pool of water. In this pool a dozen comical little brown bodies were paddling like ducks. Under the shade of adobe walls women with bare feet and bare arms, their bodies draped in scant gowns, were baking pottery or making bread. On the flat roofs other women, robed in green and black and purple, were moving about. A man in blue and pink, belted with a string of huge silver disks, was unloading an enormous dead wildcat from behind his saddle, his pony waiting with bowed head. A peculiar smell was in the air. (802)

In this passage the language is stripped of metaphor and allusion and relies on simple adjectives for its descriptive power. Nevertheless, exoticism is implied by the sentence "Behold a strange America!" Readers were encouraged to compare what Garland saw with "normal" America. Men, women, and children looked and behaved "differently": the children acted like ducks, the women were "bare," and the men wore pink and blue clothes. This was America made strange, different, but the difference was not threatening.

Garland continues this strategy of tempering the exotic with the familiar. He repeatedly notes that although he felt like he was in a dream while watching the Snake rituals, he realized that for Hopi people the rituals were part of everyday life: "Incredible, thrilling, savage, and dangerous as it appeared to us, to them it was a world old religious ceremonial." He concluded, "There is no reason why the snake-dance should be interfered with or condemned" (807). It may be that Garland saw the Snake dance as worth protecting in part because of his ideas about American literature. In *Crumbling Idols* (1894) he argued that the future of American literature depended on the recognition of American life, particularly as lived in the West, as fit for literary and artistic endeavors. The local color of the West was especially inspirational, but only as expressed and understood by natives of the region. In his account of the Snake dance, Garland began to make this move: like an ethnographer, he took on the role of interlocutor, interpreting Hopi life for non-Indian readers. In his account, Hopi people seemed more like regional folk, on the order of Sarah Orne Jewett's New Englanders, than exotic foreigners. This claim that regional difference is the source of an authentic national literature would become the dominant refrain of southwestern artists and literati over the next several decades. By reconstituting the Snake dance as a religious ritual, cleansed of oriental or Gothic strangeness, Western writers such as Lummis and Garland brought Hopis into a balance with the rest of American culture, as one more ethnic group whose main difference was religious belief, a difference Garland was willing to tolerate. Unlike Roosevelt, he could see that if Hopi people were to maintain their cultural integrity, they would need their religion. He did not want them to be just like Anglos, because they would lose their cultural distinctiveness and their usefulness as literary subjects.

Many years later another literary observer of the Snake dance summed up the ways in which Americans had come to understand the Snake dance. In 1924, while he was the guest of Mabel Dodge Luhan, D. H. Lawrence saw the Snake dance at Hotevilla. In a travel sketch that appeared in *Theatre Arts Monthly,* he distinguished three ways in which the ritual was understood by Anglo observers: as a "circus-performance," "as a cultured spectacle" (like the ballet), and as a religious ceremonial (1924, 837–38). These distinctions described the appeal of the Snake dance to tourists, artists, and anthropologists, respectively. To Lawrence the touristic appeal recalled the low-brow exoticism of a sideshow, the high-culture appreciation remade the ritual into a formally attractive arrangement of movement and sound, and the scientific approach called for an intellectual explanation of the ritual's spiritual or cultural meaning as a religion. Lawrence dismissed all three, saying that they either sentimentalized or brutalized the Indian, making "the Indian with his 'religion' . . . a sort of public pet," in other words, the savage domesticated, tamed within the terms of Western entertainment, art, or science (838). Lawrence tried to apprehend the Snake dance on the Hopis' own terms and proceeded to describe it through his own somewhat idiosyncratic understanding of "animism" and oriental philosophies. But his description of the Indian as a "public pet" suggests that Hopi people were culturally incorporated, not as full equals, but as domesticated others re-presented for public consumption.

In the years between Garland's and Lawrence's account, the cultural battle over the Snake dance and other Native American rituals continued. Although the Snake dance was never forbidden, the Indian Affairs Commission periodically tried to place restrictions on the performances. In 1921 Commissioner Charles Burke sent a series of recommendations to Indian superintendents that limited the times dances could take place and who could participate in them (Gibson 1983, 215; Lyon 1988, 256; Schultz, 1921; Sweet 1981, 85–90). This prompted a wave of activism among Anglo artists and writers working in the Southwest. Poets and writers such as Alice Corbin Henderson, Mary Austin, and John Collier, artists such as John Sloan and Marsden Hartley, the anthropologist F. W. Hodge, and many others lobbied and wrote articles arguing that Americans could only gain from preserving the rituals of Native Americans. As part of this effort, a demonstration of the Snake dance was performed in Washington on the Capitol Plaza on 15 May 1926, before Vice-President Dawes and five thousand others. The purpose was to show that Hopi ceremonies were not savage or cruel. It was reported in the *Washington Post* and the *New York Times* that Senator Cameron of Arizona found the dance no worse than the Charleston (Lyon 1988, 245). Efforts to preserve the Snake dance and other rituals coincided with the interests of tourism promoters and chambers of commerce, who began to organize annual festivals in New Mexico and Arizona, such as the Santa Fe Fiesta and Indian Market. Finally, in 1928 Deputy Indian Commissioner E. B. Merritt told the Pueblo Council that the United States "did not wish to interfere with Pueblo customs and ceremonies" (Lyon 1988, 256). It might have seemed as though the Snake dance was finally safe, that Hopi people were free to pursue their cultural practices without interference, but, as we shall see, the battle was far from over.

THE SNAKE DANCE AS A SPECTACLE

At a literal level, representations of the Snake dance circulated as commodities: as postcards and photographs and in books and magazines. And the ritual itself became a tourist attraction from which railroads and other entrepreneurs profited. But beyond the literal commodification of the representations, they circulated as part of a "spectacle" that embodied "a social relation among people, mediated by images" (Debord 1983, 4). In the spectacle of the Snake dance, Hopis did not control the making of these representations or their circulation; rather, they existed in the spectacle primarily as objects of exchange rather than subjects. Hopis quickly saw the consequences of this representational process and responded by prohibiting representation of the ritual. By examining the "spectacularization" of the Snake dance, we can begin to see how the representations crossed and recrossed cultural and institutional borders and how Hopis and others have participated in and shaped these exchanges.

An example of the "macro-economy" of the Snake dance as a spectacle and its representational proliferation is the account of Earle R. Forrest, published in 1961. Forrest was working as a cowhand on an Arizona ranch while on vacation from college when he first witnessed and photographed the ceremony at Oraibi in 1906, where he also encountered Edward S. Curtis (55). But the desire to see the ritual had been planted in him in 1899, when he was a boy in Washington, Pennsylvania. There he read an account of it in a story by Hamlin Garland in the *Saturday Evening Post.* Shortly after, he read *The Moki Snake Dance,* by Walter Hough, and then the account of the Snake and Flute ceremonies at Mishongnovi by Fewkes. He saw the dance again at Mishongnovi in 1907, but this time he was with the artist Louis Akin (a favorite of the Santa Fe Railway), who asked him to photograph the winner of the foot race so that he might paint him. It is not clear if Akin actually painted the scene, but in 1911 he was commissioned to paint murals for the Southwest room of the American Museum of Natural History in New York City. Akin died suddenly of pneumonia in 1913, before he could complete the murals, but shortly before he died he revisited the Hopi mesas, making detailed sketches for the project, including two oil portraits of Snake priests, possibly for a depiction of the Snake dance (E. Forrest 1961, 74–83; Babbitt 1973, 65).

In Forrest's account we can see how individuals who wrote about or made images of the Snake dance were connected to large and extremely powerful institutions. Images of and literature about the Snake dance were disseminated by the railroads, the popular press, museums, and academia. These representations in turn encouraged the tourist Forrest to produce his own images and, eventually, a narrative of his experience. The artist Akin, who was also a tourist, produced images intended for the railroads as well as an East Coast metropolitan museum that preserved Hopi material culture. Thus seemingly disparate institutions had overlapping interests in the Snake dance, and the representations they helped produce circulated in a vast cultural arena and became the medium of exchange in social relations among producers and consumers of the images and texts.

As the Snake dance became known the world over, it was visited by thousands of outsiders every year. Leo Crane, Hopi agent from 1911 to 1919, recounted in 1925 the difficulty of controlling the crowd at the Walpi dances. He described the Snake dance as "like staging a nervous ballet on the cornice of the Woolworth Building, knowing that fifty mice will be turned loose on signal" (249). The Snake dance had become a social event, a kind of "rendezvous" for Anglos in the know.[22] In 1922 Ethel Hickey noted in the *Santa Fe Magazine* (the railway's organ): "It is the meeting place of celebrities from all over the world, where the average man may hob-nob with the great, perhaps entirely unaware. Yet, I strongly suspect that the

Figure 13. Photographers Snapping Col. Roosevelt, *by Dwight Franklin (August 21, 1913). Photographers crowd the dance plaza at Walpi to get pictures of Theodore Roosevelt, who was there to see the Snake dance. (Roosevelt is not visible in this photograph, because it was taken near where he was seated and thus renders, more or less, his point of view.) (Special Collections, The University of Arizona Library)*

opportunity to see celebrities rough it de luxe—for everybody camps at the Snake Dance—is as strong a drawing card to many as is the dance itself" (45). The presence of Roosevelt in 1913 certainly added to the social cachet of attending the Snake dance. Figure 13 depicts the scramble of film and still photographers to get pictures of the former president and illustrates the extent to which tourists had become part of the attraction. Indeed, the spectacle of the Snake dance (and of southwestern Indian life in general) began to consume its producers. Artists who lived and worked in Taos and Santa Fe became tourist attractions themselves; in 1926 the Fred Harvey Company began its Indian Detours, and among the attractions, which included the Snake dance in the right season, was artist Sheldon Parsons's studio in Santa Fe (Bryant 1978, 452).

The pressures that the spectacularization of the Snake dance brought to bear on the dance and the Hopis very quickly became problematic—and eventually intolerable. Conflicts surrounding the performance of the ceremony involved not only the sheer number of visitors but also—and especially—photography. Photographic representations of the Snake dance seemed to proliferate exponentially. By the 1890s photographs of the Snake dance were being reproduced widely, and in many of these photographs, dozens of cameras can be seen in the hands of the hundreds of spectators. Agent Crane wrote: "Each tourist packs one of those devices sold by Mr. Eastman" (251). The presence of so many photographers was also noted in 1905 by Nell Clark Keller, writing for the *Woman's Home Companion:* when the dancers emerged, "Snap! went all the cameras." The event became a quintessential "Kodak moment" in that it offered tourists an opportunity to "capture" on film something extremely exotic, the snapshot serving as evidence of the tourists' experience. The proliferation of cameras began to cause conflicts between photographers vying for the best spots from which to shoot the public parts of the ceremony. In 1902 George Wharton James noted in *Camera Craft* that photographers were asked to

> keep within a certain line, and that no one without a camera should be permitted in their preserves. . . . Hitherto every man had chosen his own field, and moved to and fro wherever he liked—in front of his neighbor or some one else; kicking down another fellow's tripod and sticking his elbow in the next fellow's lens. (7) . . . It cannot be said that the changes are to the advantage of the photographer. They render his work less certain and effective, and it will not be long before one can write a learned and accurate paper from the standpoint of scientific ethnology on "the change in religious ceremonies owing to the camera." (1902d, 10)

Indeed, this is what began to happen. One of the changes in the Snake dance James noticed was that Hopi participants avoided the cameras when it came time to drink the emetic at the end of the ceremony.

However, Hopis did not continue to change the ceremony to accommodate photographers. Rather, they banned cameras from the Snake dance altogether. The ban came about gradually. From 1870 to 1910 there were few "formal tribal restrictions on photography of Indian ceremonies." But by the 1920s many Southwest Indian groups prohibited photography at ceremonies. Restrictions on photographing the Snake dance at Walpi began in about 1913, when visitors were charged one dollar to bring a camera onto the mesa, and "prohibition of photography of all Hopi ceremonies became almost completely effective in the late 1920s" (Lyon 1988, 238). Luke Lyon has written that he has found no photos of the Snake dance dated later than 1923 (245). Ironically, officials in the Bureau of Indian Affairs at this time agreed with the Hopis that photography should be restricted, because they thought the reproduction of images of the Snake dance encouraged the Indians to keep practicing their religion (Longo 1980).

The ban on photography came about, in part, because of the behavior of some photographers. George Wharton James admitted to having taken a photograph inside a kiva at Mishongnovi when he had been asked not to (1900c, 266). Some Anglos were more sensitive to the intrusiveness of taking photographs. Sumner Matteson, writing in *Field and Stream* in 1904, gave some advice for visitors: "It is bad enough to steal photographs of their altars and secret ceremonies, but to this some of the clans do not seriously object, so long as nothing is disturbed and they are assured that no pictures, drawings or words will ever be shown to the other Hopis, thereby exposing the secrets of their orders" (339). Indeed, as we have seen, the divulging of sacred practices was a serious transgression to Hopis, but they also considered taking photographs an act of disrespect and "resented commercial exploitation of their religion through sale of photographs" (Lyon 1988, 256). To put the dilemma in terms of the economy of the spectacle, by prohibiting photography and sketching, Hopi people could begin to escape the commodity exchange of the spectacle and to some extent break from the hegemonic relationship with their representers.

Hopis eventually closed the Snake and Antelope ceremonies to visitors altogether. But the decision to restrict the access of visitors and the making of images of the public parts of the ceremony was a long time in coming and the result of much debate among Hopis. In 1993 anthropologist Peter Whiteley pointed out:

Figure 14. Photograph of a group of Smokis performing a "Snake dance" (c. 1922). The caption to this photo reads: "Straight and tall as young pines rising in the sunlight." Reprinted from Sharlot M. Hall, The Story of the Smoki People *(Prescott, Ariz.: Way Out West, 1922), n.p. (Special Collections, The University of Arizona Library)*

> Hopis see their culture not as some abstract expression, but as instrumental: ritual dramas, for example, are performed *for* the material benefit of the world. It is only with great reluctance and significant opposition, therefore, that the priests felt they had no alternative but to close down the Snake and Kachina dances. In other words, it runs counter to Hopi first principles to restrict all outside representations of them: they are simply tired of the abuses. (1993, 147)

At the same time that Hopis began closing the Snake dance to photographers, in Prescott, Arizona, a facsimile of the ceremony was being performed by the Smokis, a secret society of Anglo businessmen and professionals (Fig. 14).[23] In 1921 they performed it as part of the city's Way Out West celebration, an exercise in civic boosterism. In 1924 the June Snake dance of the Smokis became an annual event.[24]

The Smokis performed the Snake dance as a theatrical spectacle with elaborate costumes, makeup, settings, and lighting. The authenticity of the performances extended mainly to the costumes and paraphernalia (including live bull snakes instead of rattlesnakes), not to the procedures of the ceremony. However, over time the Smokis accrued a gloss of authenticity, including their own mythology based loosely on Hopi cosmology. In 1922 Sharlot Hall wrote *The Story of the Smoki People,* which contains several poems explaining "Where the Smokis Dance," "Why the Smokis Dance," and "When the Smokis Dance," as well as "The Story of the Smoki People," which is a Smoki "origin myth" based on Fewkes's Snake legend. And more recently, in the mid-1980s, in imitation of the Hopi ban on photography, the Smokis prohibited visitors from photographing their ceremonies (although dancers could be photographed afterward) (Lyon 1988, 256).

The Smokis are part of a long tradition of American fraternal and sororal organizations engaged in "playing Indian," appropriating and reenacting various Native American cultural practices (Rayna Green 1988b; Deloria 1994). The literature the Smokis published about themselves claimed that "shrouded in the anonymity of authentic Indian dress [they] lose their identity and shed their personality of the White Man in faithful interpretation of age-old dances of their Indian neighbors" (Parker 1941, 1). As much as the Smoki rhetoric emphasized the authenticity and seriousness of their performances, they did not show respect for Hopi beliefs or cosmology, and the performances were, in fact, comic turns; as respectable members of the business elite, the Smokis played at being inferior savages. The Smokis eventually performed other Native American rituals, but that the Snake dance was the first is telling. It was the most celebrated ritual of the Southwest and also apparently the most primitive, the most other. To be able to "be" this most extreme other demonstrated the power of the performer. The Indian became entirely appropriable and controlled by the performer. As if they were bringing an ethnographic exhibit to life, the Smokis literally inhabited the space of the vanished Indian. However, as in minstrelsy, one of the problems with the Smokis' appropriation and performance was that Hopis had not vanished—they were very present.

In recent years Hopis have responded to the Smoki dances by parodying the Smokis. Peter Whiteley reports that in 1985 a group of Hopi ritual clowns performed a "burlesque" of the Smoki Snake dance using wooden snakes and executing Hollywood-style chanting and dancing. As Whiteley points out, they were "ridiculing its racism and incongruities, reasserting sovereignty over Hopi representations, parodically turning the parody back on itself, emptying it for the time being at least of its oppressive meaning and power" (1993, 150). Finally, in 1990 a group of Hopis launched a protest at the Smoki Snake dance. The Smokis responded by canceling the 1991 performance, and, for the time being at least, the Smokis no longer perform the Snake dance (127).

As representations of the Snake dance proliferated, so did the dance's social and cultural uses. The meaning of the Snake dance to non-Indian Americans has shifted over time: from profane outrage, to ethnographic curiosity, to sacred ritual, to artistic performance. Although there was a gradual drift toward tolerance of the Snake dance on the part of government authorities, all of these meanings existed at any given time. As a marker of ethnic difference, the Snake dance and its representations came to serve as a cultural battleground, where political and social issues having to do with the incorporation of Native Americans into the nation were fought, with much of the fighting being over the control of representations. The politics of representation, in collecting, in photographing, in textualizing the Snake dance, effectively objectified and silenced the men and women who participated in the ritual. The first step toward a solution was for Hopis to remove themselves from the spectacle by prohibiting the making of representations of their rituals, to cease to make themselves available for objectification. But in addition to trying to control the spread of representations, Hopis and other Native Americans have begun to "write back." By re-presenting their encounters with non-Indians in the "social spaces" provided by ethnography, tourism, and the art market, southwestern Indian people continue to reimagine and negotiate the terms of their participation in American culture.

CHAPTER 2

DISCOVERING INDIANS IN FRED HARVEY'S SOUTHWEST

In 1912 the Biograph Company released a Mack Sennett short called *The Tourists,* starring Mabel Normand. In the film Normand plays a tourist named Trixie who disembarks from a Santa Fe train at Albuquerque with three tourist friends. She gets so involved in buying souvenir pottery from the Indian women in front of the Fred Harvey Indian Building that she and her companions miss their train and have to wait for the next one (Fig. 15).

Making the best of an inconvenient situation, Trixie decides to go sightseeing at a nearby pueblo. There she attracts the attentions of Big Chief (a white actor in a war bonnet), who squires her around the pueblo. Trixie has such a good time seeing the sights with Big Chief that she gives her tourist beau the brush-off. But Mrs. Big Chief (an Anglo woman in a wig) gets jealous, which puts the "Indian Suffragettes on the War-Path." Mrs. Big Chief and a crowd of Indian women (most of whom appear to be Native Americans) determine to chase the offending tourist from the village. Trixie temporarily eludes them by hiding in an Indian blanket, but eventually Mrs. Big

Figure 15. Still photograph from The Tourists *(New York: Biograph Company, 1912). Mabel Normand, as the tourist Trixie, buys souvenir pottery in front of the Fred Harvey Indian Building, Albuquerque. (From the collections of the Library of Congress Motion Picture, Broadcasting, and Recorded Sound Division)*

Chief and the other women chase Trixie and the three tourists back to the train, which they beat on with clubs. As the train pulls out and recedes into the middle distance, the tourists smile and wave handkerchiefs.

This film accurately represents—even as it parodies—the main features of ethnic tourism in the Southwest between the turn of the century and the First World War. To begin with, the setting of the film, in and around the Fred Harvey Indian Building, adjacent to the Santa Fe depot at Albuquerque, is quite appropriate. The Fred Harvey Company, in its relationship with the Atchison, Topeka and Santa Fe Railway, was the most powerful agent of tourism in the region. During this period, the company, through its tourist attractions and publications, fostered a remarkably coherent—and persistent—version of the Southwest as a region inhabited by peaceful, pastoral people, "living ruins" from the childhood of civilization. Presumably, what lured Trixie and her tourist friends to the Southwest was the promise of an encounter with these living relics of the past. This encounter, which was thoroughly mediated by the Santa Fe Railway and the Fred Harvey Company, was a kind of reenactment of the Columbian discovery narrative. The tourists in the film journeyed out from civilization via the Santa Fe Railway and discovered the peaceful, welcoming natives at the Fred Harvey Indian Building. The Indians sold them objects of native manufacture, and, having engaged in a satisfying exchange and seen the sights (albeit after an unusually "close encounter"), the tourists returned to civilization with souvenir evidence of that encounter and tales of the region's wonders.

Fred Harvey's representation of the Indian Southwest spoke to what Renato Rosaldo has called "imperialist nostalgia," a sense of longing for what one is complicit in destroying or altering, in which the feeling of nostalgia is "innocent" and what is destroyed is simply rendered as "lost" (1989, 70). The cultural and economic incorporation of the Southwest, in which the Harvey Company and the ATSF were primary agents, caused profound disruptions and changes among Native American communities. At the turn of the century, these processes were carried out in the name of progress, with the recognized cost being the necessary destruction of primitive ways of life. Even as the ATSF conquered the region, it and the Harvey Company set about preserving the vanishing Indian. To expand on Rosaldo's idea, I would argue that Fred Harvey and the ATSF were nostalgic not for what was actually destroyed but for an Indian that never existed; in the interest of selling tickets and hotel accommodations in the region, the two corporations constructed a version of Indian life that reflected and spoke to American middle-class desires and anxieties.

The Fred Harvey Company and the ATSF created and coordinated touristic desires by rendering southwestern Indian life as a "spectacle," a cultural discourse that constructed epistemological and social relations between tourists and Indians as primarily visual; subjectivity resided with the touristic gaze, and Indians were objectified as culturally "blind" and static, available for touristic consumption (Debord 1983, 5). Whatever anxieties might have accompanied touristic desires (e.g., the fear that Indians might resist economic and cultural exploitation) were defused in the spectacle by the representation of Indians as "living ruins," simultaneously appearing from the past and disappearing from the present.

By rendering Indians as "lost" and as objects of consumption or exchange among tourist subjects, the spectacle of tourism made the experience available for the production of tourist narratives but shut down the possibility of dialogue between Native Americans and tourists. *The Tourists* works as a comedy in part because it exposes the threat of real communication. The comic misunderstanding occurs because Trixie crosses the boundary between Indian and tourist. Her mistake is to stray too far from the train and to get too close to the natives. As a parable, the film teaches that in the encounter with the primitive other, it is best to keep one's distance and not to "go native," to stick to one's own side of the tracks, so to speak. But Trixie's transgression reveals more about the implications of that warning. Even though the tourist is presented as innocent and simply overenthusiastic, her interest in the Indian man threatens a sexual liaison. This potential connection across the touristic divide is threatening, because it would admit and display the Indians' full subjectivity. The film winds up representing this subjectivity in another way: the liaison between Trixie and Big Chief is derailed by the intervention of the Pueblo women, who strenuously resist the tourist's incursion into their territory. The image of the women beating the Santa Fe train with clubs would never appear in Fred Harvey's Southwest.

THE RISE OF THE FRED HARVEY COMPANY

The story of how Fred Harvey, with his dining facilities along the ATSF and his Harvey Girls, civilized the West has become something of a frontier legend.[1] Beginning in 1876 with a single Topeka, Kansas, lunchroom, the English immigrant Harvey went on to found a virtual empire of eating establishments and hotels in the Southwest. The mythology of Harvey's lone triumph—and his paternalism—was fostered by the company itself; Harvey died in 1901, but through the 1920s and 1930s business correspondence and copyrights would be signed simply "Fred Harvey."

Although the Algeresque myth of Fred Harvey would have it that his company was the vision of one man with a single-minded devotion to quality, what is often glossed over is the Harvey Company's relationship with the Santa Fe Railway, which from the beginning was symbiotic. The railroad provided the transportation and infrastructure, and Harvey delivered standardized, high-quality services. The Santa Fe built and owned the hotels, and the Harvey Company furnished and operated them as well as dining cars, newsstands, and other shops along the railroad's route (Bryant 1974, 118). Part of the "systemized perfection" of the Harvey service depended on the Santa Fe's system of communication and its ability to ship fresh, high-quality produce and food anywhere at any time, thus freeing Harvey establishments from local limitations (Henderson 1969, 13; "How Fame Has Been Won" 1916, 32–33).

In 1895 the ATSF was sold and saved from bankruptcy. This date also marks the railroad's decision under the presidency of Edward P. Ripley to step up efforts to promote tourism in the Southwest (Dutton 1983, 93). This meant building big hotels to entice travelers to stay more than the usual one night. The Santa Fe and the Harvey Company already had some experience in this type of venture with the Montezuma Hotel, which opened at Las Vegas, New Mexico, in 1882. The healing waters of the local hot springs were the primary attraction, and the Montezuma set the standard for the Santa Fe–Harvey hotel relationship. Over the next thirty years the railroad opened hotels near their tracks throughout the Southwest, and the Harvey Company furnished and operated them. These hotels included: the Castañeda in Las Vegas, New Mexico (opened 1899); the Alvarado in Albuquerque (1902); El Tovar, Grand Canyon (1905); El Ortiz, Lamy (1910); El Navajo, Gallup (1923); and La Fonda, Santa Fe (1926) (Grattan 1980, 125–26).

To promote the attractions of the Southwest, the ATSF began in the mid-1890s to commission ethnographers, artists, and photographers to depict Indian life in the region. Following the Santa Fe's lead, in 1902 the Fred Harvey Company formed its own Indian Department, which was concerned with buying and selling Indian-made objects, coordinating the display of these objects as well as actual Native Americans, and publishing postcards, souvenir books, and pamphlets. After Fred Harvey's death, his son Ford Harvey took over the company and appointed his brother-in-law, John Frederick Huckel, to head the Indian Department. Huckel selected Herman Schweizer, a former news agent for the Harvey Company, to manage the operation in Albuquerque (Henderson 1969, 29). Huckel, Schweizer, and another Harvey employee, Mary Elizabeth Jane Colter, were largely responsible for creating the Fred Harvey image of the Indian Southwest. Although the Santa Fe handled the advertising for both the railway and Harvey, Huckel oversaw the publication of several souvenir books and hundreds of postcards, which often used ATSF artists, paintings, or photographs. Schweizer's job was mainly buying and selling Indian objects, and Colter designed several hotels as well as shops and attractions and arranged their interiors (Grattan 1980, 1–9; Weigle 1991, 120–30; Wells 1976, 32).

Over the next three decades the Harvey Company and the ATSF continued to market and display aspects of Indian cultures and in the process helped create a regional identity based on an aesthetic appreciation of Indian cultures. These practices not only encouraged tourists to visit the region but also provided a corporate image for the Harvey Company and the ATSF. Symbols of "Indianness" spread all along the railway line, through the hotels, in the decoration of the trains themselves, and in the promotional literature and corporate imagery. The Santa Fe named one of its first-class trains the *Chief,* and the corporation's emblem, which came into use in 1901, was described as "a symbol descended from pre-historic man" (Armitage 1948, 118–19) (Fig. 28). Likewise, the Fred Harvey Company adopted as its emblem the Thunder Bird, which the company claimed was part of the mythology of many of the Indians of North America (Huckel [1913] 1934, n.p.). Thus these two modern corporate entities, which were paragons of efficiency and marketing, wrapped themselves in an Indian blanket, so to speak, and used Indians to "naturalize" their activities.

THE SPECTACLE OF FRED HARVEY'S SOUTHWEST

Fred Harvey's representations of Indian life in the Southwest took two basic forms: the museumlike display of "live" Indians and their material culture and written and graphic representations of Indian life. Displays organized by the Santa Fe and the Harvey Company appeared at world's fairs and regional expositions as well as in Harvey hotels and shops. Graphic and written representations of Indians appeared in the Santa Fe's ads, calendars, time tables, and pamphlets, in Harvey postcards, souvenir books, and lantern slide lectures. These representations circulated images of and information about Native Americans within the region and throughout the nation in order to induce tourists to visit Fred Harvey's Southwest.

In forming display attractions in the region, the Harvey Company used the strategies employed by ethnographers at expositions and fairs. At the core of the Harvey display attractions were collections of Indian-made objects exhibited in museumlike settings with the occasional presence of an actual Native American demonstrating crafts or dances. Herman Schweizer was instrumental in forming the collections of Indian material culture for the Harvey Company. From 1901 to his death in 1943 Schweizer bought and sold blankets, silver, baskets, pots, and many other types of objects made by Indian people in the Southwest. He also handled Plains, Northwest Coast, and Alaskan objects, as well as Spanish and Mexican objects and artifacts from Africa, the South Seas, and New Guinea. He bought old and new objects and commissioned silver and possibly blankets and pots for the tourist trade (Adair 1944, 25–27). The sources for his purchases included Native Americans themselves, traders, dealers, and other collectors—in short, anyone who was selling (Harvey 1981, 9–10). Writing of Schweizer's collecting practices in 1963, Byron Harvey III remarked that "whole wagon loads of irreplaceable *Santos* and Indian arts were brought in for sale" (36).

Most of the objects Schweizer purchased were sold to tourists, collectors, and scientists collecting for museums. At the turn of the century all of the institutional collections of Native American material culture were in the East and Chicago, and the Harvey Company was an important supplier. By contract with the ATSF, the company had favorable shipping rates over the railroad, and boxcars full of Indian objects were shipped east. Between 1903 and 1918 Schweizer's clients included George Dorsey, who purchased for the Field Museum of Natural History; the United States National Museum in Washington, D.C.; the Carnegie Museum in Pittsburgh; the Berlin Museum; and George Heye (Harvey 1963, 38–39).

What Schweizer didn't sell to scientists, tourists, and collectors, the company kept for display. As the ATSF collected paintings, so the Harvey Company built a collection of Indian material culture. The company's ties to museums and scientists gave its collection scientific authority: in 1904 at the Louisiana Purchase Exposition in St. Louis, the Harvey Company won an award for "Aboriginal Blanketry and Basketry," and the company to some extent imitated museum methods of record keeping, documenting sources, establishing a library, and interviewing Indians (Harvey 1963, 36–37). The importance of building a collection for display was made clear by Herman Schweizer in a 1905 letter to William Randolph Hearst. Hearst, a prodigious collector, was interested in Navajo blankets and was one of Schweizer's most important customers. Even so, Schweizer had to inform Hearst that not all the company's "exhibit rugs" were for sale: "The first object in establishing this exhibit was to furnish an attraction for the Santa Fe and I believe you realize it has been a most remarkable success in that direction. That was the reason it was not considered proper to send away some of our choicest things for obviously it was intended to bring people who wanted to see or purchase them over the Santa Fé" (Schweizer 1905).[2]

This mixture of the business interests of tourism and the scientific credibility that allowed a claim of authenticity and authority pervaded the Harvey display strategies, especially the permanent display attractions in the Southwest, the most important of which were the Indian Building at Albuquerque (opened in 1902) and Hopi House, next to the Grand Canyon hotel, El Tovar (opened in 1905). The Indian Building was the first big display attraction created by Harvey, and it combined very effectively the two "regions" of the world's fair model, offering both ethnographic authenticity as well as pleasure (Weigle 1989b, 133). The building was located between the Alvarado Hotel and the Santa Fe depot along an arcade two hundred feet long. This complex was designed in the mission style with tile roofs, stucco exterior, arches, and bell towers reminiscent of a Spanish mission. Mary Colter designed the interiors; it was her first job for Harvey, and she would later design many hotels and attractions for the company.[3]

Tourists' experience at this attraction was fully mediated by the railway and Fred Harvey in a kind of train-hotel complex. Santa Fe

Figure 16. The Indian and Mexican Building, Albuquerque, New Mexico *(c. 1904). Elle of Ganado is pictured seated center, wearing the dark shirt. (Reprinted from* The Great Southwest*)*

trains stopped at Albuquerque for from twenty-five minutes to an hour, and the Indian Building (Fig. 16) was constructed so that from the depot, passengers would pass first between Indians displaying their wares in front of the building, then through the Indian Museum with its ethnographic displays, then the workroom with Indians weaving or making other crafts, and then to the curio shop, where they could purchase objects similar to those they had just seen (Grattan 1980, 13; Weigle 1989b, 125).

These displays were organized to manipulate tourists' desire to possess the objects. The visitor moved through a kind of hierarchy of desire, from museumlike displays to the shop. Upon entering the Indian Building the visitor was transformed into the collector; he or she was educated in connoisseurship and authenticity and then encountered an opportunity to buy Indian-crafted objects. In the descriptions of the Indian Building and other Harvey displays the sales

Figure 17. The Main Room in the Indian Building *(n.d.). (Reprinted from Huckel,* First Families*)*

rooms were always mentioned last, after descriptions of the collections that were not for sale, almost as an afterthought, and pictures of the salesrooms are absent from Harvey publications.

The desire to possess these objects was also promoted through the Main Room of the Indian Building (Fig. 17). Designed by Mary Colter, it strongly resembled a domestic interior and suggested how one could live with these objects. The collection on display seemed to belong to a knowledgeable collector-connoisseur, perhaps even the legendary Fred Harvey himself. The room's arrangement combined the abundance and eclecticism of the Victorian interior with the ethnographic exhibit, like a curiosity cabinet writ large. It was also a rather masculine interior; there was a Rooseveltean moose head on the wall, a canoe suspended from the ceiling, Navajo rugs on the floor, baskets hanging on the walls, and Indian pots and baskets lining the shelves. Textiles of primitive manufacture were draped tastefully about, and there were various animal skins, potted cacti, and what appears to be locally crafted furniture. The room was a textbook lesson in a Southwest rendering of an arts and crafts interior. In fact, the same photograph appeared in a 1934 edition of the Harvey souvenir book *First Families of the Southwest* and was captioned "Indian Handicraft Adapted to Interior Decoration." This style of interior decoration was a great success, and the ATSF and the Harvey Company continued to use this combination of Indian and Hispanic motifs in their hotels, trains, and attractions for the next forty years.

There were other parts of the Indian Building that intensified the economy of desire. The "vault" was known to cognoscenti to hold the best of the Harvey collection. It was not open to the public and could be visited by invitation only, presumably the invitation of Herman Schweizer. Referred to later as the "drool room," it was a place where one could look but not possess; it was the collection that helped set the standard of value for all collectible objects (Poling-Kempes 1989, 51).

The display of Indian artisans was central to Harvey displays:

> At Albuquerque in the Indian Building are a number of Navahos spinning and dyeing wool, weaving blankets, braiding quirts, and making primitive silver ornaments with their crude tools. Among them is Tsonsi-Pah, a girl of six years, whose mother instructs her when the pattern becomes too intricate. Pottery makers, apart by themselves, are moulding and decorating, and Indians from other tribes—Santo Domingo, Isleta, Laguna and San Philipe—are lounging around in their picturesque costumes. (*Indian and Mexican Building* 1904, n.p.)

In this description Indians do three things: they make things to sell, they sell things, and they lounge picturesquely. This sort of Indian presence is a hallmark of Harvey literature and Harvey representations of Indians. Indians were mainly conceived of as making objects for tourist consumption or as objects of visual consumption themselves, both as sights to be seen and as photo opportunities (Fig. 18).

Two artisans were promoted as celebrities by the Harvey company: Elle of Ganado, a Navajo weaver, and the Hopi-Tewa potter Nampeyo. In the tourist literature they were practically the only Native Americans known by name; they appeared in many tourist display settings, and their images were widely reproduced. Elle and

Figure 18. Photograph depicting Navajo weavers at the Fred Harvey Indian Building, Albuquerque (c. 1904–10). Note the "wooded" setting inside *the Indian Building, a hive of artisanal industry. (Courtesy of the Southwest Museum, Los Angeles. Photo no. N.33911)*

Nampeyo became tourist attractions in part because, as the Harvey Company claimed, they were regarded by "experts" as the best in their field. But they were also famous for being famous. In Harvey literature Elle was continually referred to as "the most renowned weaver among the Navahos," but her renown had mostly to do with the Harvey-ATSF publicity machine. In the economy of tourism the fact that "thousands of trans-continental travelers have seen this woman of the Navaho at her work" and that "no Indian, man or woman, has met and spoken to more whites than has Elle of Ganado" only served to enhance Elle's celebrity and value as an attraction (Huckel [1913] 1934, n.p.).

If Elle was an important attraction at the Indian Building, Nampeyo was the star of Hopi House, which was built near the El Tovar

Hotel at Grand Canyon and opened in 1905. Mary Colter designed Hopi House as a place where Hopi Indians would live and make craft objects that could be sold. The house was designed to look like a Hopi dwelling and, like the Indian Building, contained ethnographic displays and objects for sale, including Mexican crafts and items of Northwest Coast manufacture. The geography of Hopi House presented the same combination of ethnographic exhibits, artisans at work, and sales rooms. There was also an area whose access was limited to "special customers and important hotel guests" (Kramer 1988, 47; Henderson 1969, 30). Some of the ethnographic displays were created by H. R. Voth, who coauthored the Field Museum account of the Snake dance with George A. Dorsey in 1902.[4]

Hopi House served many of the same display functions as the Indian Building, but the emphasis was on seeing actual Hopis at home, peering into the back regions of native domestic life. John Huckel arranged for Nampeyo and ten members of her family to live at Hopi House from January to April of 1905. The Fred Harvey Company gave them room and board and "what they considered satisfactory prices for the items they crafted while demonstrating to the public." In the evenings the men demonstrated dance rituals for money.[5]

A photograph of Nampeyo and her family at Hopi House in 1905 appeared in the Harvey pamphlet *El Tovar by Fred Harvey: A New Hotel at Grand Canyon of Arizona.* It was captioned "Roof Garden Party, Hopi House" (Fig. 19) and depicts a thoroughly domesticated scene; these are not the Hopis who dance the Snake dance. The accompanying text describes the Indian life on display there:

> These quaintly-garbed Indians on the housetop hail from Tewa, the home of Nampeyo, the most noted pottery-maker in all Hopiland. Perhaps you are so fortunate as to see Nampeyo herself.
>
> Here are Hopi men, women, and children—some decorating exquisite pottery; others spinning yarn and weaving squaw dresses, scarfs, and blankets. Go inside and you see how these gentle folk live. The rooms are little and low, like their small-statured occupants. The floors and walls are as cleanly as a Dutch kitchen. The Hopis are making "piki," twining the raven black hair of the "manas" in big side whorls, smoking corn-cob pipes, building sa-

Figure 19. Photograph depicting Nampeyo and members of her family during their stay at Hopi House in 1905. (Special Collections, The University of Arizona Library)

> cred altars, mending moccasins—doing a hundred un-American things. They are the most primitive Indians in America, with ceremonies several centuries old. (Simpson n.d., 21–23)

Hopi House claimed to reveal Hopi life as it was actually lived, but that life was presented with what Dean MacCannell has called staged authenticity (MacCannell 1976, 91–107; Weigle 1989b, 125). Actual Hopi domestic life looked very different. The display presented as "natural," because it was primitive, a self-contained domestic economy. These "at home" Hopis are defined by their "un-American" activities, which are preindustrial and exotic, but also familiar in their artisanal industriousness.[6]

In addition to the displays of Indians and their material culture at the Indian Building and Hopi House, the Santa Fe Railway and the Fred Harvey Company organized displays at many national and international expositions, including the World's Columbian Exposition in 1893, the 1904 Louisiana Purchase Exposition in St. Louis, and the United States Land and Irrigation Exposition in Chicago in 1910 (Kramer 1988, 47; Trennert 1987, 142). The year 1915 was a big one for the Santa Fe and the Harvey Company. They participated in two expositions in California celebrating the opening of the Panama Canal and the anticipated economic benefits to the West Coast. The Panama-California Exposition was held in San Diego, and the Panama-Pacific International Exposition was in San Francisco.[7] At all of these events the ATSF and the Harvey Indian Department worked in conjunction with scientists to make displays that promoted the Southwest through its aboriginal inhabitants.

The entry of the United States into the First World War in April 1917 resulted in the nationalization of the railroads in December of that year. Until 1920, the railroads were run by the U.S. Railroad Administration, during which time there was no luxury train service. Accordingly, the ATSF and Fred Harvey's tourist business slowed, and all plans for new hotels were shelved (Grattan 1980, 32). After the war, the Santa Fe was faced with the increasing presence of automobiles and a diminishing number of railway passengers. The Santa Fe–Harvey response to this threat was the Indian Detour. This joint venture provided a way for the Santa Fe to extend its control over tourists through the automobile. On May 15, 1926, the first Indian Detour made all of northern New Mexico accessible to thousands of tourists. Touring cars run by the Harvey Company met railroad passengers at either Albuquerque or Las Vegas, New Mexico, and took them on one-, two-, or three-day tours of Indian pueblos, ruins, and artists' studios, and then returned them to the train to continue their journey.

As Harvey had brought southwestern Indian life to tourists at display attractions such as the Indian Building and Hopi House, on the Indian Detours Harvey took tourists directly to the Indians. The attractions included ruins, scenic landscapes, and pueblos where detourists could witness dances or buy pottery. The "Harveycars" were driven by men dressed in a sort of Tom Mix riding costume, and the tour guides, or "couriers," were all women, modeled on the successful Harvey Girls. They wore a Navajoesque costume consisting of a skirt, velveteen shirt, concha belt, and "squash blossom" necklace (Fox 1984, 29–31).[8]

The Indian Detours were relatively short lived—the Depression put a stop to much of the tourism in the region—but they held the promise of even more authentic encounters with Indians. The promotional literature promised that the detours would "open up this little known territory to the discriminating traveler" by taking the tourist "off the beaten path" of the railroad (*Harveycar Motor Cruises*). Meanwhile, as with the railroad attractions, the Indian Detour encounter was thoroughly mediated through the "thunderbird" car, the "cowboy" driver, and the "Indian maiden" guide (Weigle 1989b, 130).

As in the Santa Fe's and Harvey Company's other business dealings, the publication of literature aimed at tourists was a shared affair. For example, the Santa Fe made and paid for advertisements for both the railroad and Harvey operations. But the Harvey Indian Department also produced its own publications—postcards, books, pamphlets, and playing cards—which not only publicized the region but also functioned as souvenirs. These publications were mainly produced between 1899 and the beginning of the First World War but continued to circulate well into the 1930s, going through many editions. Most of the Harvey souvenir materials were published outside the Southwest, in Kansas City, where the company's headquarters were, or, in the case of postcards, by the Detroit Publishing Company.[9]

Postcards were a staple of Harvey publications. Fred Harvey's involvement in postcard publication began in 1899 or 1900, coinciding with the Santa Fe's and Harvey's efforts to promote tourism, and continued through the postcard "craze" in the years before the First World War (Ryan 1982, 15). By about 1903 the Harvey Company was distributing high-quality, color postcards at newsstands and hotels along the Santa Fe route. After 1907 most Harvey postcards had lengthy captions printed on the back, but in general the photographers were not credited.

Although Harvey published postcards with views of places all along the Santa Fe route, the vast majority were of the attractions in Arizona and New Mexico. The images presented landscape views of

Figure 20. Playing card depicting "Navajo Indian Silversmith" (six of diamonds), from a deck of "Souvenir Playing Cards of the Great Southwest" (Kansas City: Fred Harvey, 1911). The face of each card shows a different southwestern scene, including Indian subjects, landscapes, and Fred Harvey attractions and hotels. Frank P. Sauerwein's painting The First Santa Fe Train *(Fig. 21) appears on the back of all the cards. (Special Collections, The University of Arizona Library)*

natural wonders such as the Grand Canyon and the petrified forest, ruins of the Cliff Dwellers, inhabited pueblos, and Harvey hotels and attractions such as Hopi House and the Indian Building. Trains—going over trestles and through mountain passes—figured prominently in these views. In addition, Indian subjects from New Mexico, Arizona, and California constituted a considerable portion of Harvey postcard subjects.[10] In 1911 fifty-two of the Harvey postcard images appeared as a deck of cards, "The Great Southwest Souvenir Playing Cards," which came with an accompanying booklet of captions (Weigle 1989b, 121) (Fig. 20). These cards were probably sold to train passengers to help them pass the time on their long journey.[11]

Many of these postcard and playing card images also appeared in the 1911 souvenir book *The Great Southwest Along the Santa Fe,* which reproduced the images in full color on heavy paper bound

Figure 21. Cover of The Great Southwest. *Frank P. Sauerwein's* The First Santa Fe Train *appeared as a postcard as early as 1908. On the back of the postcard version of this image the caption reads: "Indians watching the first Santa Fe train crossing the continent, whose advent meant so little to their minds, and so much to the white man. The picture is from a famous painting."*

between embossed covers (Fig. 21). Harvey published many other souvenir books, including: *The Camera in the Southwest* (1904); *The Grand Canyon of Arizona* (1908); Karl Moon's *Photographic Studies of American Indians* (1910); and the "sister" book to *The Great Southwest, First Families of the Southwest* (1913), by John F. Huckel.[12] These souvenir books resemble albums of prints or photographs, with high-quality graphic reproductions of paintings and photographs, most in full color, many tipped in. The format is usually one image per page with a caption either beneath it or on the opposite page.

Harvey publications tended to recapitulate Harvey display attractions of Indian life. The souvenir books and postcards organized knowledge about Indians into discrete images of types of people or crafts and brief explanatory texts or captions. In the souvenir books, these displays were collected and bound for study and seemed to represent the totality of Indian and regional life in microcosm.

APPEARING AND DISAPPEARING IN FRED HARVEY'S SOUTHWEST

The Harvey spectacle of Indian life presented images of Indians that seemed to render them entirely understandable and easily classifiable. In Harvey representations, ethnographic groupings hardened into types, determined by bundles of a few characteristics and arranged along an implicit evolutionary scale, from utter savagery to a primitive version of American middle-class life. This was a moral as well as evolutionary scale, which rated Indian groups "good" or "bad" according to their hostility to civilized life. At the bottom were the Apaches, a conquered people who remained unregenerate savages (Fig. 22); then came groups like the Mojave and Pima Indians, who were very primitive but harmless and doomed to disappear; then the Navajos, whose nomadic ways made them somewhat suspect but whose industriousness redeemed them; and finally the Pueblo Indians, peaceful and settled agriculturalists who lived in houses. Among Pueblos, Hopis were deemed the "most primitive," meaning the most isolated and culturally "pure" (Fig. 23).

The Harvey spectacle represented the Southwest as a peaceful and fully domesticated region. It was not the wild, manly, cowboys-and-Indians West represented by Frederic Remington's mounted Plains warriors. *First Families,* a compendium of typical Harvey images, presented picture after picture of Indian domestic life. Men were shown doing masculine things such as hunting and riding horses, and women, when they were not depicted as mothers with children or as olla maidens carrying water, were making baskets, pots, or blankets or preparing food. This book presented a fantasy of Indian society reduced to its simplest social unit, the family, and it conceived of a rural, village utopia, with simplified, familial social relationships.

Figure 22. Apache Warrior at Navaho Rio, Arizona *(1909). This icon of the Apache as warrior-savage appeared in Fred Harvey souvenir books, on postcards, and as one of the "Souvenir Playing Cards of the Great Southwest." (Reprinted from* The Great Southwest*)*

Native American rituals were also an important part of the Harvey spectacle. Ceremonial dances, as exotic performances, were perfect tourist attractions. The Snake dance was the ritual most often represented, but other ceremonial dances, such as the Santo Domingo Corn dance, the Harvest dance at Isleta, and the Hopi Kachina dances, made their appearance in postcard images.

The central icon of Fred Harvey's Southwest was the Indian artisan. Images of weaving, pottery making, basketmaking, silversmithing, and turquoise drilling were prevalent in Harvey publications. In Chapter 3 I will go into more detail about the significance of Indian artisan iconography, but for now it is enough to note that in the tourist market, the crafts Indian artisans made were important commodities, and the tourist literature promoted them for obvious reasons. Like the typology of Indian "tribes" in the Southwest, primitive crafts were codified in a few, strict ways: basketry and pottery

Figure 23. Taking the Elevator in Hopi Land *(c. 1913). This painting by an unidentified artist imagines Hopis as children. Innocent of elevators, Hopis seemed to be simpler versions of modern Americans. (Reprinted from Huckel,* First Families*)*

making were presented as the most primitive crafts, and these were solely the province of women, especially Pueblo women, although Pimas and Apaches were sometimes shown as basketmakers (Figs. 24 and 25). Weaving appeared to be the sole occupation of Navajo women (although it was occasionally acknowledged that Hopi men also wove) and was considered less primitive than basketry or pottery. Finally, silversmithing was what Navajo men did. Even though silversmithing was not strictly a "primitive" craft, because Navajos had learned the skill from the Spanish, it came in for a lot of attention, because the Harvey Company bought and sold Navajo silver. The iconography of these artisan images seemed to urge a commer-

Figure 24. Decorating Pottery, Pueblo of Isleta, New Mexico *(c. 1900–1910). (Reprinted from* The Great Southwest Along the Santa Fe*)*

cial transaction. The images usually presented a lone artisan at work with several examples of completed objects arranged around him or her; the artisan seems to be offering the objects for sale to the viewer, who, as a tourist, was also a potential customer.

These representations of Indian domestic life, artisans, and rituals were icons that spoke to Americans' anxieties about generational continuity, the changing social roles of women, the value of labor, and spiritual "weightlessness" (Lears 1981, 220). The spectacle of these "good Indians" amounted to a prelapsarian fantasy of the premodern; they seemed to represent a time when "tradition" prevailed, when the authority of the father was unquestioned, when men were men and women were women, when people knew the value of an honest day's work, and when spiritual values were immanent. Furthermore, the positioning of these bourgeois values as primitive, or premodern, seemed to provide evidence of their universality and naturalness.

Although images of the good, peaceful, domesticated Indian

Figure 25. Postcard, "A Hopi Basket Weaver, Arizona" (Detroit: Fred Harvey, n.d.). This postcard reproduces a 1901 photograph by A. C. Vroman (Webb and Weinstein 1973, 81). (Special Collections, The University of Arizona Library)

dominated Harvey literature and displays, a parallel strain of "bad Indian" imagery persisted. Images of olla maidens, mothers and children, and contented craftspeople existed alongside representations of the "aged squaw," the Snake dance, and the wild Apache. Whereas icons of the good Indian suggested that the Southwest was a kind of American Eden, the bad Indian imagery suggested that aspects of the primitive were threatening, unassimilable, and ultimately doomed to extinction. These representations carried an exotic, frightening, or grotesque appeal that had been part of the tourist spectacle since the exposition midways of the late nineteenth century, but there was an implicit guarantee that because these Indians were tourist attractions, they were harmless. They had been captured, framed, and tamed within the tourist spectacle.

These positively and negatively charged representations constructed Indians, on the one hand, as objects of desire and, on the other hand, as objects of fear. Indians in the tourist spectacle became a locus for these emotions, which were themselves a result of imperialist social relations. The subject under imperialism desires what the other possesses *and* fears the other's subjectivity, which represents a potential threat. Constructing the other as dichotomous, splitting it in two, renders it powerless. The two Indians, one noble, the other savage, are both marginalized figures, existing in the past of the bourgeois imagination; neither is a full subject. The process of dichotomizing also defuses the fear and the desire of the subject by seeming to universalize or naturalize the ideology that is their source. The fears and desires that arise out of inequitable social relations are rewritten as repulsion and nostalgia, emotions that are indulged in the marginalized realm of the touristic spectacle.

If what *appeared* in the Harvey spectacle of the Southwest were either entirely good or entirely bad Indians, there were a number of aspects of Indian life that did *not appear.* For example, contemporary Apache life, for the most part, was not depicted. A Harvey postcard titled "In Apache Land, Arizona" shows two tepees in a desert landscape; there are no people in sight. The caption on the back reads:

> The Apache Indians were until recently the most warlike of all the Southwestern Indians and have caused the government of the United States, as well as early settlers, no end of trouble. To-day, with their number fast diminishing and with several forts on or near their scattered reservations, with the railroad as an ally, the government has no trouble with them and the Indian has turned his talents to the weaving of baskets and plaques and is at last enjoying the fruits of his labor in peace.

Not only the U.S. government and settlers but the railroad itself defeated the Apaches, whose existence in the present sounds like a pathetic retirement. This text imagines the savage diminished—but redeemed—through conquest. What is pictured on the postcard is not the peaceful present of basketmaking, reservations, and bureaucracy, but the absence of Indians, symbolized by two empty tepees.

When images of Apache people did appear, they portrayed their "warlike" past. They were images that spoke about the power of the conqueror; the Apaches were a worthy foe, but now they are defeated. Images of the consequences of that defeat, however, were not included in the spectacle; the defeated Apaches held no romantic or exotic appeal for the Harvey Company and its tourists. In this regard, it is significant also that Geronimo made no appearance in the Harvey literature. Even though he appeared at world's fairs, the company chose not to capitalize on his notoriety, perhaps because as a living Apache warrior, he might still represent a threat to tourists.

If the Apaches were a kind of "present absence" in the tourist spectacle, in the 1910s and 1920s depictions of Hispanic life in the Southwest were virtually absent from it. Although Hispanic crafts were sold in Harvey curio shops during this period, Hispanic artisans were nowhere apparent.[13] Only a few of the Harvey postcards made at this time depict Hispanic life. One, titled "A Mexican Home, New Mexico," shows an adobe dwelling with bright red *ristras* of chiles drying in the sun and a few tiny figures. Hispanos here occupy the middle distance in a picturesque Southwest landscape, but they do not inhabit it as full-fledged humans.

The disappearance of Hispanic culture was a gradual one. Early Harvey and ATSF literature was much more likely to feature images of Hispanic life. When it opened in 1902, for example, the Indian Building was called the Indian and Mexican Building. *The Camera in the Southwest* contained photographs of a bull fight, burros, Hispanic beggars, a horse and cart, and views of El Paso, but the book's text prefigured the disappearance of Hispanic subjects by claiming that

> the Spanish civilization never took hearty root in this land. It resulted only in a rude and inharmonious grotesquerie. It was earnest, and not brutal, but it failed. These pictures reveal that it pursued a course of "benevolent assimilation," and that the effort affords no historical encouragement to such a course. Degeneration seems to be the only lesson it clearly teaches. (*Camera* 1904, n.p.)

The last two sentences offer a clue as to why Hispanos did not make picturesque subjects: miscegenation. Indians were characterized as pure primitives, but people of Hispanic descent were "figures who simultaneously perverted both the purity of Indian savagery and that of European civilization" (Paredes 1977, 23). Hispanos were perceived as combining the savagery of the Indian with the bad traits of the Spanish, for example, Catholicism.

The stereotypes of Hispanic men and women as lazy, carefree, and dirty with no thoughts of the future were already well established. Early travel literature about the region is full of them (Wallace 1988, 62–69). David Weber suggests that the stereotypes were in place by 1820 and that they descended from the anti-Spanish Catholic stereotype present since colonial times. The "Black Legend" of the Spanish conquest insisted that unlike the English, who came to the New World to make a safe home for their families, the Spanish came to exploit the natives as slaves and to live in luxury (Weber 1979, 299). This anti-Catholicism is also apparent in the absence of depictions of Catholic processions, which occurred in many of the Pueblo villages.

The disappearance of Hispanos in Harvey and ATSF literature probably also had to do with the Mexican Revolution, which began officially in 1901 and lasted until the First World War. It did not serve the interests of tourism to remind tourists of the unrest at the border. However, when U.S. National Guardsmen were stationed along the border during Pancho Villa's raids into the United States in 1916 and 1917, the skirmishes provided a kind of touristic spectacle for Americans at the border, and a cottage industry of making and selling postcards of the war to bored guardsmen sprang up. One such card characterized Mexicans thus: "Types seen along the Mexican Border: The Mexican laborer (peon) is cheap, and it requires many of them to accomplish much, but there are millions to be had. They are happy-go-lucky and are unconcerned for the future" (Vanderwood and Samponaro 1988, x).

In fact, many Hispanos, like many Native Americans, participated in the area's economy as wage laborers; the railroads were built and maintained with Hispanic labor, and Hispanic workers were in high demand as agricultural laborers beginning about 1900, when big irrigation projects were underway (Reisler 1976). But Hispanic peons, peasants defined by their labor, were not exotic. Unlike Indians, Hispanos did not qualify as a primitive folk worth preserving; they were not about to disappear, and anthropologists did not study them. Their presence in the tourist spectacle threatened to reveal the infrastructure of massive capital and exploited labor that lay behind the spectacle. Furthermore, unlike Native Americans, Hispanos were numerous, and boosters for statehood in Arizona and New Mexico (granted in 1912) tried to downplay the fact that most of the inhabitants of these territories were Hispanos, not Anglos (Reisler 1976; Weber 1979). The spectacle of potential Hispanic voters was not picturesque. As a result of these stereotypes and prejudices, since the turn of the century in New Mexico Hispanos have found themselves in what Sylvia Rodríguez has called a "tri-ethnic trap," caught between hegemonic Anglo economic and political power and the "tourism-engendered Anglo glorification of Indian culture" (Rodríguez 1987, 321).

One of the only ways Hispanic Catholicism did appear in the Harvey literature was in the form of ruined churches. Ruins were important attractions in Fred Harvey's Southwest. The tourist literature continually reminded readers that there was no need to go abroad to see real antiquity. Indian Detourists visited ruins, and representations of ancient habitations such as Canyon de Chelly and the ruins of the church of the Gran Quivira were numerous.

Unlike the empty Apache tepees or Hispanic dwellings, which were the only visible signs of contemporary Apache or Hispanic life, the juxtaposition of ancient ruins with contemporary Pueblo life rendered Pueblos "living ruins." The introduction to a Harvey picture book called *Roads to Yesterday Along the Indian-detour* (c. 1926) quotes Charles Lummis: "Among the Pueblos it is possible to catch archaeology alive!" In the tourist spectacle, the ruins at Mesa Verde were presented mainly to demonstrate that living Pueblos were descendants of the ancient Cliff Dwellers. And on Indian Detours, tourists visited a ruin or two and then an "inhabited" pueblo, as if they were exactly the same, the only difference being that Indians lived in one and had abandoned the other. Representing Indians as living ruins made them seem unquestionably authentic and marvelous; rather than having lived *through* history, they emerged directly from a misty, idealized past.

THE MACHINERY OF THE TOURIST SPECTACLE

The touristic desire to experience the Columbian moment is redolent of imperialist nostalgia. A telling example of the rhetoric of this "emotion" is the introduction to the Harvey souvenir picture book

The Camera in the Southwest, which maintains a distinctly elegiac tone even as it praises the agents of progress:

> The ruins of an ancient civilization and the beginnings of a new and higher one in "The Sad Southwest, the Mystical Sunland," that is the compass of the story—the historical romance—related by the series of vivid and interesting pictures contained in this book. It is a story told to the swift eye and not to the slower ear. But to such as are able to interpret the series of pictures with historical understanding, illuminated by imagination, what a tragic fascination the book will possess—what numberless centuries of human history, of life and love, of hope and despair, of endeavor and achievement, are covered by one glance of the eye, from that picture of the light, airy, frail-looking steel bridge by which the Santa Fe railroad leaps the deep, dark chasm of the Cañon Diablo, to the rude ruins of the Cliff-Dweller's castle on another page—but geographically near-by. The one fairly stands for the new civilization of the country, the other probably as fairly for a civilization whose history has vanished in the midst of centuries—never to be recovered, or recovered only in doubtful fragments painfully patched together by the persevering archeologist. (*Camera* 1904, n.p.)

By juxtaposing an image of a train trestle with one of a ruin, the loss that this passage insists on seems inevitable in the face of progress as represented by the railroad. The violence of conquest is erased and replaced by loss or "vanishing," and the response to this process is rendered as nostalgia or "tragic fascination."

The passage also reveals the centrality of the railroad and photography in apprehending and understanding the region. In the tourist spectacle, the train and the camera were the coordinating machinery that reconciled the seemingly contradictory aims of progress and preservation. Together the Santa Fe Railway and the representations (many of them photographic) produced by the Fred Harvey Company embodied the forces of imperialism and nostalgia, erasing and preserving at the same time (Fig. 26).

Images of the encounter between trains and Indians appeared frequently in Harvey publications, and they inscribed the history of the conquest of Native Americans as inevitable. A powerful example is *The First Santa Fe Train,* by Frank P. Sauerwein. The introduction to *The Great Southwest,* which reproduced this painting on its cover

Figure 26. Pueblo of Laguna, New Mexico *(c. 1900–1910). The Santa Fe train passing through Laguna Pueblo juxtaposes the modern and the ancient. The image also appeared as a playing card and a postcard. (Reprinted from* The Great Southwest*)*

(Fig. 21), depicted the history of the Southwest as waves of European conquest: the Conquistadors, the Jesuits and Franciscans, the Americans, and the railroad: "Finally came the railroads—the greatest open trails—and with their coming time alone was required to reclaim the wilderness." In conjunction with the Sauerwein painting, this sentence compressed that history: the train conquered the Indians. The conquest was easy because Indians were perceived as ruins, already gone. In the simple juxtaposition of train and Indian, the power relationship is clear; the Indian could not comprehend, much less resist, the transforming energies of the railroad.

The train was also important in mediating the encounter between tourist and Indian and thus figured prominently in Harvey images. A widely reproduced image is the postcard "Pueblo Indians Selling Pottery" (Fig. 27), which depicts a train, a tourist man and girl, railroad employees, and a group of Pueblo women. The caption

Figure 27. Postcard, "Pueblo Indians Selling Pottery." (Detroit: Detroit Publishing, 1902). (Special Collections, The University of Arizona Library)

on the back of this postcard emphasizes the primitiveness of Pueblo culture:

> Comely Indian maidens, and aged squaws, meet the train and sell their wares. This pottery is made by hand in their crude way, moulded without a wheel, and often decorated with geometrical or symbolical designs. The Pueblo Indian is a true Pagan—superstitious, rich in fanciful legend, and profoundly ceremonious in religion. His gods are innumerable—gods of war, and gods of peace; of famine and of plenty; of sun and of rain.

Standing in for the *Niña,* the *Pinta,* and the *Santa Maria,* the train has brought the tourist to an encounter with an absolutely primitive other. In Harvey's Southwest, the uncomprehending but friendly natives greet the tourists, who learn from this postcard that the natives'

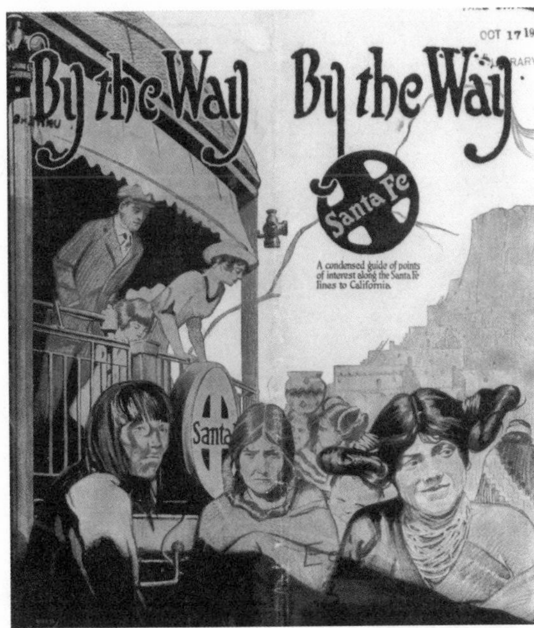

Figure 28. Santa Fe Railway promotional pamphlet (c. 1914–21). (Courtesy of Yale University Library)

civilization and beliefs are embodied in the simplicity of their pots, which the tourists can buy and carry away. The wheelless technology of the pot is implicitly contrasted with that of the train, as are the Indian women with the tourists and railroad employees.

The cover of the Santa Fe Railway pamphlet called *By the Way* (Fig. 28), which shows a tourist family looking down from the rear platform of a Santa Fe train onto a collection of Hopis in their picturesque costumes and coiffures, depicts another train-mediated encounter between tourists and Indians. That the family spectates from a protected, removed position, rather like a box seat at the theater, shows that the ATSF is not promoting the appeal of roughing it; the implication is that the tourists need not leave the train to witness the spectacle. The tourists do not mingle among the Indians, who do not return their gaze, but watch from a safe distance and then move on.

As a cultural practice within capitalism, tourism remakes the world into a spectacle through which the tourist moves freely as a

Figure 29. Indian Detour, *by John Sloan (1927); etching; 6 × 7¼ in. A comic reversal of circling the wagons, this image comments on the power of the tourist's gaze over its object. (Kraushaar Galleries, New York, photograph by Geoffrey Clements)*

consumer of goods. In Fred Harvey's Southwest, the combination of the subjective gaze and the mobility of the train afforded tourists the freedom to choose the objects of consumption. The theatricality of the *By the Way* tableau suggests the "liquidity" of social relations under capitalism and the close association between the marketplace and the theater (Agnew 1986, 6–40). The tourist subject is mercurial and mutable; he or she is at once a spectator and an actor, able to assume numerous roles. In the spectacle, the tourist plays the role of tourist, but the Indian, supposed to be authentic, does not play a role (Evans-Pritchard 1989, 102). The tourist can escape into the panopticon of the train, but the Indian is always caught in the trap of visibility. The tourist is always the subject, the receiver of information; the Indian is always the object of the gaze, a commodity to be consumed visually (see Fig. 29).

An account of visiting the Santa Fe depot in Albuquerque, from Emily Post's 1916 *By Motor to the Golden Gate,* also notes the theatricality of the encounter with Indians. Because she was traveling by automobile, Post's experience was different from that of a railroad passenger. "Stopping at the various Harvey hotels of the Santa Fé system, yet not being travelers on the railroad, is very like being behind the scenes at a theater," she wrote. "The hotel people, curio-sellers, and Indians are the actors, the travelers on the incoming trains are the audience" (160). From "behind the scenes" she went on to describe the station platform:

> You have always on picture postcards seen it filled with Indians. There is not one in sight. Wait though until ten minutes before the California limited is due. Out of the nowhere appear dozens of vividly costumed Navajos and Hopis; their blankets and long braids woven with red cloth, their headbands and beads and silver ornaments fill the platform like a flower display. Old squaws and a few young squat themselves in two rows, forming an aisle between the train and the station salesroom. Although you walk up and down between their forming lines watching them arrange their display of baskets and pottery, they are silent until the first passenger alights, and then unendingly they chorus two words: "Tain cent!" "Tain cent!" (161–62)[14]

Post's exposure of the "reality" behind the Harvey illusion comes in part out of her patrician commitment to traveling in style; she had no interest in roughing it or in trafficking with the natives or the hoi polloi on any kind of intimate basis. But her account is also interesting in that it reveals the degree to which the encounter between Native Americans and tourists was mediated and directed by the Santa Fe and the Harvey Company and the centrality of market relations in the encounter. Indians, who were usually silent in Harvey accounts, here appear as "actors" who have something to say, and from the assembled spectacle, they speak as merchants.

As presented in its publications, the Harvey Southwest was to be apprehended at a glance in a proliferation of colorful, picturesque images. What writing there was served mainly as captions to visual representations of Indian life or as anecdotal ethnographic information. According to *The Camera in the Southwest,* the modern way of understanding is through sight rather than through the words of the storyteller; the "swift eye" is superior to the "slow ear." The reader of the souvenir picture book, the armchair tourist, understood that the region was presented as a spectacle, a story readable by turning the pages and interpreting with the eye.

In Harvey's Southwest, an ancient oral culture was being replaced by a modern culture that was not so much literate as visual, a culture familiar with mechanically reproduced images. Photography was the medium that best captured the vanishing Indian. But most images in Harvey publications tended to merge photography with painting. For example, *The Camera in the Southwest* reproduced black and white photographs, but the book's cover associates the photograph with the painted image. It depicts an artist's palette with the title embossed on it. Inside, the *C* of "Camera" is a stylized camera on a tripod. In addition, Harvey postcards and souvenir books, such as *The Great Southwest* and *First Families,* reproduced paintings based on photographs or photographs with lithographically applied color. In *First Families* the images were all reproductions of paintings, by artists such as O. E. Berninghaus, J. Allen St. John, Bert Phillips, W. E. Rollins, E. Irving Couse, Charles Craig, and Louis Akin, and many of the paintings were made from photographs. The text is explicit about this, and some of Berninghaus's images are signed by him with "after photo" under his name. The use of color in these images helped to "purify" the photograph, emptied the image of the present, of the lived photographic moment, and moved the image into the lost past, that is, the ethnographic present.

Before color photography, postcard manufacturers used many methods of color lithography and halftone reproduction. After 1907, the Detroit Publishing Company, which produced Harvey's postcards, used the Phostint process. This was a time-consuming and complicated color lithography process that resulted in cards that were lavishly and brightly colored. Phostint was advertised by Detroit as "nature's coloring." Their 1912 catalogue claimed: "Phostint cards combine truthfulness and delicacy of color, taste in pictorial composition, rare choice of subject and real educational value. The colors are pure and brilliant and for the projecting lantern are unsurpassed" (quoted in Ryan 1982, 150). Harvey postcards were based on photographic images, but their color reproduction made them seem both more "real" (more natural) *and* more like paintings (more like art). Each postcard was a mass-produced image that denied its mass production; the painterly application of color made it seem individual, original, singular.

The ethnographic "accuracy" of photography, combined with the painterly, picturesque conventions, was an appropriate and useful aesthetic in Harvey representations of Indians. In blurring the line between the original and the work of mechanical reproduction, the images existed in a realm somewhere between art history and natural history, and they achieved their cultural authority through a realism that claimed both scientific and artistic authority. The painterly realism of these representations simultaneously reified and purified what was represented, which was the moment of discovery.

The conflation of photographic and painterly techniques purified these representations in other ways as well. It appears to have been a common practice in the production of Harvey images to retouch photographs and manipulate the content of paintings made from photographs in order to erase evidence of modernity and to present a more primitive image. For example, in *First Families* the watercolor illustrating the text "The Pima Women, Who Make Baskets" shows a woman and a child in a desert setting (Fig. 30). The painting is based on a 1900 photo by "A. Putnam" that was reproduced in Dorsey's *Indians of the Southwest* (Fig. 31). In the painting the woman and child are substantially the same, but they have been moved to a different setting. The shelter has been removed, as have some cloth bundles in front of it and some containers in the foreground that appear to be tin cans. In the painting the figures sit in the desert with only a yucca plant for company. This substitution makes the Pima woman and child seem even more primitive and picturesque. Even though much ethnographic information was removed with the shelter, the new setting seems more natural, more authentic. The markers of culture and history (shelter and cans) have been replaced by nature (yucca plant).[15]

Photography was the means by which Indians were "saved," but the process of rendering the ever-vanishing Indians visible in the

Figure 30. Pima Indian Basket Maker *(c. 1913). (Reprinted from Huckel,* First Families*)*

touristic spectacle constructed Indians as objects of visual consumption. The process and consequences of this objectification are quite clear in the rhetoric used by contemporary photographers working in the Southwest to describe photographing Indians. In a 1907 *Craftsman* article defending the preservation of Indian cultures, the commercial photographer Frederick Monsen wrote about the picturesque charms of the Southwest:

> The glowing atmosphere, the vast stretches of sand that fairly pulsate with light and color, the towering cliffs of rugged, rich-hued rock, and the primitive, peaceful Indian folk who still live after the manner of their forefathers in villages that seem to have been a part

Figure 31. A Pima Basket Maker, *photograph by A. Putnam (1900). (National Anthropological Archives, Smithsonian Institution)*

> of it all since the morning of the world, all these have been found to be eminently worth expressing on canvas or with camera, and the desert has taken its place as a field of unparalleled richness for the man who has *the power and the understanding* to find and express what is there [emphasis added]. (683)

The Southwest might be an artistic mother lode for the photographer or artist, but it took "power and understanding" to mine it. Thus Monsen hints that in fact Indian subjects are difficult to render. Much of this difficulty had to do with what was desired and expected of Indians in representations.

In *First Families,* John F. Huckel wrote the caption to the illustration *A Hopi St. John,* a watercolor by O. E. Berninghaus based on a photograph depicting a mother and two children. Huckel emphasized the natural picturesqueness of Indians:

> Unconsciously the primitive people group themselves with an effect pleasing to the eye of the artist—"they make the picture"—to a degree that deliberate posing can seldom reach. . . . The little figure with leg gracefully poised, a mystical smile illuminating his face, might well be a St. John by one of the old masters.

But in a 1913 letter to F. W. Hodge, director of the Southwest Museum in Los Angeles, Huckel remarked about the images in the book:

> In this volume I have tried to select subjects showing the Indians in natural, unconscious attitudes. As you know, when their pictures are taken they immediately pose.

And Karl Moon, who contracted with the Harvey Company to sell his photographs of Indians at the Harvey hotel, El Tovar, noted in his catalogue:

> It has been my wish to keep my pictures free from evidence of the white man, even the camera man, so that the awkward self-consciousness and artificiality, that too often is apparent, might give place to that freedom and ease that is so natural and pleasing a part of the Indian. (Moon n.d., 1)

What was demanded of the represented Indian was "naturalness" and "freedom and ease," elements of the picturesque. But with the knowledge that they were being observed, Indians might become self-conscious and the desired "unconscious" effect would be lost. Thus the awareness of being observed, the power to see, the very state of subjectivity, made the Indian unfit for representation.

This was where Monsen's "power and understanding" came in. It took both mastery and intimate knowledge of Indians to capture them. Ideally, intimacy alone should suffice, and this might involve a certain amount of "playing Indian." In a 1907 issue of the *Craftsman* Monsen and the painter Louis Akin each wrote an article praising the other's work. Both Monsen and Akin had lived among Hopis for a time, and Akin remarked that one must gain Indians' friendship and "coax" them into becoming unselfconscious in the presence of the camera and the sketchbook: "Before I could understand the Indian, I had to learn how to 'get behind his eyes,'—to think as he thought, to live as he lived, and to become, so far as was possible for a white man, an accepted member of his society" (Akin 1907, 684). The ability of the artist or photographer to play Indian assumed his superior evolutionary position, which allowed him to practice a "catholicity of taste" (Monsen 1907, 685). The photographer or artist was able to master two cultures, his own and the Indian's.

In the representation of Indian women, the power of the photographer becomes at once clearer and more complicated. In a 1900 *Overland Monthly* article copiously illustrated with his own photographs, George Wharton James called Indian women "Copper Cleopatras" and argued in terms fraught with orientalism that the white man was in the best position to appreciate all types of female beauty:

> It is a singular fact, noticed by more than one ethnologist, that the more limited the scope of choice, and the lower in the scale of civilization, the more restricted are the estimates of beauty. The higher the civilization, on the other hand, the wider the ideas of beauty. The cultured, traveled American or European can see beauty in the Turkish woman, the maid of Bethlehem, the Tartar wife, or the Circasian slave. (1900b, 199)

Concomitantly, to the Mojave Apache "the coarse, heavy, painted faces of his women are far more attractive than the paler, thinner faces of the white women. His is one standard; that of the white man is another. The Moki man sees little beauty except in the faces of his kind" (200). The white man had the power to see with the eyes of the Indian and judge the "Moki" by her standards, but not vice versa. Not only did Indians lack the power to possess anything other than their own culture, but as objects of desire they could not even desire something other. The power to desire and possess everything in the world was solely the prerogative of the white man.

If intimacy and playing Indian failed to fulfill photographic desire, one brought more powerful strategies into play. The inequitable power relationship between photographer and Indian is evident in the metaphors of hunting that pervade writings by photographers, especially after the introduction of the roll-film box camera, which gave the photographer greater mobility and enabled him to work almost without detection. In a promotional pamphlet called *With a Kodak in the Land of the Navajo* (c. 1910), Frederick Monsen recalled the pre-Kodak days:

> Our method was something like this: the Indian was secured and seated, my assistants standing by ready to hold him should he attempt to run away. Then the big black camera was brought into action, and the long, murderous looking lens was pointed straight at his heart, with myself at the other end covered with a great black cloth and apparently about to pull the trigger which would usher poor Lo into eternity. You can imagine the effect on the poor ignorant, superstitious Indian, who had probably never faced anything worse than a Winchester rifle. The hackneyed expression, "Look pleasant, please," must have sounded like a death sentence to the poor aborigine, who, on being released from his torture and apparently immediate death, must have considered it the narrowest escape of his life. Can you imagine securing a natural portrait under such conditions? (n.p.)

Monsen's description calls to mind Sumner Matteson's photograph of Hopis being photographed and interviewed by ethnographers (Fig. 6). Monsen was much happier with the flexibility that a Kodak allowed him, but the hunting metaphor persisted: "Long practice in focusing has made it possible for me to do it almost by instinct, as a rifleman will hit the target when firing from the hip or at arm's length almost as often as when the weapon is sighted, and my subjects seldom know when they are photographed" (1907, 687). The Kodak is clearly a superior weapon in the hunt for Indians.

George Wharton James also used hunting rhetoric:

> To the student and the photographic artist nothing is more interesting than to watch for and endeavor to catch these flitting moods of expression on the Indians' faces. The pursuit has all the fascinations of the difficult hunt. It is as easy to catch the illusive [*sic*] chamois by running him down, as an expressive photograph of a wild Indian. (1903b, 13)

James claimed seldom to pose an Indian and referred to Indian babies as "field cupids":

> And now, like all other hunters, I prize most the game I find hardest to get. For as the years roll on the Indian becomes more and more "civilized," and now he "works" the photographer for all he is worth, or all he thinks he is worth, and it costs a small fortune to accomplish much with a camera where one is a stranger. (1902c, 58)

The economy of desire governed James's hunt. A wild, unposed Indian was most valuable because he was most rare, and presumably the photographer took these photos for free. Least valuable was the photograph for which the subject was paid. Apparently Indian children and babies were easier to capture without the struggle of paying them. Also, playing the role of the hunter was another way of playing Indian, of getting behind the Indian's eyes, as Akin put it. In hunting Indians with a camera, the photographer reenacted a version of the buffalo hunt, the vanishing Indian being analogous to the nearly extinct buffalo, and the photographs became trophies of the hunt. Like life groups in museum displays the photographs preserved (or taxidermied) the Indian.

THE TOURISTIC EXCHANGE

In most tourist accounts, what Indian people thought about tourists was almost never examined. Most guidebooks and promotional materials depicted Indians as ever hospitable to the uninvited tourist "guests"; Indians were just there, like part of the landscape, to be observed for free (Fig. 32). There are, however, a few narratives that reveal how tourists imagined Indians' receiving objects from the "civilized" world. The most interesting—in that they depict the process of representation as an exchange—have to do, again, with photography. In a 1927 *Couriers' Instructional Bulletin* for tour guides on the Indian Detour, one of the "miscellaneous questions" tourists had asked was: "How do the different pueblos divide the funds derived from fees charged for the taking of photographs (as at Acoma—$5) among such a large population?" Elizabeth DeHuff, who was in charge of the couriers, wrote an answer: "Nobody knows how the money is expended. It is one of the Indian secrets, differing perhaps

Figure 32. Photograph depicting an Indian Detour car "encountering" Pueblo women selling pottery (c. 1929). (Photo by Edward Kemp, courtesy Museum of New Mexico, Neg. No. 47185)

in each pueblo." She went on to describe the trouble that once arose when one faction in a village was paid and the other was not: A "regular riot occurred in the pueblo between two factions over a single dollar given for the privilege of taking pictures. The side that received the dollar evidently refused to divide fifty-fifty with the other side." She concluded that she was not sure if the "'rake offs' or tips" went directly into the pockets of pueblo leaders or if "they may be used in a communal fund to be expended for the common good" (DeHuff 1927, n.p.).[16]

Another example of Native American reactions to an encounter with photographic technology is in a 1921 account published in the *Santa Fe Magazine* about a group of Hopis seeing a movie for the first time. The movie was *The Mollycoddle* (1920), starring Douglas Fairbanks as the mollycoddle who regains his manly vigor in the Southwest. The climax of the movie depicted the destruction of a Hopi village by a landslide. What would the Indians do when they "saw" their village destroyed? The unspoken assumption in the article was that the innocent eyes of the Hopis would not be able to tell the movie from reality. According to the article, when the movie was shown, the reaction was first silence and then laughter, which the writer said was probably not amusement: "It had knocked them dead. . . . We had given them the best that the white man had in the way of a miracle; we had shown them a spectacle which had amazed some of us, a spectacle which is making hardened movie fans sit up stiff in their seats all over the world today. But we had not shaken them away from their old beliefs" (Bechdolt 1921, 22–23).

One more account of the "primitive" response to photography is instructive. In *With a Kodak in the Land of the Navajo,* Frederick Monsen related the following story:

> An Indian will look at his photograph and recognize it an image of himself. He realizes that he is still complete physically; hence this picture must be part of his soul, and if he should die his soul would be incomplete—hence his objection.
>
> Apropos of this, I remember having surreptitiously secured a photograph of a fine old Navajo—a man whom I had approached on the subject, but who had sternly refused all bribes. The following day I missed one of my Kodaks and, knowing that these Indians were not inclined to theft, I could not account for its disappearance. The second day after the loss a young Indian friend informed me that he knew where the Kodak was. That afternoon I found it on the crest of a mesa, where it had been placed on top of a Navajo shrine or altar as an offering to the Nature gods. Thus I found the camera not only satisfactory to men, but fit for the gods. (n.d., 24–25)

It is not clear that the person who placed the camera on the "shrine" meant it as an "offering," but the white man's story of the encounter with Indians demanded this explanation (as did the interests of Kodak).

All three of these narratives tell essentially the same story, and they reaffirm the power of the observing visitors over the Indians. In each the Indian reaction is typically primitive, which is characterized as uncomprehending, simplemindedly literal, and childlike. What happens when you give Indians a camera or money or a moving image of themselves is that they cannot comprehend these objects' symbolic meanings or functions and hence cannot "possess" them. The objects of civilization making the journey into primitive society are imagined to be extremely powerful and disruptive. The story is similar to the legend of Indians' trading away Manhattan for twenty-four dollars' worth of beads and recalls the disruptive power of the Coca-Cola bottle in the film *The Gods Must Be Crazy* (1981). Furthermore, the silence of the Indians is an important feature in all these accounts. The tour guide, the photographer, and the movie makers all presume to explain Indian motives without asking any Indians for an answer or an opinion. Their silence in the tourist literature parallels their "blindness"; they do not possess the power to see tourists, nor can they speak.

The exchange between tourists and Native Americans did not produce mutual communication. Mutual communication occurred back home, between the tourist and his or her audience. As Indian-made objects (or representations of Indians) traveled out from the region, they became benign sources of knowledge, valuable but not destructive or threatening. Removed from the site of the touristic encounter and taken home, souvenirs—be they postcards, snapshots, or a pot purchased from an Indian artisan—became objects loaded with meaning, sources for narratives of the region. The tourist narrative is a story of a quest for contact with authenticity and gains its authority from the journey into and return from the realm of the other. As vehicles for touristic narratives, the Harvey postcards, playing cards, and picture books made especially appropriate souvenirs. They recapitulated the spectacle of the Indian Southwest as a series of attractions and could function as "museums of Human nature" that constructed meaning and organized knowledge of the other (Foucault 1977, 202; Haraway 1986, 23).

As an armchair tourist, the reader of Harvey souvenir publications could create a variety of narratives. For example, the picture book *The Great Southwest* could be read as a geographic journey west from Colorado, through New Mexico and Arizona, to California, or it could be read thematically, according to landscape or attraction. Postcards could be collected and arranged into an album, like cartes de visite or snapshots. Postcards were especially effective at verifying the tourist's experience and bearing narratives; bought on site in the realm of the other and mailed to friends and relatives back home, the postcard bore an inscription by the tourist and an authenticating postmark (Stewart 1984, 138).

What the spectacle of Indian life in Fred Harvey's Southwest offered was not a connection with authenticity that would bring an end to nostalgia and longing but the maintenance and celebration of difference and distance, which produced nostalgia and longing. Ethnic tourism is a discourse that demands that tourists make meaning out of the disjunction between the tourist subject and the other. Out of this distance and the desire or nostalgia it creates, interpretation is required; the distance creates a space within which the tourist can establish his or her authority. What the tourist narrates is not only a story of "discovery," with souvenirs perhaps metonymically prompting the narrative, but also the narrative of the tourist's own subjectivity. Thus the touristic encounter becomes an event through which one establishes one's subjectivity in relation to an other.

Sightseeing and collecting souvenirs might seem to satisfy the imperialist nostalgia that motivated ethnic tourism in the Southwest. But ironically, the past (or simplicity or authenticity) that the primitive represents and that is so desired always slips from one's grasp: tourism constructs authenticity in such a way that it is never attainable. Sightseeing is doomed; the very presence of the observer spells the end of the authenticity of the observed. The same is true of the collector, whether ethnographer or tourist; in the act of collecting, the collectible disappears from the world of its origin and the experience of collecting it is no longer available. Collecting brings about a literal depletion of the culture one desires so desperately, which makes one desire it all the more—a process similar to the erasing and preserving powers of the train and the camera. The unfulfillable desire that drives collecting may be why it is often referred to as a pathology. Similarly, tourism is a kind of pathology in that the touristic journey must be enacted time and time again.

The touristic economy of desire also speaks about the energies of capital. Just as capitalism needs natural and human resources, so it needs cultural otherness to maintain its own cultural practices. Ethnic tourism is one of the mechanisms by which capitalism, as it eliminates different systems of production, incorporates cultural difference as otherness—as primitive, old-fashioned, or quaint (Williamson 1986, 112). But only difference that is perceived to be disappearing is celebrated. Other differences, such as class inequalities in modern cities, are in no danger of disappearing—or being preserved as tourist attractions. To continue to function, ethnic tourism in the Southwest has had to maintain a constant Indian disappearing act. So far it has been very successful; for the past one hundred years tourists have been hurrying to the region to see authentic Indian culture before it disappears.

RE-PRESENTING THE TOURISTIC ENCOUNTER

The tourist spectacle of Fred Harvey's Southwest denied the subjectivity of Native Americans by representing them as vanishing, silent, and blind to modernity. But of course, Native Americans are aware of and have a very great interest in the "outside" world, and Indian artists and artisans have long depicted tourists in their work. However, these types of representations have not been widely collected by non-Indians, nor have they received much scholarly attention, because they are not perceived to be authentically Indian (Evans-Pritchard 1989, 90).

Land of Enchantment, a 1946 watercolor by Woodrow Crumbo, a Creek-Potawatomi artist, reimagines the Fred Harvey version of the touristic encounter and comments on it in terms of the spectacle and exchange (Fig. 33). In the painting, all three tourists wear eyeglasses and intently inspect a Navajo woman and girl, who do not return their gaze but peer obliquely from lowered faces. In contrast to the tourists, the woman and girl are covered up; the little girl is enfolded in a blanket, and the woman stands behind the blanket she is selling. They seem to be trying to deflect the tourists' gaze, which suggests an attempt to resist the inequitable social relations present in the encounter.

This painting recalls other depictions of the touristic encounter, including Trixie's in *The Tourists;* the Santa Fe Railway pamphlet, *By the Way;* and John Sloan's etching, *Indian Detour.* In all these images, female tourists either predominate (as in the Sloan image) or are

Figure 33. Land of Enchantment, *by Woodrow Crumbo (1946); watercolor on paper; 17 3/4 × 23 1/2 in. (The Philbrook Museum of Art, Tulsa, Oklahoma)*

closest to the Indians being observed (as in the Santa Fe pamphlet). Women tourists in these representations are most active in the encounter and exchange: in the case of *The Tourists,* it is Trixie who selects the souvenir pots to buy (her tourist beau pays for them), and in the Crumbo watercolor, it is the woman who is most closely inspecting the rug. Her husband stands back, presumably preparing to pay. The touristic encounter might recapitulate the masculine discovery narrative, but the exchange—the purchase of souvenirs—inscribed the gendered nature of consumerism on this narrative. The humor of *Land of Enchantment* hinges on the woman's role as consumer. Her largeness, the profusion of her accessories, and the smallness of her costume, call attention to her as a consumer and an object of display. The tourist women in these images are not simply observers of the spectacle of Indian life but, like the Indian women they purchase souvenirs from, are part of what is on display. Even though they are the primary consumers in these images, they too become consumed by the spectacle.

The question of what exactly is for sale here is also interesting: it is surely blankets, but because the girl and the woman are so closely covered by the blankets, they are almost part of the merchandise. Thus, viewing the Indians through their "spectacles," the tourists can hardly distinguish Indian from commodity. Furthermore, the broken Land of "Enchantment" sign indicates that the land is not inherently mystical or wondrous but is in fact under the spell of the tourist spectacle and commodification.

Finally, although the exchange of blankets for tourist dollars seems impending, the painting indicates that another exchange has already taken place. A doll, apparently representing a white cavalry officer, peeks out from the little girl's blanket.[17] There are a number of ways to interpret the presence of this doll. It could be seen as a "trifle," like the beads traded for Manhattan and thus a harbinger of the destruction of the girl's culture. But the fact that she possesses a representation of the other culture opens up a crack in the hegemony of the exchange. It suggests that she might be creating her own narratives, that she is not simply an object of exchange but is also a subject, capable of creating meaning. The image stops short of suggesting the possibility of dialogue, but it hints at the possibility of meaningful interpretive activity on both sides of the encounter.

Crumbo's image rewrites the Columbian encounter to reveal its commercial underpinnings. An exchange may be taking place, but the Navajo woman and girl are not available for objectification. In resisting the touristic gaze, they will not become objects of desire; they, and the Land of Enchantment, are not accessible or possessible. Instead, it is the tourists who are curiosities available for inspection; they are what is "discovered" in this version of Fred Harvey's Southwest.

CHAPTER 3

THE SPECTACLE OF INDIAN ARTISANAL LABOR

From the late 1890s to the 1920s, much of the information about Native Americans of the Southwest that circulated in ethnographic reports, popular magazines, and tourist literature was about their crafts, particularly basketmaking, Pueblo pottery, and Navajo blankets and silverwork. Markets emerged nationwide for Indian crafts; books and magazine articles described and evaluated Indian crafts, educating the public in the connoisseurship of craft objects; and Indian artisans and the objects they made were displayed in museums and at expositions regionally and nationally.

At the center of this spectacle of Indian craftsmanship were two figures: the collector-connoisseur and the Indian artisan. As a model of bourgeois subjectivity, the collector, via acts of possession and narration that organized knowledge about Native Americans and their crafts, constructed and authorized his own subject position. As represented in the spectacle, the Indian artisan produced not only collectible objects but also authenticity, which was located in the primitiveness of Indian hand labor. The collector-connoisseur demonstrated and explained this authenticity and made it available to non-Indian Americans for a variety of cultural uses.

The spectacle of Indian artisanal labor revived a republican myth of artisanal labor at a time when work in the United States was becoming increasingly industrialized and corporate. The immediacy of Indian craftwork—its relatively unmediated methods of production—seemed to provide an antidote to the alienated labor of industrial production. The practice of "primitive" crafts became central to reform strategies such as the arts and crafts movement and manual training in education. And because the Indian artisans represented were predominantly women, the spectacle spoke to issues surrounding women's labor in American society. Furthermore, the spectacle of Indian artisanal labor, which was constructed by non-Indian ethnographers, writers, and artists and reflected and reaffirmed American bourgeois values and identity, had lasting consequences for the Native American artisans of the Southwest. Represented as primitive craftspeople, bound by nature and tradition, they continued to be marginalized from the centers of cultural and economic power.

In this chapter, one artisan, the Hopi-Tewa potter Nampeyo (c. 1860–1942), will appear several times. I have chosen to discuss Nampeyo in particular because she was the first—and for years the only—Native American artisan to become well known by name, and her contacts with science, tourism, and the art market are representative in the development of the spectacle of Indian artisanal labor in the Southwest. Pictures of Nampeyo appeared in a variety of publications and circulated widely, and she was promoted as a tourist attraction by the Fred Harvey Company. Her pots were purchased by scientists for museums of natural history, by tourists as souvenirs, and by collectors of Indian art.[1]

THE DEVELOPMENT OF MARKETS FOR INDIAN CRAFTS

Native Americans in the Southwest have engaged in economic exchanges with Europeans since the Spanish Entrada, but it was not until the mid-nineteenth century that a market economy was firmly established and began to expand in the region. In 1821 the newly independent Mexican government legalized trade with the United

States, which opened the door for a flood of Anglo-American interests. Early traders from the United States exchanged manufactured goods and staples such as tobacco, coffee, flour, and sugar (as well as liquor and guns) for pelts and buffalo robes. U.S. annexation of the Southwest territories from Mexico in 1848 did little to change the nature of trade in the region. Native Americans continued to trade in villages and with pack trains that moved through the area. However, in 1868, when the Navajos were moved to their reservation, the structure of the area's economy changed. In an effort to "civilize" Indians, the U.S. government licensed traders to set up posts on the reservation; in addition, unlicensed traders operated posts along the reservation's borders. The economy was based, as before, on credit and barter, but the permanency of these posts brought Native Americans more firmly into the national economy. In exchange for food staples and manufactured goods such as tools and fabric, traders received livestock, agricultural goods, wool, and craft objects such as pots, blankets, and baskets. Traders depended on contractors in Santa Fe and other commercial centers to provide them with goods to trade and a market to turn goods into cash (McNitt 1962, 3–68). At the posts serving Navajos, a system of pawn based on silver jewelry came into practice. To get through lean times before sheep shearing, a person could leave his or her jewelry in pawn at the store in exchange for store credit.

Two of the most prosperous and influential reservation traders were Thomas Keam, who established his post twelve miles east of the Hopi First Mesa in 1875, and Lorenzo Hubbell, who set up a post at Ganado, Arizona, in 1876 or 1878 and later founded a virtual empire of trading posts (McNitt 1962, 201). Through the 1880s and 1890s Keam, Hubbell, and other traders were the mediators between Native Americans and ethnographers, photographers, artists, and tourists who visited the area. Visitors often stayed at the trading posts while they did their research or used the posts as bases of operation.

Traders were instrumental in establishing national markets for Indian-made goods. Some of their best customers were ethnologists, who bought not only provisions for their expeditions but also Indian-crafted objects for their collections. In addition to creating a direct demand for traditional objects by buying them from traders and the Indians themselves, ethnologists helped to create a national ethnic art market. As Nancy Parezo has pointed out, one of the effects of ethnographic collecting was the "transformation of native material culture into marketable ethnic art" (1986, 16). The objects ethnologists took from the Southwest to universities and museums in the nation's cities were valued because they were perceived to be either already or soon to be scarce. Taken out of their original context and put into museums or displayed at international expositions, they became exemplary artifacts that set the standards for authenticity. By publicizing the existence of these rare commodities and establishing their value, ethnographers and anthropologists played a key role in the markets for these objects. Private collectors began buying objects using the grounds for authenticity and value set by ethnologists (Wade 1985, 167).

The relationship between the potter Nampeyo and the Smithsonian ethnologist Jesse Walter Fewkes, who excavated at Sikyatki in 1895 and 1896, illustrates the connections among artisans, ethnologists, and the ethnic art market. In the *17th Annual Report of the Bureau of American Ethnology,* published in 1898, Fewkes wrote:

> The most expert modern potter at East Mesa is Nampéo, a Tanoan woman who is a thorough artist in her line of work. Finding a better market for ancient than for modern ware, she cleverly copies old decorations, and imitates the Sikyatki ware almost perfectly. She knows where the Sikyatki potters obtained their clay, and uses it in her work. Almost any Hopi who has a bowl to sell will say that it is ancient, and care must always be exercised in accepting such claims. (660)

By 1898 the market for authentic Indian pottery was well established, enough so that Fewkes felt compelled to issue a warning about false claims as to the provenance of pots. But Fewkes did not admit his own complicity in potters' finding "a better market for ancient than for modern ware." In fact, some of the ambiguity concerning authenticity was caused by ethnologists themselves: in 1896 Walter Hough, Fewkes's assistant at the excavation of "Old Cuñopavi" on Second Mesa, bought some of Nampeyo's pots to exhibit alongside ancient ceramics in the National Museum in Washington, D.C. Another irony of the revival style of pottery produced by Nampeyo and other potters is that it helped to displace the traditional local pottery, the so-called Polacca Polychrome, which had been judged decadent and of low quality by ethnologists (Wade 1985, 174).

As ethnologists descended on Native Americans of the Southwest, so did the railroads. The completion of the Atchison, Topeka and Santa Fe Railroad's route to California in the early 1880s marked the beginning of the swift expansion of national markets for Indian-made goods and the increasing presence of cash in the local economy. By about 1885 mass-produced goods were widely available to the people of the region, and as a result, they began replacing many locally made objects. For example, as Native Americans began using metal vessels, many potters stopped making ceramic vessels for their own use (except for religious objects or specialized cooking or service ware) and began to make objects for the non-Indian markets. The Santa Fe's and Fred Harvey's promotion of tourism in the Southwest created a market for Indian-made curios and souvenirs. Via the railroad and Harvey attractions, tourists and collectors came into direct contact with Indians and gave them cash for their crafts. By 1900 in some pueblos, potters were making and selling almost all their pottery directly to tourists for cash (Brody 1976, 74). Increasingly, Indian-crafted objects appeared not only in museums and at exhibitions but also in department store windows, in train stations, and in middle-class homes in the East and the Midwest (Fig. 34).

Outside markets began to determine the sorts of Indian crafts that were produced as many Native American craftspeople made what demand dictated. Because purchasers ranged from museums of natural history to individual collectors, department stores, and tourists, a wide variety of goods could be produced. In general, the markets split between the poles of the art market and the curio market, with the art market making the most limiting demands on what sorts of objects were acceptable as authentic. Nevertheless, only a few types of objects dominated both markets. Much of southwestern Native American material culture, such as musical instruments, weapons, agricultural implements, clothing, tanning and leatherwork, and ceremonial paraphernalia, did not find a national market. Baskets, pots, rugs, and silver jewelry were by far the objects most in demand, possibly because these objects could easily find places in middle-class American households and were considered utilitarian as well as decorative. Amy Richards Colton, writing in the *Garden and*

Figure 34. Photograph depicting Navajo blankets for sale in the window of the Marshall Field department store, Chicago (1899). The card in the window reads: "Interesting Collection by Lieut. Davison U.S.A. of Navajo Blankets Representing all the different weaves from the [illegible word] to the present period. Entire collection for sale. No single pieces can be sold. Oriental Rug Department. 3rd Floor Main Bldg." Department-store windows resembled ethnographic museum displays in that they presented objects of desire available to viewers but preserved and tantalizingly out of reach behind glass. (National Anthropological Archives, Smithsonian Institution)

Home Builder in 1926, pointed out that in the Southwest one could find "a great variety of household objects, having real decorative value." She recommended that pots be used as flower vases, lamps, or garden pots and that baskets be used for "scrap-baskets" or simply for "decorative charm." In addition, she noted that Navajo rugs were useful as floor coverings, and belts and scarfs could make interesting bellpulls, borders for curtains, valences, or runners for tables (Colton 1926, 31–32).

A brief survey of some of the changes in the production of Indian craft objects will illustrate the extent to which non-Indians controlled the markets for these goods and how market demands influenced production. The most obvious case in point is the Navajo blanket, which was initially a garment, but which national markets transformed into a floor covering and wall hanging. The Navajos, since their arrival in the region around 1500, had learned weaving from the Pueblos and found it an economically expedient way to use the wool from the sheep they herded. Navajo women wove blankets for their own use as well as for trade with other Indians and Europeans. With the arrival of the traders, the market for rugs rapidly expanded, and traders were quick to suggest to weavers designs that would sell. Some traders, such as Lorenzo Hubbell, tried to control quality, which fluctuated wildly, especially when traders sometimes bought rugs by the pound. But it was the traders, dealers, and collectors, rather than the weavers, who decided what the standards of quality were. Under the influence of collectors and the arts and crafts movement, high-quality rugs were defined as those woven on upright looms and made with hand-spun yarn and natural (not aniline) dyes. These rugs were expensive to produce and had a very small market. On the other hand, tourist demand was high, and in the tourist market these high-quality characteristics mattered less, so many weavers made rugs using Germantown yarns and found ways to increase production to meet the demand. Designs also changed under the influence of non-Indian demand. In the mid-nineteenth century, Navajo blankets were usually woven in broad horizontal stripes. As they came to be used as rugs, their designs began to include borders and other features reminiscent of oriental carpets. In general, as demand increased, quality went down, so that by 1900 there was a consensus among preservationists that the weaving of Navajo rugs was a dying art (Lummis 1899, 9–10). By 1920, however, there was a "revival" of the craft initiated by collectors such as Mary Cabot Wheelwright (who owned the Indian Craft Shop in Boston), the Fred Harvey Company, and some traders. In this revival the standards were based on the "classic" blankets of the prereservation era of the mid-nineteenth century (Rodee 1981).

In contrast to the Navajo rug, a demand for Pueblo textiles did not develop in non-Indian markets. Pueblo men, especially the

Hopis, continued to weave textiles for internal consumption and for trade with other Pueblos, but as they increasingly turned to wage labor, they left weaving. Unlike Navajo society, in which the primary work was herding and a surplus of wool was produced, Pueblo society did not have the potential for a large export production (Kent 1976, 99).

Silver was also a trade item from the beginning of its manufacture by Navajos, who learned how to work it from Mexican *plateros* after the middle of the nineteenth century (Adair 1944, 3–6; Bedinger 1973, 20). Silver in the form of coins and jewelry was the medium of exchange among Navajos. Before 1890 Navajos did not make silver for sale to non-Indians, although some whites traded goods for silver and bought dead pawn. The Fred Harvey Company bought pawned silver from the traders to sell to tourists, but these pieces were often considered too heavy for non-Indian tastes, so in 1899 the company began ordering lighter jewelry specifically for tourist consumption. Eventually the Harvey Company got into the business of providing precut turquoise stones and silver to the traders, who then gave it, along with design specifications, to the Navajo silversmiths to make into jewelry. By the 1920s the manufacture of "Indian" jewelry was a huge business and was conducted by non-Indians in Gallup and other places. After 1918, to meet the demand and to earn cash, Navajo women began to make silver jewelry (Adair 1944, 9–25). The Hopis, Zunis, and the Rio Grande Pueblos learned silversmithing from the Navajos, but it was not commercialized to the same extent among the Pueblos until the 1920s, when demand for silver jewelry increased and buyers looked for other sources. Zuni silver work became popular, and production increased accordingly. At Zuni in 1920 there were eight silversmiths; there were ninety in 1938 (Adair 1944, 135–36).

In contrast to Navajo weaving and silversmithing, pottery and basketmaking were practiced before the arrival of Europeans. The interest that ethnologists and traders showed in ancient ceramics led to a revival of ancient designs and techniques. Nampeyo was credited with beginning the revival in Hopi pottery when she began copying designs and techniques found in pottery at the Sikyatki ruins. Whether Nampeyo was the first potter to revive the Sikyatki style is a matter of debate, but the story of Nampeyo as its originator became part of a "marketing myth" (McChesney 1994, 6). As in the revival of classic Navajo textiles, the Anglos responsible for the invention of these "traditions" looked to a period before European conquest for their standards of quality and design.

Whereas the art-oriented market for pots tended to value antiquarian features, tourist ware was often miniature and figurative—partly because potters made smaller objects to increase their output and partly because tourists needed small, easily transportable souvenirs. As a result, a new genre of figurative ceramics developed. For example, the popular Tesuque "Rain God" was possibly suggested by Jake Gold, a Santa Fe dealer, who wholesaled them to curio dealers throughout the United States (Babcock and Monthan 1988, 14). Tourist items were often nonutilitarian objects or miniatures of useful ones, and the more "exotic" they were perceived to be the better.

Indian-made baskets were also in demand as souvenirs and collectibles. The last half of the 1890s witnessed a craze for collecting baskets, especially those made by California Indians such as the Maidu, Pomo, Hupa, and Yurok. Large collections of baskets were amassed very quickly by collectors such as George Wharton James and Charles Lummis. Although these collectors desired "traditional" baskets, Indian weavers also incorporated nontraditional forms and designs into their baskets for the tourist and other markets (Connor 1896; Washburn 1984). Photographs of the interiors of trading posts show them hung on the walls as decoration, and they were in demand as household objects of decoration and utility (Fig. 35).

THE COLLECTOR-CONNOISSEUR

As the markets for Indian-made objects expanded and diversified, as objects circulated variously as scientific data, collectibles, and curios, connoisseurship—knowing how to determine an object's authenticity and value—became important. All the markets—ethnographic, art, and tourist—demanded some form of authenticity, a bundle of characteristics that usually included that the object be handmade by a Native American in an "Indian" style. The articles about southwestern Indian crafts that filled national and regional periodicals at the turn of the century focused almost exclusively on the production techniques and design of Indian objects; the ethnographic signifi-

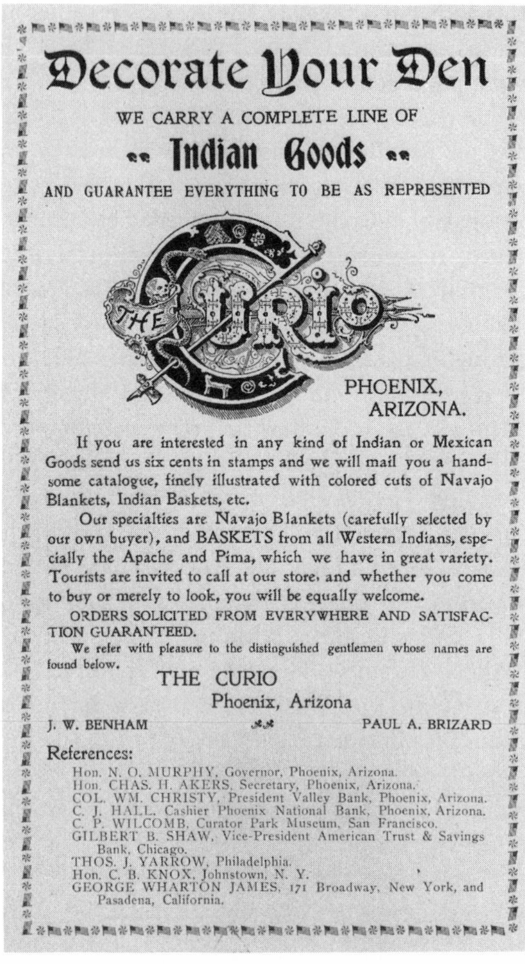

Figure 35. Advertisement that appeared in George Wharton James's Indian Basketry *(1902). The Curio, an establishment in Phoenix, Arizona, sold mail-order "Indian Goods" for decorative uses in bourgeois homes. "Dens" were appropriate places for "Indian corners." Note also the "references" that speak to concerns about the objects' authenticity.*

cance of baskets, pots, blankets, and jewelry was usually mentioned only in passing, if at all.

The proliferation of books and articles about Indian crafts was in part a function of the expanding markets for them, but the information that circulated is interesting also in what it reveals about the construction of expertise and authority. The authority to define these objects as more or less authentic resided with non-Indian scientists and collector-connoisseurs, and in the processes of connoisseurship, a kind of personal authenticity accrued to the collector (Whiteley 1993, 134). Most authoritative were the standards of authenticity set by scientists such as Otis Tufton Mason, George Dorsey, and Walter Hough, who wrote for the popular press. But there were also lay collectors, such as George Wharton James and Charles Lummis, who brought a missionary zeal to educating the public about the Indians of the region and the objects they made.

The career and writings of George Wharton James (1858–1923) exemplify how the collector-connoisseur constructed and maintained his authority. James was a collector, writer, and photographer who eventually settled in Pasadena, California. After emigrating from England in 1880, he worked on and off as an itinerant Methodist preacher in western Nevada and southern California (Maurer 1986, 5). His career as a minister ended in 1889 when he and his wife divorced. Then, like many before and after him, James discovered the rejuvenative powers of the deserts of New Mexico and Arizona. During the 1890s and through the 1910s he wrote and lectured widely on the Southwest and its Native American cultures, natural history, and Spanish missions. From 1903 to 1904 he published *The Basket, the Journal of the Basket Fraternity or lovers of Indian Baskets and other good things.* His books on Indian blankets and baskets, which were profusely illustrated with his own photographs of Indians and artifacts from his collection, were models of connoisseurship.

In 1901 James wrote an article for the *Chautauquan* called "Indian Basketry in House Decoration," an exercise in the appreciation of Indian baskets. In it James argued that not only were Indian baskets decorative and so had a place in the "civilized" household but also they had moral meaning and the power to shape character. James was something of a strenuous primitivist who believed that the "white race" had much to learn from the Indian, that the softening and feminizing effects of civilization should be balanced by the vigor of the Indian way of life, and that one way to understand Indian culture was to study its objects (James 1908). In the *Chautauquan* article he suggested that "every well-appointed house might appropriately arrange an Indian corner. Here baskets, pottery, blankets, arrow-points, spear-heads, beads, wampum, belts, kilts, moccasins, head-dresses, masks, pictures, spears, bows and arrows, drums, prayer-

Figure 36. Indian Corner in Library of George Wharton James, Pasadena, California, *photograph by George Wharton James (1901). (Reprinted in James, "Indian Basketry in House Decoration")*

sticks, boomerangs, katcina dolls, fetishes, and beadwork might be displayed with artistic and pleasing effect" (620–21). James's own Indian corner included Indian artifacts as well as framed landscapes and books (Fig. 36). In this type of collection, similar to a nineteenth-century curiosity cabinet, objects were assumed to embody the knowledge and way of life of their makers; through the basket one could know the Indian and, more important, preserve a disappearing way of life—a basic assumption of contemporary ethnology and archaeology. As James noted: "These baskets, thus looked at, become the embalmed mummies of the mentality and spirituality of ages that are past—of a civilization that would soon otherwise be lost" (620).

But James also romanticized the meaning of these objects: the Indian basket was "to the aborigine what the cathedral was to Europe in the middle ages: the book of record of aspirations, ideals, fears, emotions, poetry, and religion." He went on to quote Victor Hugo:

"The book has killed the building!" (620). This evocation of literacy is interesting. James assumed that among nonliterate people, the objects they made were as expressive of meaning as books, but that civilization, as represented by its literacy, had destroyed the production of these beautiful and meaningful objects. His declaration presupposed that craftwork (making baskets or cathedrals) was somehow more true or authentic than writing and reading. And by equating nonliterate Indians with illiterate medieval peasants, he located Indians and their authenticity in the distant past and in a class apart from his middle-class readers. It is significant that James's Indian corner was in his library. His baskets were placed alongside books and framed pictures of landscapes, some of which appear to depict Roman ruins. In this setting, these baskets and objects constituted a special library or storehouse of knowledge of a culture in ruins.[2]

As a collection of relics, James's Indian corner, like other collections of Indian artifacts and souvenirs, recapitulated the structure of imperial conquest and embodied a nostalgia for what imperialism had destroyed. As in the touristic encounter, which reenacted a kind of Columbian moment, the collector-connoisseur reenacted a fantasy of discovery and exchange that hinged on a desire to possess objects from vanishing cultures. John L. Cowan wrote in 1912 about collecting Navajo blankets, "No doubt the most satisfactory of all ways to buy them is direct from the squaws on the reservation" (114). Rather than buying the object from a dealer or trader, the collector made direct contact with the maker of the collected object and in the process assured its authenticity. In the burgeoning art market for Indian artifacts, authenticity demanded that one collect things that were no longer made, not things Indians made for sale. "A true collector does not wish a basket made to sell" (James 1902a, 16). The literature of connoisseurship is full of stories of how the collector saw an object in the possession of an Indian and the Indian would not sell. Often the stories of successful collecting featured objects the Indian craftsperson planned to be buried with.[3] At this point, the economy of desire set in for the collector; that which one couldn't have increased in value. In the end the collector usually succeeded in cajoling or bribing the Indian to part with the object of desire. But by its very nature collecting destroyed what was most desired, and the collector had the satisfaction of possession but also the longing for what could not be possessed: Indian life in the ethnographic present, the very thing the collector helped to destroy. As in James's writings about photographing Indians, collected baskets become trophies of the hunt.

Like ethnographic writing, collecting objects "textualized" them; the object was taken for a sign, but understanding its significance required interpretation by the collector subject.[4] James seemed to be aware of this process of narration when he explained the practices of collecting in terms of literacy. He may have bemoaned the fact that the book killed the cathedral (or the basket), but as a collector-connoisseur he was consummately literate. The comparison of collected objects to texts appears in an anonymous article in *Brush and Pencil* in 1905:

> One may view an olla or a basket and admire, in a casual way, its graceful contour, its peculiar coloring, its odd designs, and turn away with but a slight thrill of pleasure. Let the maker of that article interpret the significance of those colors, pattern, and shape, and he has found a feast for his soul. There are poems, histories, and creeds woven into every Indian basket and imprinted upon every decorated piece of pottery. ("Art of the American Indian" 1905, 84–85)

Indian objects might seem strange to the non-Indian, but if they were understood as "poems, histories, and creeds," they would become more familiar to a literate culture. And although the Indian artisan might serve as the informant in detecting the meaning of an object, the ability to appreciate Indian culture was solely the reserve of the civilized, literate individual and reaffirmed the power of that position.

Indian craft objects, as object lessons, had a powerful moral meaning for their students. In a photograph from James's *What the White Race May Learn from the Indian* (1908) (Fig. 37), the author is depicted showing a Paiute basket to a white woman and a boy, presumably her son. The three are seated in a middle-class Victorian parlor whose furnishings offer a revealing contrast with the assembled baskets. The lace curtains, plushly upholstered seating, lamp, and neoclassical sculpture atop the china cabinet establish the home as one of bourgeois respectability and feminine domesticity. The baskets are displayed for the benefit of the camera, but their presence on the floor and their design motifs declare them to be objects foreign to this environment. The china cabinet with its collection of painted

Figure 37. The Author Describing the Symbolism of the Paiuti Basket Design, *by unidentified photographer (1902). George Wharton James (*left*), the collector-connoisseur, enacts the scene of interpretation in a bourgeois home. (Reprinted in James,* What the White Race May Learn*)*

porcelain dishes emphasizes both the familiarity and the strangeness of the baskets; the baskets could be understood as the dishes of another culture, but their form and construction declare their difference. One is tempted to imagine the baskets in the china cabinet and the porcelain objects on the floor. If the baskets were inside the cabinet, they would become another group of objects, along with the sculpture and lamp, that symbolize the collected knowledge of civilization. But it is doubtful that the woman and boy would be inclined to look at the porcelain dishes in the way they look at the baskets.

James, however, might agree that the porcelain dishes embodied the culture of middle-class Americans, and he might even say that they showed clearly what ailed it. James believed that the main lesson the white race had to learn from the Indian was to follow a life of vigor and strenuosity. If we compare the room in this photograph with James's Indian corner, it is clear that part of what was wrong with civilized life had to do with gender. The parlor seems overly feminine in contrast with the Indian corner and its masculine primitivism. The Indian corner evokes the outdoors and activity, the parlor confines one indoors; baskets are flexible and strong, china is brittle and fragile. In James's photograph it may be too late for the woman, who looks bored, but the boy is his mission. The male collector, through his expertise and vigor, will provide the antidote to feminized civilization. But in the *Chautauquan* article James reaffirmed the site of cultural transmission as being the "ladies' club" and suggested that such clubs form a "loan collection" of baskets, so that a members could give talks on their construction and meaning: "Such a talk could be followed by a general discussion and exchange of ideas that would prove to be profitable and instructive to the whole company" (1901a, 624).[5]

If the collection constituted a storehouse of information about Indians that required the connoisseur to reveal, it also reflected the individuality (and the class standing) of the collector. James pointed out that unlike the "parvenu" who ostentatiously decorates his home, the "man of wide sympathies, broad culture, and refined mind, unconsciously reveals himself in the chaste, appropriate, and yet widely differing articles of decoration and art with which he surrounds himself in his home." The Indian corner is more than just a display of conspicuous consumption; the collection is itself representative of the mind and knowledge of the individual: "Decorations and furnishings, also, are, in a measure, indexes to the mind of their possessor" (1901a, 620).

In owning certain types of objects, the collector is the archetype of "possessive individualism," a modern, Western conception of the self as owner. As much as James and others claimed that by studying the objects of primitive cultures they would come to a greater understanding of humankind, the collection itself was structured to reveal the bourgeois individual, redefined as universal. James Clifford has argued that collecting is probably a universal behavior, but conceiving of identity as a sense of wealth is probably not. In some cultures collecting objects is done in order to redistribute them. "In the West, however, collecting has long been a strategy for the deployment of a possessive self, culture, and authenticity" (Clifford 1985, 238–39).[6]

In addition to constructing the self as "possessive," the practice of collecting also speaks to the self as "narrated." Like the touristic narratives of experience prompted by souvenirs, the collector-connoisseur's interpretation of Indian cultures reveals that the authority of the subject is constructed in relation to a distant (and different) object. In *On Longing,* Susan Stewart writes, "Narrative is seen . . . as a structure of desire, a structure that both invents and distances its object and thereby inscribes again and again the gap between signifier and signified that is the place of generation for the symbolic" (1984, ix). The scene of George Wharton James's interpreting the basket for the woman and her son enacts the structure of signification; James's narrative and his authority emerge out of the distance between the basket in his hand and its referent, Paiute culture. In unlocking the meaning of the basket, he bridges that gap, but he also maintains it; the distance necessitates James as the interlocutor who will explain "what the white race may learn from the Indian."

THE INDIAN ARTISAN

In the spectacle of Indian artisanal labor the pendant figure, the other, to the collector-connoisseur was the Indian artisan. Whereas collector-connoisseurs appeared in the spectacle as writers—the voices of authority on Indian crafts—Indian artisans primarily appeared as anonymous figures in illustrations. As in other representations of Native Americans during this period, artisans appeared physically but did not "speak." Images of four types of southwestern artisans predominated: weavers, basketmakers, potters, and silversmiths. The weaver was almost invariably a Navajo woman seated before her loom with a half-completed rug on it (Fig. 38), although Pueblo men were sometimes depicted weaving textiles. Silversmithing was less frequently discussed in the literature of Indian crafts, but in tourist materials, images of Navajo men at their bellows and Pueblo men drilling turquoise were common (Fig. 39). Representations of women weaving baskets and molding and decorating pots appeared often in ethnological and popular writing and in paintings. Although basketmaking was practiced widely, it tended to be associated with Apaches, Hopis, and Native Americans of California (Fig. 40). Pueblo women making pottery became an icon for the region, and Nampeyo was photographed and painted dozens of times (Fig. 41).[7] All of these

Figure 40. Postcard, "A Year's Labor—Indian Ollas, Arizona" (Phoenix: Berryhill, n.d.). The purchaser or receiver of this postcard might be moved to wonder what a year of his or her labor would look like. As was typical of touristic representations, accurate ethnographic information was irrelevant; the caption mislabels the baskets as "ollas," and the unidentified women are Apaches. Purified of ethnographic specificity, the image is a powerful icon of "authentic primitive labor." (Courtesy of the Arizona Historical Society/Tucson. Photo no. 48174)

Figure 38. (above left) *Photograph depicting a Navajo weaver working at her loom, by Adam Clark Vroman (1901). (Courtesy of the Southwest Museum, Los Angeles. Photo no. N.33942)*

Figure 39. (left, below) Turquoise Bead Maker, *by E. Irving Couse (1925); oil on canvas. This painting was reproduced as a Santa Fe Railway calendar in 1926. (Santa Fe Railway Collection of Southwestern Art)*

Figure 41. Nampeyo Decorating Pottery, *photograph by Edward S. Curtis (1900). (National Anthropological Archives, Smithsonian Institution)*

images tended to be formulaic in their presentation of artisans: they were either at work and lost in concentration or displaying a selection of completed wares.

Representations of Native American artisans were self-reflexive primitivist icons that seemed to provide answers to a variety of Anglo-American concerns about labor. In American society at the end of the nineteenth century the meaning of work was in a crisis. Factory and office work were perceived as alienating and meaningless, separated from ethical and moral rewards. American sociologists were influenced by the criticisms of Marx, Durkheim, and Weber, who examined the alienation brought about by the division of industrial labor. In contrast to industrial work, which was rigidly structured by the boss and the clock, was mechanized, urban, repetitive, mindless, proletarian, centralized, and unskilled, artisanal labor was character-

Figure 42. Beshthlagai-ithline-athlsosigi, famous Navajo Silversmith, *photograph by A. F. Randall (c. 1885). (National Anthropological Archives, Smithsonian Institution)*

ized as autonomous (but not excessively individualistic), "by hand," rural, traditional, classless, satisfying, local, and skilled. The spectacle of Indian artisanal labor presented a fantasy of authenticity and autonomy united with work in which individuals crafted the world and themselves, not in alienated isolation but with a clear understanding of their purpose and place in the universe.

The photographic portrait of the Navajo silversmith Beshthlagai-ithline-athlsosigi (Slender Maker of Silver) by A. F. Randall (c. 1885) is a powerful icon of individual autonomy and moral authenticity (Fig. 42).[8] He is seated alone before a painted scenic backdrop and cactus props. He wears and displays objects of his own manufacture, including a bridle, a concha belt, and silver buttons on his leggings. A leather pouch is opened to reveal his tools, and a rifle rests next to the bridle. Here is another version of the modern "possessive individual" whose identity is known through the objects he possesses. In the same way that Slender Maker of Silver holds these objects, he *has* an identity: Navajo silversmith. But unlike the collector, whose subjectivity is constructed by way of acquisition and narration, this artisan's identity is literally of his own making. With the exception of the firearm, he presumably made these markers of identity with his own hands and from his own design. A similar image is the photograph of Nampeyo made by Edward S. Curtis in about 1900 (Fig. 41). Like Slender Maker of Silver, Nampeyo is surrounded by her tools and objects she has made. These images depict *homo faber* and assert that creativity is what makes humans human.

The portrait of Slender Maker of Silver recalls that of another famous silversmith (Fig. 43). John Singleton Copley's *Portrait of Paul Revere* (1768–70) depicts an individual whose identity is recognizable in the same way, as someone who, with the use of his hands and a few tools, has crafted an authentic identity and the world itself, as represented by the globe of the teapot he is about to inscribe. Revere prefigures the ideal citizen of the American Republic, an individual with the power to shape society through his labor and his vote. But his power and autonomy are not limitless. In the myth of the artisan, the artisan of the republic is not an artist in the romantic tradition; he is not an excessively individualistic genius but acts and exists within circumscribed social structures that limit his creativity. He produces objects of utility that meet societal demands, rather than things that please only his own imagination. His autonomy is balanced and tempered by the limitations of the implied small scale and secure structure of artisanal society. He will think independently but will act in concert with his fellow citizens.

The corollary to the myth of the artisan in democratic ideology is that of the artist as inauthentic and unnatural, the maker of artifice, the teller of lies, a monster of individualism. Louis Akin's 1904 painting *Hopi Weaver* tempers that image by making an analogy between artist and artisan. The painting depicts a Hopi man sitting before a loom that has been strung with warp strings and has some of its weft but as yet no woven pattern (Babbitt 1973). The weaver is like the artist before a blank canvas, and the image mystifies the creative process (the weaver's back is turned and he appears to be communing with Indian muses). In this primitivist fantasy the artist-as-

Figure 43. Paul Revere, *by John Singleton Copley (1768); oil on canvas; 35 × 28½ in. (Gift of Joseph W. Revere, William B. Revere, and Edward H. R. Revere; courtesy, Museum of Fine Arts, Boston)*

artisan comes in from the margins of society and becomes a useful and respected citizen. In primitive cultures individual artists in the romantic sense—those alienated from society in the individualistic pursuit of genius—did not seem to exist. Instead the divisions between craft and art blurred into a unity in which the schisms between art and industry, the individual and society, civilization and nature were healed.

That artisanal iconography and ideology were revived in the figure of Indian artisans such as Slender Maker of Silver, Nampeyo, and the Hopi weaver also reflected anxieties about the effects of immigration and urban labor radicalism (Rodgers 1974, xii). Images of Indian artisans offered a vision of a preindustrial economy, a time before the Western frontier closed and before European and Asian immigrants "swarmed" American shores. As it was becoming increasingly clear that the development of the American West would depend on the metropolis for capital and cheap immigrant labor, the spectacle of Indian artisanal labor resurrected an ideology that declared precisely the opposite: that the rural artisan and the farmer were the backbone of the nation's economy (Slotkin 1985, 36–47). Furthermore, although Pueblo and Navajo social structure was praised by much of the popular literature for being community- or family-oriented, its small scale could never suggest urban communism. Indian artisans seemed to strike a perfect balance between community and individualism and were comforting images to an urban middle class concerned about social cohesion in a society increasingly divided into disparate classes (Gilbert 1977, 5).

To a large extent what made these "folk" Indians seem familiar was their work. At Fred Harvey's Hopi House, where Nampeyo and her family demonstrated craft making in 1905 and 1907, tourists could see how these industrious (but not industrial) primitive people, as they crafted by hand moccasins, fabric, baskets, and pots, literally made their world. This sort of labor, the making of useful objects, was familiar to tourists, but that it was set aside as a tourist spectacle indicated that it was a relic of the past. At Hopi House skilled hand labor was museumized as something civilized people did not do any more. In an increasingly consumer-oriented marketplace, Americans *bought* what they needed. This quaint spectacle of people making what they needed reinforced the difference between now and then, us and them, even as it inspired a longing for the immediacy and authenticity Indian labor represented.

Whereas the Pueblos and Navajos seemed to be paragons of artisanal industry, other ethnic groups in the Southwest were depicted in less flattering ways. The good Indian–bad Indian dichotomization persisted in depictions of Native American artisans. An illustration from the Harvey souvenir book *First Families of the Southwest* (1913) depicts "An Apache Grand Dame Weaving a Supply Basket" (Fig. 44). The text describing this image illustrates how ideas about labor helped define ethnic stereotypes:

> It is stretching the imagination to connect this peaceful scene of household industry with the word Apache, for that name has come to mean everything cruel and bloodthirsty to the last degree . . . the tribe as a whole has been greatly maligned.

Figure 44. Weaving an Apache Granary, *painting by unidentified artist (c. 1913). (Reprinted from Huckel,* First Families*)*

> The old mother peacefully, contentedly weaving herself into a basket is an Apache, every drop of her blood, as much as Victorio or Geronimo when they were murdering settlers and baffling the United States government. Yet, with all the evidence of her domesticity, this Apache matron is by no means a paragon. For one thing she is a gambler to the marrow—gambling is a national pastime among the Apache men and women. . . . All of the Apache women make baskets, some of them water-tight to be used as jugs. (Huckel n.p.)

While praising the quality of Apache baskets, the text suggests that artisanal industry among the Apaches was not really industrious, it was something done when the Apaches were not gambling—an activity subversive of the work ethic. The weaver is presented as a comic sport; the picture suggests that she is weaving herself into a corner she won't be able to get out of, indicating an inability to plan ahead. However, a granary is used for storing grains and vegetables and is an object that is a direct result of careful planning and concern about saving food for the future. Furthermore, as an inversion of the "olla maiden" icon, the image objectifies the woman as a substance contained by the basket she is "weaving herself into."

Apaches appeared in the spectacle of Indian artisanal labor as savages who lacked a work ethic. Unredeemed by their labor, they were positioned as the necessary evil twin of Pueblos, and so constructed, their work had no moral meaning or effect. Apaches, unlike other Native Americans in the region, were not allowed to escape history; the recent deeds of Victorio and Geronimo dogged every representation of Apache culture. When he appeared at the Louisiana Purchase Exposition in 1904, Geronimo was set to "work" making souvenir bows and arrows and selling his autograph. Within the spectacle of the exposition, Geronimo produced (useless) relics of his warrior past as well as representations of himself, which contributed to his commodification as a celebrity.

As we have seen, Hispanic people were for a long time invisible in the tourist literature. Anti-Catholic and racist attitudes toward Hispanos had much to do with this absence, but so did their role as workers in the region. Both Hispanos and Native Americans worked as wage laborers for the railroads and in agriculture, but whereas some Indians were stereotyped as artisans, the "Mexicans" became peons, a peasant class, and were reviled as lazy and submissive, characteristics that made them unfit for citizenship. Like the Apache grandmother, Hispanos were understood as living only for the moment and therefore as incapable of improving their lot. The spectacle of peonage (or urban industrial labor) could not satisfy longings for authentic, meaningful labor, and unlike artisanal labor, wage labor actually supported the structure of the local economy. To turn this into a tourist attraction would have threatened to reveal the oppression and exploitation of workers on which the economy depended.

In the 1920s there was some Anglo interest in the Spanish colonial past in New Mexico, but Hispanos did not widely "appear" as artisans in representations of the region and its people until the 1930s. By the mid-1920s, as Hispanos lost much of their grazing land and as tourism became New Mexico's biggest industry, they began to market more of their traditional crafts, such as weaving and wood carving. Their efforts were aided by Anglo interest in preserving these "vanishing" crafts. Thus Hispanic culture could be "seen" only at the point certain aspects of it were perceived to be disappearing. This strategy reveals what Suzanne Forrest has called the "myth of the melting pot," which stipulates that "ethnic and national differences enriched a nation culturally as long as they were not allowed to impede it economically or politically" (1989, 34). In other words as long as Native Americans and Hispanos could be perceived as powerless (or disappearing), they could be seen.

IMAGINING PRIMITIVE LABOR

The ability of Indian artisans to stand as ideological icons lay in the claim that authenticity resided in the primitive mind and in primitive culture. Primitive cultures were authentic, primitivist reasoning went, because primitive people enjoyed a relatively unmediated relationship with the ultimate reality of nature and the universe. Whereas the civilized mind was capable of mental abstraction (as well as alienation and neurosis), Indians were understood to have a more direct—a literally hands-on—relationship with the world.

The centrality of hand labor in characterizing the primitive mind was the subject of much scientific discourse. As W. J. McGee, one of the organizers of the Indian School exhibit at the 1904 Louisiana Purchase Exposition, wrote, "Experience has shown that among all aboriginal peoples the hand leads to the mind" (Gilbert 1977, 101). Frank Hamilton Cushing's study of Zuni pottery illustrates how central craft was to ethnologists' understanding of Indian cultures (Fig. 45). Assuming that the material culture of a group revealed important information about it, Cushing described the "culture-growth" of Zunis by examining the pots they made (Cushing 1886). Eventually Cushing developed his theories about the importance of hand work in an article for the *American Anthropologist* published in 1892 called "Manual Concepts: A Study of the Influence of Hand-Usage on Culture-Growth." Using evidence from his study of Zunis, he postulated three stages of intellectual development: the biotic, the manual, and the mental. The biotic was the earliest stage, when humans were barely human but had developed hands, which they used in climbing and fending and defending. The next stage, the manual, was

Figure 45. Frank Hamilton Cushing Demonstrating Pottery-making Technique *(c. 1890s). Cushing was painted and photographed many times posing in Indian paraphernalia and reenacting ritual postures (Truettner 1985). By engaging in an imagined union with the primitive artisan, Cushing, like the collector-connoisseur, could claim an authentic experience and special knowledge. (National Anthropological Archives, Smithsonian Institution)*

when humans began to develop "extranaturally," when they acted upon (made) the environment rather than just reacted to it. Cushing asserted that the mental stage of human development depended on "the ascertainment of *truth*. . . . I think that man is what he is, even racially to a certain extent, through this same use and using of his hands" (1892, 289–90). This hierarchical schema of development assumed that manipulation of the environment was a determining factor in cultural evolution. Cushing asserted that humans are fundamentally makers, that the way they use their hands frames the mind and forms both mythic concepts and religious beliefs, and that in

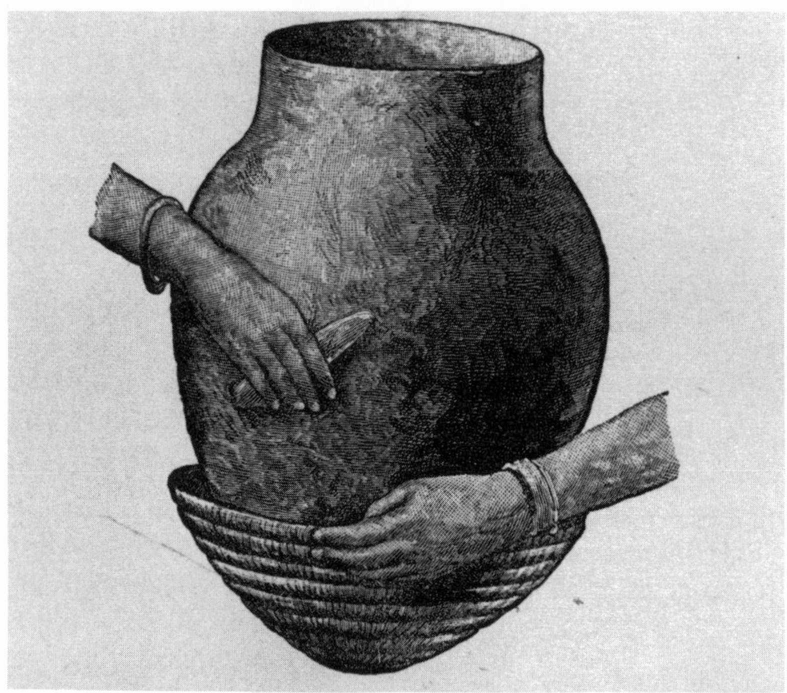

Figure 46. Basket-bowl as Base-mold for Large Vessels *(c. 1886). (Reprinted from Mason,* Woman's Share in Primitive Culture*)*

primitive cultures such as the Zuni one can see "survivals" of the earlier manual stage (291).

Figure 46 is from Cushing's article "A Study of Pueblo Pottery as Illustrative of Zuñi Culture-Growth" (1886). It shows the final step in molding a water vessel. This illustration and another, "Clay Nucleus in Base-mold, with Beginning of Spiral Building," continued to be reproduced in publications by Otis T. Mason and George Wharton James and others for more than twenty years. This engraving was meant to show the process of manufacture, with more clarity than even a photograph. The vessel is removed from its context and only the important facts are depicted: disembodied hands, scraper, clay, and basket base. The texture of the clay is rendered in great detail.

The missing body and head of the maker emphasizes that the focus here is on the hands, which seem not even to need the head. But as the hands make the pot, so they will make the mind. Hands and clay are the source of thoughts and ideas, the origins of Indian culture and society.

Because they were perceived to be survivals of the manual stage of cultural evolution, Indian artisans seemed to provide scientists with opportunities to discover the conditions of invention and creativity. William Henry Holmes and Otis T. Mason were especially interested in the creative process and the evolution of ornament. The evolutionary scale was understood to extend from people to design, which, like individuals, was organic and had a youth, maturity, and old age. Likewise, crafts had an evolutionary history in which, it was argued, basketry was the "mother" of pottery, and Indian crafts existed in a hierarchy that classified them as decorative rather than fine arts (James 1902a; Mason 1899, 1901). These scientists assumed that because Indian crafts were primitive, by definition simpler, then the processes of creativity would be more apparent. In 1890 William Henry Holmes argued that the "artistic sense" was present to some extent in the minds of all people:

> In the early stages of culture its exercise is not wholly an intellectual, but rather what I prefer to call an instinctive act, and under favorable conditions it so remains far into the stage of culture known as civilization; it does not cease to be measurably unerring in its action until intellect essays to perform the work of instinct—until men begin to think out results instead of feeling them out. (1890, 137)

In other words, the decorative instinct was somehow more true and beautiful (i.e., more authentic) among primitive people because they did not interrupt the creative process with thought. They thought with their hands.

This perceived lack of mediation between maker and object made Indian-crafted objects important because they exhibited singularity. In the age of mechanical reproduction, in which the hallmark of mass-produced objects was their sameness, objects that showed singularity and the mark of the maker's hand were highly valued and, as we have seen, had many uses for their collectors. In *The Theory of the Leisure Class* Thorstein Veblen noted that the valuation of handmade objects was a leisure class preoccupation, because mass-produced objects were perceived as common, and it is this commonness that the leisure class objected to. He also argued that in this preference for the singular, marks of imperfection, or the marks of the hand, became "honorific" ([1899] 1979, 161–62).

The primitiveness of Indian craftwork and objects (in their singularity and authenticity) could be appropriated to define the Southwest as a region, a place of handmade objects, not industrial commodities, a utopia redemptive of urban ills. Julius Gans, a Santa Fe dealer in Indian arts and crafts, ran on every page of his 1920 catalogue this helpful reminder: "Remember! Indians never make two things alike. We prepay all express and parcel post charges." In this way the Southwest became a source of singularity and authenticity, which was then exported via the postal system and railroads to the rest of the nation. Or the rest of the nation could come to the region to experience "firsthand" this authenticity, to witness the making of the objects in collections elsewhere. Tourists could also read about Indian crafts in souvenir books such as the Harvey Company's *First Families of the Southwest,* in which John F. Huckel wrote of Nampeyo's work: "In making pottery the Indian uses neither measure, model nor potter's wheel. All is done from memory and with the hands. A few tools, hardly more than sticks and brushes made from yucca leaves, are the instruments." This is as if to say that Native American artisans simply reached out to the natural environment and through the use of only memory and their hands constructed these objects.

This passage identifies two locations of authenticity: nature and memory. Inspired by nature, the Indian's hands (and mind) supposedly transferred the idea directly to the object: "The Indian artist works without pattern, model—other than nature—and without rule or compass. The conception of the brain is brought directly to the place it is to occupy" ("Art of the American Indian" 1905, 86). If tools were used, they were simple and natural; Indian-crafted objects seemed to grow more than be made. Charles Lummis, in a *Land of Sunshine* article about Navajo blankets, described the world of Indian artisanal labor as comprising only "the stolid women working at their crude 'looms,' whose only machinery is the hanging of the warp-cords from a pine bough; the wonderful patterns of the lightning and the morning star, the clouds, the earth, the sky" (1899, 11). Indians were considered natural artists—without training and with a close, unmediated relationship to the natural world: they made "patterns supplied from the keen observations taken in by their Indian eyes when they were birds with the birds and squirrels with the squirrels" (Bartlett 1900, 595).

Under the rubric of cultural evolution, it was assumed that in a nonliterate culture, memory served to conserve cultural forms and traditions, and tradition did not allow for individualism or rapid change. Indian objects looked the way they did because of primitive tradition. Rather than being the result of individual imagination, designs were handed down from mother to daughter, from father to son, and were distinct from village to village. A favorite subject of the painter E. Irving Couse was the handing down of craft knowledge from one generation to the next. His painting, *The Turquoise Bead Maker* (Fig. 39) is one of many examples.[9] The primitivist understanding of Indian design was that it originated in nature, received its forms based on the Indian's spiritual cosmology, and was passed on via an oral tradition. As Olive Wilson wrote in 1920: "The designs are the outgrowth of the religious conceptions of the Indian, with whom everything in nature is hallowed by association with divine powers" (28). These characteristics, closeness to nature and obligation to tradition, authenticated the Indian artisan's work by grounding it in the universal (nature) and the local (tradition), but the individual's autonomy was limited by the supposed immutability of these structures. So even though Indians never made two things alike, tradition dictated that neither did they vary too much.

Some writers, though, gave Indian artisans credit for having *thought* about what they were doing. Charles Lummis wrote of Navajo silversmiths: "Some of these men, absolutely untutored except by tradition, almost without facilities, show remarkable taste and skill. A little mud forge, a hammer, a simple punch, a three-cornered file, a stone or bit of iron for an anvil, a little clay for a crucible and some solder, *and* brains—and there is your aboriginal smith" (1898, 58). George H. Pepper wrote of Navajo blankets in 1902: "It is not machine work, where each thread is counted by a complicated mechanism, and where each design is mathematically perfect; the forms and figures are evolved while the work is in progress, and drawn in their entirety upon the kaleidoscopic mirror of the mind alone" (34). I will come back to the issue of creativity and design, but what I want to point out here is the importance to these writers of the immediacy of craftwork. In general the literature about Indian crafts focused on the last steps in the process of manufacture: earlier steps—such as sheepherding, shearing, and dyeing; digging clay; gathering vegetable matter for basketmaking; and obtaining silver—were rarely depicted or discussed. Focusing on the point at which the finished object was in sight made the process of manufacture seem more immediate; earlier steps in production and distribution were glossed or ignored, and we are left with the image of the Indian who reached out to the natural world and crafted a nearly finished object.

ARTISANAL CRAFT AS A TOOL OF REFORM

At the turn of the century many American scientists, educators, and reformers marshalled evidence based on their understanding of primitive cultures to support the value of hand labor as a powerful tool of reform. The ideology of the arts and crafts movement, which was concerned with correcting the abuses of industrialization, including bad design and alienating work, promoted the idea that the individual could be revitalized and re-created through craftwork. The movement, as theorized by Ruskin and Morris and popularized in England and the United States, evoked a nostalgia for a craft society based on apprenticeship, stability, and close social relations. It emphasized smallness and decentralization in production and promoted the village as the ideal site of production. The Indians of the Southwest seemed to epitomize arts and crafts ideals; they lived in small villages or family groups, and because they were primitive, it was assumed they had never experienced the alienation of industrial work. But the arts and crafts movement was an urban movement whose promoters were middle- and upper-class Anglos who had the leisure to pursue crafts as hobbies.[10]

Another reformist strategy that emphasized the moral value of manual labor and that invoked the figure of the Indian artisan to naturalize its ideas was the manual training movement in education, which asserted that manual labor had the power to reform the mind. Like the arts and crafts movement, manual training was mainly concerned with urban problems, particularly the "Americanization" of immigrants, freed slaves, and Native Americans, and the rehabilitation of delinquents and the mentally ill. The theory also assumed that because industrial and office work were empty of meaning, reform meant that the worker was compelled to bring meaning to the work, rather than that the work itself needed reforming. The way to do this was to train future workers in handicrafts of the past, which was where these values resided, and in the process workers would somehow transfer the ethic of manual labor to their work in society (Gilbert 1977, 98–103).

Many educational theorists at the turn of the century believed that children recapitulated the development of civilization and thus should be made to progress through these "natural" stages throughout their education. One way to do this was to teach them decorative arts. Like children, the decorative arts occupied a less developed position in a progressive hierarchy that culminated with the fine arts. It was also believed that art training would promote good behavior and good workmanship. Basketmaking proved to be a popular answer: materials were cheap, and both boys and girls seemed to like it (Tinsley 1904, 8) (Fig. 47).

Social and educational reformers often promoted "playing Indian," a complex of primitivist activities that were becoming institutionalized in education and leisure pursuits at the turn of the century. Leisure was increasingly regarded as a problematic field of activity; if work was meaningless, workers had to look to leisure to produce meaning in their lives. Learning Indian crafts as hobbies seemed to provide a way to instill moral and ethical values via a kind of leisured labor. In organizations such as the Woodcraft Indians and Camp Fire Girls, middle-class white girls and boys learned "Indian" outdoor and craft skills in order to counteract the debilitating effects of modern urban life.[11] This sort of activity was thought to offer access to authentic experience in a world regarded as insincere and weightless; the experience of temporarily taking on a primitive identity would supposedly help to ground the individual's identity in an ultimate, primal reality, in a world of one's own making.

Figure 47. Oh, This Is Fun! *(c. 1904). (Reprinted from Tinsley,* Practical and Artistic Basketry*)*

As middle-class white children were learning Indian crafts, Indian children were learning European crafts. The ideals of manual training were widely applied in Indian education, initially with the goal of Americanizing Native Americans. At the Carlisle Indian School in Pennsylvania, Native American girls and boys learned cabinetry, tinsmithing, harness making, and other "American" skills (Fig. 48).[12] Constance Goddard Du Bois, in a 1904 *Craftsman* article with the awkward title "The Indian Woman as a Craftsman," described the recent introduction of Venetian lace making among the Mission Indians near San Diego: the white man's industry no matter how "exotic or inappropriate in theory, becomes a means of salvation both to life and character" (391). In yet another cross-cultural twist, an American yarn manufacturer provided instructions on how to *knit* and *crochet* one's own Navajo blankets (*Fleisher's Manual* 1912).

Figure 48. Tin Shop at Carlisle Indian School, *photograph by John Choate (c. 1879–1902). At the Carlisle Indian School, Native American students learned "civilized" skills. Here boys learn to make the tin vessels that would replace "traditional" pottery vessels. (National Anthropological Archives, Smithsonian Institution)*

Navajo weavers began using these same "Germantown" yarns in their blankets in the 1880s (Amsden 1934, 184–85).

Many reformers, however, criticized government efforts to assimilate Indians through this kind of education. John L. Cowan, in *Out West* in 1912, wrote: "The attempt to metamorphose an Indian into a white man is usually fatal; and the non-reservation schools maintained by the Government for the 'education' of its wards have made more 'good Indians' (assuming that a 'good Indian' means a dead one) than a long series of Indian wars" (115). He argued that Navajos' blanketry and silverwork made them less dependent on outsiders. In the coming years, the movement among Anglos to revive and preserve Indian crafts would gain momentum. One of the perceived benefits of this strategy was to improve the economic lives of Native Americans. In his 1934 book *Navaho Weaving: Its Technic and Its History,* Charles Amsden echoed Cowan in arguing that education was no great success in adjusting the Indian to the "American economic scheme": "For few Indians can step out of school and take their place in the American community except as day-laborers. In the advancement of the Indian his native crafts thus far have been the most helpful, for they allow him to remain himself, to express himself, while at the same time they have an economic value" (v).

Another important reform issue that the spectacle of Indian artisanal labor addressed was the "problem" of idle womanhood. At the turn of the century, middle-class American women seemed to lack a productive role in modern society; they appeared to be primarily consumers in the national economy. Many reformers believed that industrialization had stripped women of their work, and they pointed to various times in the past when a family-centered economy had prevailed (Rodgers 1974, 197). In *Woman's Share in Primitive Culture* (1899), ethnologist Otis T. Mason argued that women were the originators of the arts and of civilization itself. This was plain to see in primitive cultures, in which women continued to control what they invented: agriculture, clothing, language, art, religion, and, as mothers, the perpetuation of society itself. The editor's preface to Mason's book explained the evolution of the gender division of labor:

> Division of labour began with the invention of fire-making, and it was a division of labour based upon sex. The woman staid by the fire to keep it alive while the man went to the field or to the forest for game. The world's industrialism and militancy began then and there. Man has been cunning in devising means of killing beast and his fellowman—he has been the inventor in every murderous art. The woman at the fireside became the burden bearer, the basket-maker, the weaver, potter, agriculturalist, domesticator of animals—in a word, the inventor of all the peaceful arts of life. (viii)

Charles Lummis, in "The First American Potters," followed Mason's lead but used the masculine pronoun to describe the female potter:

> The potter has come to be given a humble consideration in the procession of nations; but it is well not to forget him. He is the dean of

> domestic artisans—the eldest son of the inventor of Home. Before him, humanity was a wanderer; he arose with the dawn of the idea that it might be better to reside; and by giving his contemporaries useful furniture which would break if they went tramping again, he seriously helped to clinch the mode of life upon which all civilization rests—and which half of the civilized world already forgets did not begin with the creation. (1900, 50)

George Wharton James was also a reader of Mason and dedicated his *Indian Basketry* (1902) to him. In this book James pointed out that woman's work, "from the very earliest ages of human history, has tended towards the health, the comfort, the knowledge and the culture of mankind. She has not been merely the wife, the mother, the nurse of man, but the teacher in many arts which man now proudly and haughtily claims as his own 'sphere'" (1902a, 15).

The literature on Indian crafts presented a past in which women were still in control of a family-based economy. Most of the images of artisans depicted a strict division of labor along gender lines and tended to show Indian women engaged in household or distaff arts. Images of domestic Pueblo interiors were popular and often featured women grinding corn. Art and labor seemed united in Indian life, and the corn grinding song was the perfect example. Writing in 1913 in the *Craftsman,* ethnologist Natalie Curtis told about hearing a woman at Laguna Pueblo sing corn-grinding songs throughout the day:

> So, like the Hindus, whose "ragas" belong to certain seasons of the year, this brown-skinned child of nature had "a song for every time of day," and the rhythm of her grinding-stones seemed in tune with the turning of the planet. I thought of our complex city life, and of the songs of the paid singers to whom we listen when our day's work is *done;* singers whose art, with all its beauty, is yet but a gas-lit luxury for a few. And I had a new respect for the Pueblo woman who awoke with the sun and toiled with the sun and sang with the sun, all her life in harmony with the cosmic world about her.[13]

Images of Indian women at work depicted a world of domestic industry, and in the iconography of pottery making and basket weaving it was a domestic world reduced to its most primal elements: women and vessels. Pictures of Nampeyo at work show her alone either shaping pots or decorating them. It was alleged that her husband

Lesso decorated pottery and was instrumental in collecting designs, but he was never shown in published photographs actively making or decorating pots. Similarly, other kinds of women's work were not usually depicted: child care, food preparation (except corn grinding), adobe building, or farming. The images of women with pots, including representations of "olla maidens," alluded to women as creators, as childbearers, as vessels. This metaphor of primal origins served to naturalize the idea that a woman's place was originally—and should continue to be—in the home.

In *What the White Race May Learn from the Indian,* George Wharton James suggested that if the race were to survive, white women should take Indian women as an example, because they were not ashamed of manual labor. A result of this sort of primitivism was that Indian crafts were practiced by middle-class Anglo women and children as a form of therapy and education, activities outside the workplace. These crafts were not paths to economic independence or political power, but they were thought to bring a sense of authenticity and virtue to women and workers in their leisure. Furthermore, learning to appreciate the aesthetics of Indian crafts by practicing or collecting them taught middle-class Americans, especially women, how to be knowledgeable consumers, and as good consumers, their choices could influence production.

Depictions of Indian artisanal work domesticated and to some extent "feminized" Indians of the Southwest. Representations of women dominated, and in the Southwest images of women artisans persisted on postcards and in other materials long after the bonneted Indian "warrior" had usurped all other images of Indians in other regions (Albers and James 1984, 35). The Southwest appeared to be a region where men and women performed domestic tasks in peace. Tourist representations of Pueblo life often remarked on how gender roles, defined by non-Indian standards, were reversed. Huckel in *First Families* described "Indian Women Who Command the Household" and explained matrilineal Pueblo women's rights thus: "While the women do the housework and some of the lighter farm labor, the men aid in the heavier domestic duties, gather the fuel, make moccasins for the women, weave blankets and in fact do the sewing, knitting and embroidering for the family" (n.p.). Navajos' gender roles seemed to follow Western standards. Nevertheless, although there were hundreds of images of Navajo women weaving, Irving Couse's widely reproduced paintings for the Santa Fe Railway depicted men weaving Navajo blankets. He also painted Indian men decorating pots. In what seems to have been a personal preference, Couse painted very few women (Woloshuk 1976, 85). Usually his male weavers and potters were bare-chested and squatting, and there were often children with the men. Many of Couse's paintings are reminiscent of the paintings of George de Forest Brush, which show an academic interest in painting the nude and participate in the tradition of oriental exotica. Couse's and Huckel's depicting Indian men doing "women's work" defused the threat of the Indian as "warrior" and assured visitors to the region that the Indians there were thoroughly domesticated.

LIMITATIONS OF THE ARTISAN STEREOTYPE

By the 1920s the movement to preserve Native American cultures, led by scientists, art colonists, and dealers, pushed to keep the Native Americans of the Southwest "Indian." But the terms of this identity, as well as the valuation of Indian artisanal labor, were determined by non-Indians. The image of the Indian artisan may have seemed a friendly or kind conception, but only because it mirrored bourgeois values; the spectacle of Indian artisanal labor elided difference by incorporating Indians into the Euro-American past and mythology by making them into a "folk" (McGovern 1990, 494). Although this made them accessible and allowed middle-class Americans to "play Indian," Native Americans could not "play civilized" and still be "Indians." Furthermore, the dichotomy between primitive and civilized was strictly maintained; other more dialogic or complicated modes of being were not "visible" in the spectacle.

Native Americans were imagined as makers of their world, but not producers and consumers in the national economy, which they were. Native American artisans would never become capitalists; they would never make enough money to hire other people to work for them. If Indian artisans were marginalized as preindustrial producers, neither could they become consumers of manufactured goods. Describing the effects of the pottery revival in Jemez Pueblo, a writer in *El Palacio* wrote in 1926: "Women with figures erect and with jars of their own making gracefully balanced on their heads once more wend their way to the springs, and the sight of some sister who still struggles, stoop-shouldered, with the burden of a tin water bucket in each hand brings smiles of realization to their faces" (Halseth 1926, 149). Tin buckets were cheap and durable, but their very presence threatened to disrupt the mythological artisanal economy.

Even the desire for consumer goods was forbidden to Indians. In the literature of the arts and crafts movement, it was a common complaint that the working class's proximity to industrial production created a constant demand for "degraded" goods. Constance Du Bois wrote in the *Craftsman* in 1904, "The modern appreciation of good handicraft which is gaining ground among the intelligent few, can not offset the degrading tendencies of a commercialism whose watchword is cheapness; the imperative desire for which is forced upon the many by the conditions of a struggle for existence which includes as necessities a thousand artificial wants" (392). There is a paradox here: Native Americans desired mass-produced goods, which reform-minded middle-class Americans considered cheap and shoddy; non-Indian Americans desired handmade Indian goods, which were relatively expensive to produce. Middle-class whites could be catholic in their desires, but Indian people were expected to be culturally blind and uncorrupted by desires beyond their own cultures.

The literature on Indian crafts avoided representing the complex economic realities affecting Native Americans in the Southwest. One of the few exceptions is an article by George Pepper called "The Making of an Indian Blanket," which appeared in *Everybody's* magazine in 1902. Pepper had been head of the Hyde expedition among the Navajos for three years and was employed by the American Museum of Natural History when he wrote the article. In it he pointed out that if a Navajo blanket could talk, it would tell of hardship: "How many instances of suffering might be cited—patient cripples, weak and emaciated men and women, feeble with age and exposure, subsisting on corn and water, watching day by day the progress of the blanket where completion will mean coffee and a few of the luxuries that we would class as necessities!" (42). Compared with Constance

Du Bois's comment on the working-class demand for manufactured goods, this passage shows how different the notions of luxury and necessity could be. Pepper continues:

> Then the blanket is finished and the journey to the trading store begins. The squaw knows from experience what she should receive for her work, and therefore demands a certain amount as her just dues. The trader, hard-hearted and grasping, as a rule, takes from his money-pouch perhaps one-half the blanket's value in silver and throws it upon the counter. The squaw realizes the injustice of the act, but also knows full well that there is but one alternative, and that is to ride perhaps a score of miles to the next store, and that, too, without the slightest prospect of better treatment when she reaches it. Then comes the thought of the anxious ones at home, and she realizes how great will be the disappointment if she returns empty-handed. Long she ponders, then conquering the ever-increasing anger that threatens to gain the mastery over reason, she takes the proffered coin. She is able to buy but half the goods that she had hoped to get, and the trader realizes from one hundred to three hundred per cent. on each article that she buys. (42)

Melodramatic perhaps, but Pepper's is one of the few representations that shows an Indian artisan to be less than happy and that portrays the realities of the market economy and its exploitation of Native American artisanal labor. The value of the blanket is wholly in the hands of the trader and the market; the woman's labor is ultimately rendered in terms of a few groceries.

Although writing a moving plea for the plight of the Navajo weaver, Pepper placed the preservation of traditional techniques and products above the welfare of Native Americans. The solution was not to reform the means of production but to educate the buyer, thus keeping the control of production in the hands of the middle-class consumer. Pepper implored buyers not to accept poor quality blankets, especially those made with Germantown yarns:

> A saving of labor to the Indian, 'tis true, but oh, how much the beauty and artistic merit of their work has suffered! . . . Where is that inexplainable something that draws us with irresistible desire to the native work? All have vanished, and we behold in the Ger-

> mantown blanket a textile not truly Indian, but merely an exhibition of his abilities as a weaver. (43)

Why not just give them machines? he asks.

> May the sun never rise upon the Navajo and behold him in more modernized condition in his blanket work than at the present time. On the contrary, let us hope that the efforts that are now on foot may grow to such proportions that the modern influence may be swept away completely, and primitive ideas and primitive work be once more the dominant factor in his weaving industries. (43)

The point was not to make the production of blankets economically viable for the Navajo weavers but to preserve at any cost the present methods of production. Oddly enough, Pepper almost completely devalued the weaver's labor, at least in terms of the value of time. The weaver was expected to produce a wholly traditional product without regard to what she could expect in return, without regard to the value of her labor. The "saving of labor" was worthless compared to the end product. To Pepper and other collector-connoisseurs, the talents of the weaver were secondary to the "Indianness" of the product; thus even if the Germantown blanket was finely designed and woven, it was not as valuable as one whose wool had been hand spun and dyed. This scale of value assumed that Indian craftspeople would somehow set themselves apart from the exigencies of supply and demand. Rather than assessing and meeting demand, Pepper asked the Native American artisan to hold out for the buyer who had good taste and deep pockets, who could afford to pay a high price for an object that required so much labor.

The economic consequences to Native American communities of the expanding crafts markets are too complex to go into in any detail here. But generally speaking, the history of Native American responses to the craft markets has involved continual cross-cultural negotiation and exchange. The literal exchange of crafts for cash brought artisans and their communities a certain amount of economic autonomy, but the cultural consequences of these exchanges were deeply felt by all southwestern Native American communities (Wade 1986; Brody 1976). One of the most striking, and obvious, consequences, one that is not often questioned, is that artisanal labor has continued to be one of the most viable forms of work available to Native Americans in the Southwest. Native Americans of the Southwest continue to "appear" primarily as artists and artisans.

The limitations of the Indian artisan as a subject are closely related to the issue of artistic creativity and ideas about individualism and work. In the 1920s the rhetoric in the literature and representations of Indian craftwork began to reclassify Indian craftspeople as artists, making more apparent the conflict between individualism and "Indian" identity. The career of Nampeyo is again illustrative. Although Nampeyo was widely known as the greatest potter in the Southwest, she did not sign her pots. In fact, Pueblo potters did not sign their work until after 1920. Apparently the first potter to do so was Maria Martinez of San Ildefonso. Until the 1910s all potters were nonprofessional and anonymous, with the sole exception of Nampeyo. Nampeyo's fame may have been initiated by her contacts with ethnologists such as Jesse Walter Fewkes, but her involvement with the Fred Harvey Company made her known to the nation. The only other Indian artisan to become nationally known before 1920 was the Navajo weaver Elle of Ganado, whom the Harvey Company also promoted. The signing of pots came into practice because of market demands: as pottery became more valuable and more collectible, some buyers wanted to know who made the objects they bought, and the identification of some artisans as especially talented made their works more valuable. The Harvey Company affixed labels to the pots Nampeyo made at Hopi House in 1905. These small black and gold stickers read, Made by Nampeyo, Hopi (Kramer 1988, 49). The special quality of Nampeyoness enhanced the value of these pots. Other potters eventually learned this lesson: Maria Martinez, it is said, would sign the works of other potters in her village, because if the pots had her name on them they brought higher prices (Marriott 1948, 243).

Unlike industrialized societies, in which the fruits of industrial labor were not identified with their makers, in Pueblo villages labor was not anonymous, and, more important, the value of objects was not determined by who made them. When non-Indians began collecting Indian-made objects, it was generally enough for collectors to be able to identify the Native American group the object came from.

But gradually, collectors demanded to know which individuals made which objects, and signing became necessary. As the ethnic art market developed, quality could be assured by buying a brand name, so to speak. Signatures lent authenticity to objects, and Indian artisans began to be recognized as individual artists. But the ethnic identity of the artisan, as understood and defined by the art market, posed strict limitations on what could be produced. Expectations in the markets for Indian-crafted objects were that the objects would retain their "Indianness" more than exhibit individuality. The Indian artisan could be declared an artist as long as he or she did not leave behind traditional qualities. Nampeyo was called an artist in part because she excelled within the bounds of what was determined to be her ethnic tradition. Some changes in design were tolerated, but radical changes in either design or production technique were not allowed. I am not suggesting that Western individualism was the only (or even a viable) alternative for Nampeyo and other Native American artisans. However, as an "Indian artist," Nampeyo remained an "other" to an implied (non-Indian) artist subject. This dichotomy offered only one extremely limited way to understand her and her work.

Contemporary discussions about Indian design bring to a head the question of Indian subjectivity. It was said that Nampeyo began making revival ware in 1895 when her husband Lesso and fourteen other Indian men were hired by Jesse Walter Fewkes to help him excavate the ancient site at Sikyatki. Lesso, the story goes, brought some sherds of ancient pots home to Nampeyo, who then began working the designs into her own pots. (An almost identical story is associated with the San Ildefonso potter Maria Martinez, her husband Julian, and the scientist Edgar Lee Hewitt some fifteen years later.) In fact, that Fewkes had any direct influence over Nampeyo's decision to imitate ancient pots is doubtful (Frisbie 1973, 235; Wade 1985). It is true that Lesso worked for Fewkes and that he and Nampeyo asked him for permission to copy designs from sherds, but she had taken an interest in sherds earlier and was probably making pots with designs from Sikyatki as well as Zuni by 1892 (Colton and Colton 1943; Judd 1951; Nequatewa 1943). There is some evidence that she was encouraged by the trader Thomas Keam to make pots based on ancient designs, because they would sell. So Nampeyo participated quite early in her career in the non-Indian market for pottery by making the types of pots that were in demand (McChesney 1994, 6).

In the *Smithsonian Institution Annual Report for 1895*, Fewkes wrote of Nampeyo:

> The best potter of the East mesa, an intelligent woman from Hano, named Nampio, acknowledged that her productions were far inferior to those of the women of Sikyatki, and she begged permission to copy some of the decorations for future inspiration. The sight of this dusky woman and her husband copying the designs of ancient ware and acknowledging their superiority was instructive in many ways. (Frisbie 1973, 237–38)

What I find instructive about this scene is that it was dropped from the legend of how Nampeyo got her designs. The image of Lesso and Nampeyo assiduously collecting sherds on their own and copying designs with pencil and paper is what is not told until after her death, when Anglos interested in her work began building Nampeyo's reputation as an artist and giving her more credit for autonomous creativity (Judd 1951; Ashton 1976). In the untold story, Nampeyo and Lesso behave like ethnologists collecting artifacts and use the tools of literacy to copy the designs. This type of activity begins to look very much like "civilized" work and not the spectacle of Indian artisanal labor.

Toward the end of her life, more and more connoisseurs and scholars asserted that Nampeyo was more an originator than a copyist. Her reclassification as an artist rested on the ability of critics and scholars to demonstrate that she had expressed her individual imagination in her designs, that she had the capacity to innovate. Her elevation to artist began with the publication of *The Pueblo Potter* (1929), by anthropologist Ruth Bunzel. Bunzel's teacher at Columbia University was Franz Boas. Like Boas and many other anthropologists, Bunzel asserted that decoration was universal behavior: "The world contains no peoples so crude in culture that they lack a decorative art" (1). She aimed to make the case that art is not just individual expression, but is cast within narrow limits that are socially determined. To do this she concentrated her study on the decorative style of pottery made at Zuni and Acoma, where pottery making seemed to be closest to its aboriginal conditions.

She also examined the revival of ancient designs as practiced by Nampeyo and other Hopi women. She found that the women indeed gathered sherds at the Sikyatki ruin, but the sherds were fragmentary: imagination was required to make a whole design from them. She concluded that modern potters did not slavishly copy the Sikyatki wares. She noted a "decorative vitality" in Hopi work and gave the potters credit for an

> unfailing freshness and variety of design. Since, as we have seen, this endless variety of designs is not copied from Sikyatki prototypes, we must conclude that this surprising exuberance is due to the very high development of the inventive faculty among the Hopi women. These potters constantly invent new patterns, or rather new variants of typical Sikyatki patterns, because it is as easy as painting the old ones and very much more enjoyable. When we compare this vitality with the artistic sterility that immediately preceded it, we conclude that inventiveness is not a peculiarly Hopi gift of mind, but rather that the introduction of a new medium of expression released an apparently inexhaustible stream of artistic creativeness which found no outlet in the old cramped style. (Bunzel 1929, 56–57)

In possessing the qualities of freshness, inventiveness, newness, and vitality, these potters begin to sound more like modern artists. And indeed Bunzel reconstructed an understanding of Pueblo tradition that was more like the Western fine art tradition. She identified Nampeyo and Maria as two potters who originated new directions in pottery, new styles: "One of the qualities of genius is the ability to experience mentally what has not been experienced sensually, and to embody this unique experience in tangible form. When such a person functions in the field of art, he may produce those sudden mutations in style that mark the history of the arts among all peoples" (Bunzel 1929, 88). Thus like Western art history, the history of ceramics in the Southwest was a gradual development in the same general direction with punctuations of sudden change brought about by individual genius. By giving Nampeyo and Maria credit for personal preference and imagination within the tradition itself, Bunzel gave them characteristics of the modern individual. In Bunzel's account, the primitive and the Western traditions were two expressions of the same thing, but the relativistic description of decorative practices more firmly justified the practices of the West. Bunzel was not interested in the influences of the market in the pueblos and on the reservations; she was looking for eternals, for universals in human psyche, and like so many before and after her, she looked to the primitive to find authenticity. What she found instead was a mirror image of the self, and in the process she created her own authority.

By the time of Nampeyo's death in 1942 the modernist appreciation of "primitive art" had completely changed the rhetoric used to describe the Indian artisan's work. Mary-Russell Colton and Harold Colton wrote in 1943 of Nampeyo's ceramics:

> Her work was distinguished from that of Hopi potters by a sense of freedom and a fluid flowing quality of design, together with an appreciation of *space* as a background for her bold rhythmic forms. Nampeyo's interest did not confine itself to design and its application, but also included the basic forms of her pottery; she introduced the beautiful low wide-shouldered jars characteristic of Sikyatki and other fine forms not heretofore in use. . . . Nampeyo's greatest contribution to the art of her people was a release and stimulation of creative ability from a decadent and hide-bound tradition. (44–45)

Here Nampeyo is the prototypical modern artist and liberator of her people. But her "contribution," the release from "decadent and hide-bound tradition," involved an appropriation of ancient designs; this liberation led to the past, not into modernity.

Under the rubric of modernism, Indians began to reflect non-Indian desires about cultural nationalism and artistic production. Increasingly, American artists, writers, and cultural critics saw Indian artisans as models for what was authentically American and essentially artistic. But, as I shall argue, this kind of modernist primitivism could not cure the perceived ills of American modernity.

CHAPTER 4

MODERNISM, PRIMITIVISM, AND *THE AMERICAN RHYTHM*

Reviewing the 1913 Armory Show of European and American art for *Outlook* magazine, Theodore Roosevelt compared Marcel Duchamp's *Nude Descending a Staircase* to a Navajo rug in his bathroom at home and found the rug "infinitely ahead of the picture" (1913b, 719). Roosevelt was reaffirming progressive-era assumptions about the civilized and the primitive. The primitive was something to evolve beyond; a painting that looked like a Navajo rug had no place in an art exhibit.

In her 1923 book *The American Rhythm,* which compared modern free verse or imagistic poetry and Native American songs, Mary Austin also compared the primitive and the modern. But unlike Roosevelt, Austin found the similarities to be within the natural order of things. She was convinced that "American poetry must inevitably take, at some period of its history, the mold of Amerind verse" (42). Rather than a regression to a savage state, this development appeared to Austin to be both a healthy return to the nation's authentic literary roots *and* a turn toward the modern.

In the ten years between the Armory Show and the publication of *The American Rhythm,* modernism, as an aesthetic and as a cultural critique, gained considerable currency among a generation of American artists and writers. Many of these men and women diagnosed modern American culture and society as being sick, or at least deficient. They perceived a number of problems: the staleness of the "genteel tradition" in American arts and letters, a mass culture with no depth or soul, rampant materialism and commercialization, and an overriding spiritual "weightlessness"—all of which were part of what T. J. Jackson Lears has identified as a crisis of cultural authority (1981, 4–54). The answers to these problems seemed to many Americans to be found among "primitive" societies, especially among Native Americans. Indian people, particularly the Pueblo groups of the Southwest, seemed to be without modern problems or urban ills, individuals living rich spiritual lives in harmony with one another and with nature.[1]

As a "cultural cure" for modernity, primitivism, the belief in the superiority of seemingly simpler ways of life, was a familiar response (Altieri 1989, 57; Shi 1985, 148). The primitivism of the 1920s recalled the ancient ideal of the simple life and echoed the romantic primitivism of the early nineteenth century. Among American reformers of the progressive era, Indian life had provided a model for the notion of the strenuous life, and Indian handicrafts had appealed to arts and crafts sensibilities. Progressive primitivism promised to reinvigorate culture in the areas of leisure and child rearing, but the primitive, as a stage to move beyond, had no place in the realm of high culture. Hence Roosevelt's dislike of modernist painting.

MODERNIST PRIMITIVISM

In the second and third decades of the twentieth century, many American artists and writers claimed that their abstract paintings and free verse poems had an essential aesthetic affinity with Indian designs and songs, and they borrowed the forms of Indian graphic and verbal expressions to use in their own works. Painters such as Emil Bisttram, Ernest L. Blumenschein, John Marin, Jan Matulka, and B. J. O. Nordfeldt, who depicted Southwestern subjects, used abstract

Native American forms in their paintings (Broder 1984; Udall 1984). In 1914 Marsden Hartley painted a series of *Indian Compositions,* abstract assemblies of geometric shapes incorporating Indianesque figures, such as eagles, tepees, and feathers (Fig. 49). At about the same time, writers such as Mary Austin, Amy Lowell, Alice Corbin Henderson, Witter Bynner, Vachel Lindsay, Max Weber, and Carl Sandburg began writing poems that suggested Indian "songs" or used Indian motifs.[2] An example of this Indian-inspired verse is Alice Corbin Henderson's imagistic poem "Fiesta," from her book *Red Earth* (1920). The poem depicts part of a Pueblo ceremonial dance, a favorite subject of artists and writers working in the Southwest:

> The sun dances to the drums
> With cottonwood boughs
> On head and ankles.
>
> The moon steps softly
> In a turquoise tablita.
>
> The stars run to pick up
> The eagle feathers
> Dropped by the dancers. (35)

What distinguished this modernist primitivism from earlier poetic and artistic depictions of Indian subjects was a kind of aesthetic "playing Indian." The relationship between the Indian and the modernist poet or artist was different from that of earlier primitivists, such as George Wharton James and other collector-connoisseurs, who "hunted" for Indian objects, or painters such as Louis Akin and E. Irving Couse, who made realistic renderings of Native Americans that drew analogies between the artist's and the artisan's work. Akin and Couse used a realistic, academic style in their works, choosing not to paint like a "primitive" would. Modernists such as Hartley also believed that they and the Native Americans they depicted were engaged in similar activities, but they appropriated Native American aesthetic idioms.

Whereas the Indian artisan was a significant icon among pro-

Figure 49. Indian Composition, *by Marsden Hartley (c. 1914–15); oil on canvas; 47 3/16 × 47 in. (Frances Lehman Loeb Art Center, Vassar College, Poughkeepsie, New York; gift of Paul Rosenfeld; 1950.1.5)*

gressive primitivists, among modernists it was Native American rituals and chants, especially those of the Southwestern Pueblo groups, that best served their aesthetic and cultural interests.[3] For painters as well as poets, the dances of the Southwest offered the appeal of rhythmic movement and repeating patterns and seemed to display a unity of spirituality, communality, and aesthetics. Dances had always been favorite subjects for painters, but the modernists engaged the idiom of abstraction and emphasized the dances' formal elements of repetition, color, and pattern, aiming to convey a sense of movement and rhythm (Figs. 50 and 51). This artistic and poetic interest in Native American chants and dances was informed in part by the increased production in the last two decades of the nineteenth century of ethnographic studies of Native Americans. At the turn of the century translations of Native American songs by ethnographers and folklorists were widely published in professional journals, popular periodicals, and anthologies.[4] The ethnographic and folkloric interest in songs was paralleled by a craze for popular songs with Indian motifs in the first two decades of the century.[5]

Figure 50. Dance at Taos, *by Ernest L. Blumenschein (1923); oil on canvas; 24 × 27 in. (Collection of the Museum of Fine Arts, Museum of New Mexico; gift of Florence Dibbell Bartlett, 1947)*

Although there was widespread popular interest in Native American arts and rituals, modernist primitivism was very much a cosmopolitan phenomenon. In the United States, modernist aesthetics began to be discussed and practiced in literary and art circles in New York and Chicago in the 1910s. New York of the 1910s and 1920s was undergoing an artistic and literary "Little Renaissance" (Wertheim 1976; Heller and Rudnick 1991). Magazines such as *Camera Work,* the *Dial,* and the *Soil* expressed interest in primitive art from around the world, and galleries such as Alfred Stieglitz's 291 and the Washington Square Gallery exhibited both modern and primitive art.

Figure 51. Antelope Dance, *by B. J. O. Nordfeldt (1919); oil on canvas; 35 5/8 × 43 in. (Museum of Fine Arts, Museum of New Mexico; museum purchase with funds donated by Friends of Southwestern Art/Archaeology Society, 1920)*

In literary circles, magazines such as the *Smart Set, Seven Arts,* and the *New Republic* published modernist poetry (Wertheim 1976, 5). In Chicago, Harriet Monroe and Alice Corbin Henderson edited *Poetry* magazine, an important and influential forum for modernist verse. The February 1917 issue of *Poetry* was devoted to Native American–inspired poetry and offered "interpretations" from "American-Indian motives" using "subjects and rhythms drawn from aboriginal life and song" (Monroe 1917, 251).[6]

For American artists and writers, interest in Native American aesthetics was in part an extension of European modernist interest in primitive art. In fact, it was African art that first caught the attention of American modernists. European artists, most notably Picasso, had visited the Trocadéro Museum in Paris and, inspired by African sculptures there, began incorporating these motifs into their work. In November 1914 the 291 gallery presented an exhibit of African sculpture, but it wasn't until 1931 at the Exposition of Indian Tribal Arts that Indian-crafted objects were shown in New York as art.[7] Furthermore, many early American modernist paintings of Indian subjects tended to be stylistically derivative of European modernist painters. Nordfeldt's *Antelope Dance* (1919), for example, shows the influence of Cézanne (Fig. 51).

In this milieu of ethnographic, popular, and artistic interest in Indian arts and rituals, and the increasing influence of modernist aesthetics as a lens through which to see them, Mary Austin published *The American Rhythm,* a manifesto for the central role she believed Native American "poetry" should play in American literary life. Austin's interest in Native Americans was lifelong. After the success of *The Land of Little Rain* (1903), her book of sketches of life in California's Owens Valley, she published translations of Native American poetry in many periodicals (Castro 1983, 17). During this time she also wrote a collection of stories for children called *The Basket Woman* (1904). In these stories Seyavi, the Paiute "Basket Woman," narrates tales to a white boy named Alan and is a creative figure analogous to Austin herself (Viehmann 1994, 163–68). In 1911 her play *The Arrow Maker,* about the unrequited love of an Indian woman shaman, was produced in New York at the New Theatre and was subsequently published (Langlois 1988b, 79–81).[8]

American Indian subjects became increasingly important to Austin's work, and *The American Rhythm* is her most comprehensive book about Native Americans. The book begins with a long essay, "The American Rhythm," which discusses the nature of poetic rhythm and "Amerindian verse" and the state and future of American poetry. Generally, Austin's argument was that Native American songs and ritual dances were examples of purely American poetic expression and, therefore, modern American poets should take them as models. She also outlined an evolution of poetic expression, in which "Amerind" verse forms were living examples of a primitive stage of poetic evolution. Following the essay are a number of "Amerindian Songs Reëxpressed from the Originals" and a selection of "Songs in the American Manner," poems of Austin's own creation. The

Amerindian songs appear to be from Native American groups all over North America and include ritual chants by groups as well as individuals. In the essay Austin says that most of the poems were written before 1910 and published between 1910 and 1914. In 1930 a second, revised edition of *The American Rhythm* appeared.[9]

Some of the Indian songs Austin "reëxpressed" were "Warrior's Song," "The Eagle's Song," "Medicine Songs," "Papago Love Songs," and this "glyph":

> A girl wearing a green ribbon,—
> As if it had been my girl.
> —The green ribbon I gave her for remembrance—
> Knowing all the time it was not my girl,
> Such was the magic of that ribbon,
> Suddenly,
> My girl existed inside me! (1930b, 107)

Austin used the term *glyph* to describe a kind of imagism in Native American expression, "a type of Amerind song which is lyric in its emotional quality and yet cannot be completely expressed by the simple lyric cry" (53). Apparently, Austin's reexpressions were very loose translations. In the essay she recalled that this poem was based on a song by someone called Washoe Charlie, who lamented the absence of his sweetheart. What he sang to her was this: "The Green ribbon, when I saw a girl wearing it, my girl existed inside me" (53). It is not clear if Charlie was speaking in English, or if Austin translated it from his language.

In *The American Rhythm,* only a few of Austin's own "Songs in the American Manner" take Indian themes. One poem, "Women's War Thoughts," is about the First World War, and there is the strongly imagistic "Fifth Avenue at Night." Also included are "New Mexican Love Song," "On Hearing Vachel Lindsay Chant his Verse," and "Song of the Maverick":

> I am too arid for tears, and for laughter
> Too sore with unslaked desires.
> My nights are scanty of sleep

And my sleep too full of dreaming;
The frosts are not cold enough
Nor the suns sufficiently burning:

The hollow waves are slack
And no wind from any quarter
Lifts strongly enough to outwear me.
My body is bitter with baffled lusts
Of work and love and endurance.
As a maverick, leaderless, lost from the herd,
Loweth my soul with the need of man encounters.

For I am crammed and replete
With the power of desolate places;
I have gone far on faint trails
And slept in the shade of my arrows;
Patience, forgiveness and might
Ache in me, finding no egress,
And virtues stale that are too big for the out gate.

I would run large with the man herd, the hill subduers,
I would impress myself on the mold of large adventure
Until all deeds of that likeness
Should a long time carry
The stripe of the firstling's father.

For I am anguished with strength,
Overfed with the common experience,
My feet run wide of the rutted trails
Toward the undared destinies. (1923, 112)

To Austin and other modernists, Native American "art" and "songs" seemed modern in their formal qualities; they looked like abstract paintings or sounded like imagist poems. Carl Sandburg, writing about the songs recorded by Frances Densmore among the Chippewa, commented ironically: "Suspicion arises definitely that the Red Man and his children committed direct plagiarisms on the modern imagists and vorticists" (1917, 255). But most modernist works are only readable as "Indian" when they mention or describe Indian subjects, such as the dance described by Alice Corbin Henderson in "Fiesta," the tepees in Marsden Hartley's *Indian Composition,* or the "trails" and "arrows" of Austin's "Song of the Maverick." The poems clearly have other poetic roots; Austin's poem owes its verse form and inspiration to Whitman, and Henderson's poem is in the tradition of imagism. Although the alleged affinity between Indian and modern art forms is not always evident, it was insisted upon in the criticism and essays of many modernists.

CULTURAL NATIONALISM AND REGIONALISM

Modernist interest in primitive art may have been a largely imported idea, but the turn to the American Indian gave this primitivism a strong nationalist spin. The question of what shape American arts and letters should take was perennial and had plagued artists and writers since Independence, but at the turn of the century cultural nationalism became an urgent issue to many artists, writers, and critics.

Part of this concern had to do with determining who exactly was an American. Increased immigration raised questions about ethnicity and national identity. In 1916 Randolph Bourne pointed out in "Trans-National America" that the United States was not a melting pot but a heterogeneous culture, and Waldo Frank addressed the issues of plurality and national identity in *Our America* (1919). In an ethnically diverse society, what constituted American identity?

By the 1920s the answers to that question were tied increasingly to the anthropological notion of culture. Drawing on Werner Sollors's thinking about cultural identities of consent and descent, Walter Benn Michaels has written, "The distinctive mark of culture is that it must be both achieved and inherited" (1990, 231). There is always a tension between these two ideas, but in the United States in the 1920s, being an American was coming to be perceived less as a political, achieved identity and more as something one was born into. Michaels argues that in 1924 the passage of the Johnson Act, which limited immigration, and the Citizenship Act, which made Native Americans citizens, delimited American citizenship as less achievable than inherited; the Johnson Act made it harder for immigrants to become citizens, and the Citizenship Act answered the question of how to make Indians Americans by declaring that they already were (Michaels 1990, 222–23).[10]

In *The American Rhythm* and other of her writings, Austin determined the Indian to be essentially American, but the parameters of this identity shifted back and forth between achieved and ascribed characteristics. Austin believed that Indian cultures could provide the basis for a national culture, because Indians, being intimately tied to nature, were products of the American environment and thus expressed what was truly and essentially American.[11] This environmental determinism was also at the heart of Austin's theories about American poetry. She argued that poetry had its source in movement and rhythm, which in turn was rooted in human beings' responses to the earth. In her book about the Southwest, *The Land of Journey's Ending* (1924), Austin wrote:

> Man is not himself only, not solely a variation of his racial type in the pattern of his immediate experience. He is all that he sees; all that flows to him from a thousand sources, half noted, or noted not at all except by some sense that lies too deep for naming. He is the land, the lift of its mountain lines, the reach of its valleys; his is the rhythm of its seasonal processions, the involution and variation of its vegetal patterns. If there is in the country of his abiding, no more than a single refluent color, such as the veiled green of sage-brush or the splendid wine of sunset spilled along the Sangre de Cristo, he takes it in and gives it forth again in directions and occasions least suspected by himself, as a manner, as music, as a prevailing tone of thought, as the line of his roof-tree, the pattern of his personal adornment. (1924b, 437)[12]

Austin acknowledges some sense of racial determinism, but the influence of the land overcomes the influence of race. By locating the source of Americanness in the environment, Austin found a literal common ground for all the nation's inhabitants. The experience of being American and expressing Americanness could be *achieved* by everyone if they took the Indian as an example and paid close attention to their particular American environment. In this way, Americans, and especially American artists, could become "natives."

Elsewhere, however, Austin waffles on the issue of racial versus environmental influence. In an essay on "aboriginal" American literature in *The Cambridge History of American Literature* (1921) she wrote: "The homogeneity of the Amerind race makes it possible to detect environmental influences with a precision not possible among the mixed races of Europe" (630). Although she argued that the "mixed races of Europe" in America should take the Indian as a model, this passage suggests that the ability to tune into the natural environment is a racial prerogative of the "pure" American Indian and an impossibility for others of "impure" lineage. I will return to how playing Indian seemed to resolve this dilemma for Austin, but for now it is enough to point out the interplay between racial and environmental sources in the construction of Austin's notion of American and in the figuration of the Indian as pure.

The United States' entry into World War I was another spur to cultural nationalism. During and after the war the rhetoric about the Americanness of Indians became more heated and fervent. Austin and others who had previously promoted Indian art often expressed a kind of gratitude to the war for forcing American artists and writers to "come home." Marsden Hartley, who had complained about the "fetish for Paris" among American artists, wrote: "The war has accomplished this for the painter, it has demanded originality of him. It has sent him back to his own soil to ponder and readjust himself to a conviction of his own and an esthetics of his own" (1918b, 341; 1918a, 333).

The anti-European nationalist rhetoric of Austin and Hartley implied a kind of cultural colonialism. They saw themselves as oppressed by the traditions of Europe, and they called for artistic independence. But as much as artists and writers wanted to free themselves from European cultural colonialism, their cultural situation inevitability produced ambivalence. Facing what now might be called a postcolonial dilemma, they realized that even though they thought American art should grow from its roots in the American environment, it was also a product of traditions imported from Europe. They rejected "Plato and Shakespeare by way of New England" while claiming affinity with the roots of the European tradition, and they often compared Native American arts with those of other vanished cultures: Egyptian, Hebrew, and Greek (Hartley 1918b, 342). Austin believed that Native American dances had much in common with ancient Greek theater. By likening Native American cultures to ancient Western civilizations, these writers implied a similar trajectory for American culture, prophesying that, like ancient Greek civilization, it would blossom into its own distinctive tradition.[13]

The work of Austin, Hartley, Henderson, and others amounted to a rewriting of the history of American arts and letters. *The American Rhythm* is in many ways a creation myth for American literature. In the introductory essay Austin argues that literature evolved from tribal ritual to poetry and drama. Thus the songs and dances of American Indians become the earliest American texts. By rejecting Europe and claiming the Indian as the founder of American art and literature, Austin was able to claim a new, independent beginning for American culture.

Austin's revision of American literary history, which reconstituted Indian songs and chants as a kind of American folk expression, was not a completely new move. The eloquence of the Indian was an old and popular idea. Thomas Jefferson included Chief Logan's speech of 1774 in his *Notes on the State of Virginia* and compared it to Greek oratory. The inclusion of the speech in McGuffey's reader in the mid-nineteenth century placed Indian speech within the American literary tradition (Pearce 1965, 78–79). Austin made a similar gesture in the *Cambridge History of American Literature.* In this passage Native American oratory sounds very much like Puritan plain speaking:

> The language being native, there were no words in it derived from scholastic sources, no words that were not used all the time by all the people. It was not even possible for poet or orator to talk "over the heads" of his audiences. There was a kind of sacred patter used by the initiates of certain mysteries, but the language of literature was the common vehicle of daily life. (611)

Like Puritan sermons, Indian chants and songs had the power to sway the tribe and the deities. The scene Austin describes is an image of a community that shared not only a common "sacred" language but also, more important, a common "literature"; Austin identified literature as the primary vehicle by which a nation imagines itself as a community.[14]

The Indians in this passage may seem like Puritan orators and the souls of democracy, but some writers within the American literary tradition seemed more "Indian" than others. For example, the modernists did not claim Longfellow's *Hiawatha* as part of the tradition of authentic American verse. Austin criticized Longfellow for using a Finnish verse form to tell his story. But she praised Abraham Lincoln's oratory as an authentic example of the American rhythm (1930b, 15-16). She also said that Walt Whitman was on the right track, but that "his capacity was on every side limited by his intelligence, which was adolescent and gamboling" (18). Whitman was an important touchstone in locating the authentic American voice; Marsden Hartley claimed that Whitman could be "a precipitant likewise for American painting" (1918b, 342). Whitman is an obvious and appropriate forebear for these modernists in his verse form and his championing of democratic principles, and in many ways Austin's "American Rhythm" essay echoes Whitman's *Democratic Vistas* as a manifesto for an original American culture.

Although Austin's literary history embraced Indians within American tradition, it generally assumed an evolutionary progress that distinguished between the primitive and the modern; tribal ritual and modern literature were not equal modes of expression. In another passage from *The Cambridge History of American Literature,* Austin described the appropriate uses of Native American expression:

> The permanent worth of song and epic, folk-tale and drama, aside from its intrinsic literary quality, is its revelation of the power of the American landscape to influence form, and the expressiveness of democratic living in native measures. We have seen how easily some of our outstanding writers have grafted their genius to the Amerind stock, producing work that passes at once into the category of literature. And in this there has nothing happened that has not happened already in every country in the world, where the really great literature is found to have developed on some deep rooted aboriginal stock. The earlier, then, we leave off thinking of our own aboriginal literary sources as the product of an alien and conquered people, and begin to think of them as the inevitable outgrowth of the American environment, the more readily shall we come into

> full use of it: such use as has in other lands produced out of just such material the plays of Shakespeare, the epics of Homer, the operas of Wagner, the fables of Æsop, the hymns of David, the tales of Andersen, and the Arabian Nights. (633–34)

To Austin the main value of American Indian literature was not that it was a lasting and viable voice unto itself, but that it could be used to revitalize a somnolent Euro-American tradition.[15] Through the process of "grafting" European tradition onto the "deep-rooted" native "stock," a new modern American literature would grow. This begins to sound like literary eugenics and suggests how these Native American literary origins could become the *inherited* legacy of modern non-Indian American writers.

American modernists identified themselves with another colonial subject, the Indian, but in their appreciation of the primitive, history and the political aspects of the artist-Indian relationship tended to disappear. Native Americans *were* a conquered, if not exactly an alien, people, but in her desire to find a usable literary past, Austin ignored the ongoing political relationship between Indian people and the rest of the nation. Because Austin and many other artists and writers worked to secure Native American civil rights as well as to preserve Indian arts, the oppressed status of Indian people in the United States must have been clear to them. But the Indian they cited as a model for the American writer or artist was not the historically oppressed Indian but the pure primitive who seemed to exist outside any political or historical reality. As in ethnographic writing, there is the sense that as American poets brought the Indian into literature, that as the Indian was "written," Native Americans vanished. And furthermore, this was a necessary transformation. The Indian was usable *only* as a past.

Related to the Indian's role as a symbol of national identity was his role as a figure of regional authority and authenticity; regionalism and nationalism in the 1920s were two sides of the same cultural coin. Robert Dorman has identified three regionalist cultural movements in the 1920s that invoked the Indian: New Mexico and Arizona, Oklahoma, and Nebraska witnessed cultural awakenings in which local art and literature were seen as a source of a "regionalist civic religion," which would act as a cure for the cultural ills of the whole nation (1993, 55–80). The Southwest, more than any other region in the United States, seemed remote and exotic, and this cultural "distance" gave writers and artists who could identify their work with it an authority that rested on the authenticity of the other. By identifying with the region's Native American inhabitants, Austin and other southwestern artists and writers could imagine themselves outside the mainstream of popular and genteel culture, in a region of the handmade, the unique, and the authentic.

One of the themes of cultural regionalism during the 1920s was a rejection of mass culture. In 1929 Austin wrote that ultimately it was the "disposition of the people" to reject mass culture and to embrace regional particularity (1929a, 477; 1932). In 1922 ethnologist Natalie Curtis had made the anti–mass culture appeal of the Southwest even more explicit:

> Although New Mexico is so foreign to the character of much of our country that visitors have been known to talk of going back to New York or Chicago as "returning to America," it is, nevertheless, a very real part of these United States, with a distinct utterance of its own. A land lives through its artists even after the people themselves have perished. That type of Americanization which is largely a matter of mail-order-house clothes and crockery, of chewing-gum and "movies" will soon wipe its erasing hand across the South-west like a well-meaning but ignorant servant who, zealously "setting to rights" an artist's studio, dusts off his pastels. One can not sufficiently prize this growing literature of the South-west which reminds us of the worth and beauty of a section of America that is still free from machinery and—marvellous to relate—free from billboards as well. (1922, 468)

Curtis distinguishes between the mass culture of "mail-order-house clothes," "chewing gum," and "movies" and an implied other, more authentic regional culture that is analogous to an artist's pastel, free of mass-culture influences. The art analogy is interesting, because it locates the region's singularity within the realm of the aesthetic. Many of the artists and writers who worked to preserve traditional Indian arts and crafts usually mentioned the worst aesthetic offenses of popular culture as evidence to justify their efforts. Austin, Hartley, and others called for the artist to look to Indian dances and songs for inspiration, but they did not have in mind the many popular Indian songs, such as "Oh, That Navajo Rag" (1911), "Wigwam Stomp," and "Indianola" (1918), that appeared in sheet-music form from the turn of the century through the 1920s.[16]

Of course, what these arguments about the Southwest's superior aesthetic value were also speaking about was class. In Curtis's passage, mass culture is figured as the "ignorant servant." As much as artists were "othering" themselves in their alliance with the region or with Native Americans, they occupied an elite realm. They maintained strict boundaries between art and mass culture, and their promotion of regional culture suggested a certain anxiety about losing cultural control and authority (Mullin 1993, 163–74).

In a related move, modernists also set themselves against the avatars of genteel culture, such as the chautauqua movement and the YWCA, which opposed the Indian dances as immoral. Austin was active in working to preserve Hispanic and Indian arts in New Mexico, and she was a principal figure in the defeat of the establishment of a chautauqua in Santa Fe. To Austin, the chautauqua represented an intrusion of an older version of high culture that had been diluted and made palatable for the middle class. By keeping the chautauqua out of Santa Fe, Austin and the other art colonists preserved Indian traditions and defended their own cultural authority (Austin 1926b; Gibson 1983, 211–16; Sloan 1924).

As in their discussions about the cultural influences of Europe, Austin and other writers and artists who lived and worked in Santa Fe and Taos felt a tension between the desire to escape the "dictatorial" influence of the American metropolitan centers and the need for their approval. Writers and artists such as Austin, John Sloan, Marsden Hartley, and Georgia O'Keeffe carried on the nineteenth-century tradition of art colonists who summered in a location remote from the city. They moved easily between the two landscapes; the city and the desert seemed to satisfy complementary needs, such as the availability of authentic regional subject matter and access to national markets. Austin wrote stories about southwestern Indians, and she wrote a novel about New York bohemian life, *No. 26 Jayne Street* (1920). In her poem "Fifth Avenue at Night" (one of her "Songs in the American Manner") she contrasted the busy New York avenue with the calm of the desert.

Austin had a profoundly ambivalent attitude toward the centers of the art and publishing markets, especially New York. As had Mabel Dodge Luhan and Alice Corbin Henderson before her, Austin eventually rejected the city in favor of the region; she moved to Santa Fe permanently in 1925. Austin had long resented the fact that all the critical appraisals and definitions of American literature seemed to come from a few people in New York, whom she said regarded American cultural geography as "a country centered in New York, with a small New England ell in the rear and a rustic gazebo in Chicago; the rest of it is magnificently predicated from a car window" (Austin 1920, 129.) Even though Austin continued to move in cosmopolitan circles in Santa Fe and New York, she often expressed anger at her sense of having to give in to critics and editors in the East. Mostly this boiled down to her not liking their criticism, and she tended to claim a regional authority whenever things didn't go her way.[17] In truth, her cultural authority rested as much on metropolitan approval as on regional authenticity.

In a 1920 article for the *Nation,* "New York: Dictator of American Criticism," Austin's anticosmopolitanism took an ugly anti-Semitic turn when she declared that Jews had no right to be the arbiters of American culture. Citing Waldo Frank as an example, she asked, "Can the Jew, with his profound complex of election, his need of sensuous satisfaction qualifying his every expression of personal life, and his short pendulum-swing between mystical orthodoxy and a sterile ethical culture—can he become the commentator, the arbiter, of American art and American thinking?" (129). This rhetorical question raised again the issue of American cultural identity in terms of consent and descent. To Austin, the Jew and the Indian signified opposing models of cultural authority (and authenticity). The Indian, racially pure and a product of the natural American environment, was authentic; the Jew, also a racial type, but "foreign" and a product of the metropolis, was patently inauthentic. Thus New York was not really American, whereas the Southwest was, and Austin, by aligning herself with the region, appeared to be truly "native American."

Austin often represented herself as an outsider, an interlocutor "clamoring on the doorstep," someone who speaks for the region and demands to be heard in the centers of empire (Said 1989, 210). Austin's strategy was similar to that of other regional writers (and anthropologists) of the 1920s and earlier. In the national literary and art markets, the authenticity of regional literature and art and the authority of the regional writer and artist were the result of a "foray into otherness" (Stewart 1989, 51). By interpreting the Indian Southwest to the rest of the nation, Austin became the interlocutor in a national dialogue about the region. But she was not merely "provincial"; her authorial legitimacy came from this "in-between," transient position. She could move in both worlds, but she needed for there to remain a distance between them; she needed the center *and* the periphery to remain in a colonial relationship in order to maintain her authority.[18]

Conceived of as culturally static and ahistorical, Indians of the Southwest seemed unquestionably authentic. But even as Indians served as a locus for regional and national identity, it is clear that the cultural authority maintained by those who claimed affinity with them was contingent on a web of shifting and complicated boundaries —between races, ethnicities, class, regions, insiders, and outsiders— and that these relationships between Indians and artists and between artists and centers of cultural power were precisely historical.

PRIMITIVISM AS A CULTURAL CURE

In addition to serving the interests of cultural nationalism and regionalism, modernist primitivism offered answers to several other perceived cultural and social problems. Austin wrote in *The Land of Journey's Ending* of the Pueblos of the Southwest:

> Living in such fashion, the pueblos, at the time Spain found them, had no rich, no poor, no paupers, no prisons, no red-light district, no criminal classes, no institutionalized orphans, no mothers of dependent children penalized by their widowhood, no one pining for a mate, who wished to be married. All this is so much a part of their manner of living together in communities, that three centuries of Christian contact have not quite cured them of their superior achievement. (1924b, 244)

The Indians Austin describes seem to be less children of nature than geniuses at social engineering and urban planning. Austin had in common with critics such as Randolph Bourne, Van Wyck Brooks, Lewis Mumford, and (even) Waldo Frank the belief that modern existence was dangerously fragmented. Individuals, they believed, felt alienated from the rest of society, which was increasingly split along ethnic and class lines. They also shared the idea that the cure for this malaise was cultural, that it might be possible to reform American culture in such a way that would answer spiritual, personal, and social needs.[19]

Much American ethnography of the 1920s was a critique of American culture. The works of Edward Sapir, Ruth Benedict, and Margaret Mead implied that primitive cultures could be models for American society. In his 1924 essay "Culture, Genuine and Spurious," Edward Sapir outlined the characteristics of "genuine" culture (in opposition to the "spurious" culture of modern civilization). Genuine culture was "inherently harmonious, balanced, self-satisfactory," a culture in which "nothing is spiritually meaningless" (1949, 314–15). Sapir and others believed that genuine culture was increasingly absent in American life, that human spirituality and well-being had been sacrificed to industrialization and machines. He held up the Indian as the product of genuine culture and the "telephone girl" as the product of modern American culture. Sapir argued that the Indian's "salmon-spearing is a culturally higher type of activity than that of the telephone girl or mill hand simply because there is normally no sense of spiritual frustration during its prosecution, no feeling of subservience to tyrannous yet largely inchoate demands, because it works naturally with all the rest of the Indian's activities instead of standing out as a desert patch of merely economic effort in the whole of life" (316).

There was, however, a strain in modernist cultural critique that embraced the machine as authentic. The machine, like the Indian, could be construed as a primitive other. Take, for example, Francis Picabia's *Portrait d'une jeune fille américaine dans l'état de nudité* (Fig. 52), which was published in Stieglitz's *291* magazine in 1915. Picabia's precise, mechanical rendering of a spark plug is an icon of the modernity of America, a literalization of Sapir's "telephone girl." The machine becomes a kind of body without a head, without language, without thinking—a model of action, purity, simplicity, and unambiguity. This image was a version of modernism that valued the

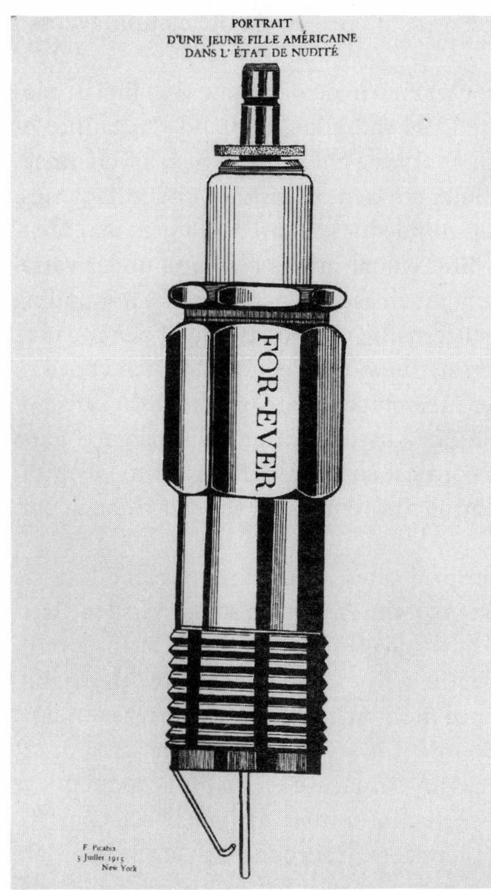

Figure 52. Portrait d'une jeune fille américaine dans l'état de nudité, *by Francis Picabia (1915). This "object-portrait" appeared in 291 magazine (July–August 1915). (Art and Architecture Collection; Miriam and Ira D. Wallach Division of Art, Prints and Photographs; The New York Public Library; Astor, Lenox and Tilden Foundations)*

primitive, authentic qualities that resided in modernity, not in vanishing societies.[20]

What was it that made Indian culture seem especially genuine or authentic? Writing in *Our America* in 1919, Waldo Frank described prehistoric American tribes as "fashioners of beauty, masters of communal order, worshipers of a true God" (107). This trinity of characteristics was repeatedly echoed among modernist primitivists who represented Native Americans as natural artists, good citizens, and spiritually authentic. These qualities converged in the ritual dances of the Pueblo Indians, which were at once aesthetic, communal, and spiritual events.

Native American dances seemed to demonstrate that Indian people did not suffer from alienated individualism and the failure of communal life. Social relations among Native Americans were imagined to be preindividualistic and based on kinship and village ties. Austin believed that "group-mindedness" antedated personal identity and that in the dance "individual minds combine under variations of emotional stress very much as the dust grains on a sounding board are marshaled into patterns by the vibrations of the musical chord" (1930b, 19). By contrast, "mob-mindedness," which called to mind labor strikes and other urban problems, came from the effect of one person on the group (24). But Austin's critique of urban problems overlooked the presence of political conflict; her answer to labor unrest was a kind of reimagination and renewal of the self through cultural practices.

In addition to a desire for a sense of community, modernists were concerned about the state of the American soul. Marsden Hartley complained that Americans had erroneously placed their faith in science and progress. In 1922 he wrote: "So it is we have the highly deified and wholly worshipped mechanical era. Electricity is our new found deific principle. Therefore it is science and not religion or art has become our modern necessity" (1922a, 117). In his account of the Snake dance, D. H. Lawrence made a similar critique of science: "To us, science is our religion of conquest. Hence through science, we are the conquerors and resultant gods of our earth. But to the Indian, the so-called mechanical processes do not exist. All lives. And the conquest is made by the means of the living will" (1924, 845).

In contrast to the American worship of science and its practices, Indian dances seemed to exemplify spiritual authenticity. The dances represented good relationships not only among individuals within the community but also between people and the universe, or Allness, as Austin called it. The Indian dance ritual was understood to be prayer in motion:

> The Amerind makes poetry because he believes it to be good for him. He makes it because he believes it to be a contribution to the well-being of his group. He makes it to put himself in sympathy

> with the *wakonda*, the *orenda* or god-stuff which he conceives to be to some degree in every created thing. Finally—and on almost every occasion—he makes it to affect objects that are removed from him in the dimension of *time and space*. (1930b, 34)

Thus ritual dance, or "poetry," was at once a magical practice (analogous to science) and a kind of therapy.[21]

In speaking of Indian "drama" or "dance," "song" or "poetry," modernists conflated the aesthetic and the spiritual. Austin, Hartley, and other modernists believed that art could fill the vacuum of spiritual weightlessness. Alice Corbin Henderson argued in 1923 that the spirituality apparent in Indian dances could be a model for every American artist:

> In the childhood of the world, in which these dances live, there is no distinction between art and religion; and for the artist, too, it may be said that the distinction does not exist. . . . It is not at all impossible that we may come to realize that the cause of the childlike, peaceful and civilized Pueblo Indians is the cause of every American artist, the cause of art itself, as against the materialistic tendency of the age and its lack of vision. . . . If, from these Pueblo dances, we could regain something of this older unity, this essential faith, would it not add greatly to our art, which seems to suffer from this lack of any spiritual source or background? (1923a, 114–15)

In Henderson's argument art would answer society's spiritual needs. If Indians practiced their religion in artistic forms, then artists could practice their art in spiritual ways. Borrowing the practices of Native Americans would provide artists, and by extension all Americans, with a way into, access to, a vital spiritual life.

The model that modernists invoked of the Indian as communal and spiritual rested on certain assumptions about the nature of the primitive. One of its most important characteristics was that the primitive was the essential, whole human being. The overriding theme of modernist representations of Indians was the interrelated ideas of universality and holism. When Mary Austin described the origins of dance rituals in *The American Rhythm*, she might have been describing her own time: "Man learned to resort to the dance when he felt helpless or fragmentary, when he felt dislocated in his universe" (26). It was assumed that Indians, as primitives, did not separate or categorize experience but had a wholly integrated sense of themselves and the world. Thus modernists tried to strip away what they perceived as the differentiating excesses of modern experience, to get at what was universally human. They believed that beyond self-consciousness and differentiation was a way of being that all humans had in common and that Indians were already in touch with.

Indians did not seem to suffer from the mind-body dualism that many modernists complained was the legacy of the American Puritan tradition. Rather, the primitive mind and body functioned harmoniously with each other and with nature. In 1922 Marsden Hartley declared that the body was central to artistic expression and criticized Western Christian tradition for denying physical pleasures:

> All primitive peoples believe in and indulge the sensuous aspects of their religions. They provide for the delight of their bodies in the imagined needs of the soul. . . . When a man can so attune his body that every part of it not only aspires but accomplishes the perfect fusion of the song, the poem, and the dance, then he may be said to achieve the perfect notion of what a real religion should be, what the spiritual universe is meant to signify, and more especially to the esthetic consciousness; it is the cosmic significance to the poetic soul raised to its most convincing height. (1922a, 113)

In Native American ritual dances not only did the mind and body function together with the universe but also the song, the poem, and the dance were united.

Likewise, modernist ideas about the primitive mind characterized it as whole and undivided. Because Indians were supposedly not subject to the distractions of civilization, they were not jaded to sensations. Austin wrote that a primitive state of mind is "a state of acute, happy awareness." She believed that civilization had forced upon us "a selective intensity of observation such as rarely occurs in primitive experience" and remarked that the Indian doesn't see better than white man, he sees more (1930b, 28–29, 82). This point was crucial in supporting her argument that Indians were more sensitive to the American environment. It also echoed Spencerian ideas about cultural evolution in that it posited an Indian whose mental state was in many respects immature and undeveloped and "rarely rose above the level of sensation" (Stocking 1968, 117). In *The American Rhythm* Austin wrote that "psychologically the state called primitive is one of deeply imbricated complexity" (28), which suggests that the primitive mind is like a flower bud; it has the parts of the civilized mind, but they are not yet fully realized.

Austin was writing at a time when new ideas about human psychology were in circulation. Freud's work was becoming widely known in the United States, and Jung was working out his ideas about the mythological roots of indigenous culture and creativity. Austin expressed strong ambivalence about Freudian notions of the subconscious but suggested that some mental region like the subconscious might be the source of poetry, "since [poetry] so obviously cannot be produced by effort of the intelligence" (1930b, 28). As she looked to the cultural region for authentic American expression, Austin looked for the sources of poetic creativity in some primal corner of the mind. Consciousness seemed impure and inauthentic; it interfered with the purer truth of older, simpler mental functions. Because it was more primitive, the Indian mind was assumed to lack a fully developed sense of self-consciousness and seemed to operate at some simpler level, without the interference of an ego (Austin 1927b, 745).

Indian arts also appeared to be unified: "All Amerind poetry . . . presents itself as three-plied movement and melody and words" (Austin 1930b, 46). Suggesting a unity of form in all Native American arts, some writers argued that the patterns of dance were repeated in baskets, pottery, and sand paintings: "Many of the South-western songs are shaped in the conventionalized ceremonial song-pattern of the desert tribes—a pattern paralleled in woven baskets, in pottery-designs, and in the altar-pictures wrought with coloured sand" (Curtis 1922, 468).[22]

This sense of holism and integration extended to Indian social organization; unlike American society, the Pueblo Indians were "sole among the peoples of the earth, a society in which there is no partition between cultural and economic interests" (Austin 1924a, 35). Instead, artistic expression in Indian society seemed to inhabit all aspects of life, from "Corn Grinding" songs, to a "Song for the New-born," to "A Song in Depression."[23] The image of the singing Indian woman grinding corn echoes Sapir's model of the "salmon-spearing" Indian, whose labor was not alienated from other aspects of his life.

All of which is to say that modernist primitivism conceptualized the production of artistic expression, graphic and verbal, as something all Indians did naturally. Or rather, that everything Indians did was art, that art was not a specialized skill but was central to Indian culture. There was no form of expression or communication among Indians that did not come to seem like art. They sang while they worked; their prayers were dances; their dances were poetry in motion.

The presumed centrality of art in Indian culture was, in part, a function of the romantic association of creativity with the primitive, children, and the mentally ill (Price 1989, 47). But the idea that art was able to cure modernity also rested upon a concept of culture that replaced faith in a Creator with faith in human creativity. To modernists not only was the Indian an archetypal artist but also the Indian artist (and by association, the modern artist) was a kind of shaman, a promethean figure of considerable spiritual and cultural authority. As Hartley wrote in 1922: "It is the artist who is permitted to understand a great many things, for he is despite himself part priest and part actor. These are the primal instincts of the type, the power for reverence, and the power for re-presentation" (1922a, 118). This must have been good news to the many writers and artists who complained that "today in this unreverential age the artist is the excrescence," "an interruption in the business of living, . . . something queer, . . . something not belonging."[24] By taking the Indian as a model, the modernist primitivist was able to imagine the artist in dialogue with his or her public, in a society in which individual expression was instantly understood by everyone and was in fact an act of communion with society and the universe.

However, among modernists there remained a feeling that society must rise to the level of the artist and not the other way around. One of the duties of art and artists was to save the masses from mass culture. Although much was made of the "group-mindedness" of Indian society, in the ideology of modernism, it was the individual artist-shaman who emerged as a cultural leader (Austin 1924a, 35). The modernist turn to the Indian did not represent the success of the community but was a way for artists to claim authority in their own communities, which seemed to be increasingly engulfed by a mass culture they could not control.

THE INDIAN AND AESTHETIC AUTHENTICITY

Modernist primitivism was never about practicing Native American belief systems. It was, rather, about an aesthetic practice that would lead to spiritual experience. The poem or painting demonstrated the authority and authenticity of the artist's experience, and looking at the painting or reading the poem became an authentic experience itself. Modernist aesthetics shared with romantic ideology the belief that art was the result of an individual's experience of an essential reality (Williams 1958, 39). Modernist poets and artists were driven by a desire to get beyond the surface of things, to get at an inner, structural truth. Marsden Hartley identified the path to this aesthetic authenticity as spiritual and individual: "Until he [the artist] has imbibed something of the character and quality underlying and inherent in the superior spectacle of spiritual veracity, he can not hope to do more than feebly copy the tritest of externals which any half naked eye can observe" (1922a, 118). Mary Austin realized that writing poetry called for a kind of elemental connection between the individual and a higher reality: "Thus poetry becomes the means by which men and their occasions are rewoven from time to time with the Allness; and who is there to tell me that this, in art, is not the essence of modernity?" (1930b, 57).

The necessity of directly connecting with something absolutely real was at the core of modernist poetics. Ezra Pound's principles of imagism exhorted poets "to use the language of common speech, but to employ always the *exact* word, not the nearly-exact, nor the merely decorative word" and "To produce poetry that is hard and clear, never blurred nor indefinite."[25] And the poet Amy Lowell defined imagist poetry as "a new technique relying on vivid images and clear and colloquial language to describe experience" (Wertheim 1976, 100). This aesthetic authenticity called for a stripping away of excess, of anything that got between the individual and experience. The first things to go were the genteel Victorian poetic and artistic conventions, which were considered stale and inauthentic, intrusions on essential reality. Noting the disappearance of "the fetish of conventional rhetoric in painting," Marsden Hartley wrote, "It is the same with poetry, which is rapidly dismissing its 'isms,' and we see genuine individuals appearing with their own relationships to things, and their own methods of expression" (1918b, 340). Free verse was free because it liberated the poet from the conventions of meter and rhyme and opened up possibilities for originality and authenticity.[26]

The modernist passion for direct expression reiterated the romantic idea that language itself was a kind of obfuscating mediation, that it was fundamentally inauthentic. Rousseau described "humanity's transition from a natural to a civilized state as a consequence of the acquisition of language." He understood language to be a form of symbolic mediation that separates humans from their true being by allowing them to play social roles (Handler 1989, 354–55). Authenticity in human expression seemed to exist only in a presocial state. In the modernist valorization of the universal, language was also problematic because it was one of the main differentiating structures of human experience. In 1894 Alice Fletcher wrote about Indian music:

> Language is intellectual, the tool of the mind, primarily, to speak broadly; and the languages of the earth represent many and various forms of structure. If a more universal common structure prevails in vocal folk-music, may not the reason be that the emotions of the heart of man are more in common the world over than are his intellectual ideas? These separate, while the former unite the human race. (199)

This anti-intellectual motif echoes ancient ideas about "headlessness . . . as a means of bypassing routine existence and the mediation of language . . . a means of getting to the essential" (Torgovnick 1990, 148). This calls to mind the illustration in Frank Cushing's treatise on Indian handcraft of disembodied hands molding a clay vessel (Fig. 45) and Picabia's *Portrait d'une jeune fille américaine dans l'état de nudité.* Both these illustrations are images of headlessness, of primitive energy and instinct, and imply that the modernist understanding of primitive art assumed that it was not so much thought as felt or "perceptually conceived" (Torgovnick 1990, 150–51).

Mary Austin viewed the body as the source of preverbal authentic expression. She believed in "the physical basis of poetry" and argued that because rhythm is the most primitive element in poetry, the primary basis for poetic expression resides in the human body (1930b, 8). "What," she asked, "is the familiar trochee but the *lub*-dub, *lub*-dub of the heart, what the hurrying of the syllable in the iambus but the inhibition of the blood by the smaller vessels?" (11). In Austin's poetic cosmology, blood and breath rhythms were the organizing principles behind all human expression. And again, "What experience is older or comes closer to the life of man than his Two-handedness? Taker and Holder: the play of them, one into the other; strike with the right, cover with the left; thus he conceived his Universe, two-handed" (8). This is a compelling and elegant argument. She found in the stress between the two-handedness of humans a binary push-pull, the possibility of infinite stresses, waves, swings: "It was back to the foot pace on the new earth, ax stroke and paddle stroke. So it is that new rhythms are born of new motor impulses" (12–13).[27]

Beginning with the body and "Consciousness" as a foundation, Austin described the poet's creative process as moving from sensory experience to rhythmic expression to language:

> Experience presents itself as One; existing by itself in Consciousness. The experience completely transpires; the autonomic centers are stirred, giving rise to motor impulses. Rhythm ensues and with rhythm the esthetic sense is quickened, evoking order and arrangement. Words are perhaps the final evocation of the intelligence, taking possession of the experience and decorating it appropriately. (1930b, 53–54)

This passage seems to describe both an individual's creative process and the origins and evolution of language and human expression. Thus poetic ontogeny recapitulates phylogeny. Stimulus comes from "experience" of the world, with the human response first occurring in the body and eventually stimulating a language response.

Given her understanding of language as a late development in the evolution of poetry, it makes sense that Native American ritual dances would hold special appeal for Austin. They seemed to her to embody a moment in cultural evolution when humans still used their bodies to express things, before language dominated expression. Furthermore, Austin argued that the dances' effectiveness as prayer operated through a kind of mimesis. The Indian sought to understand the cosmos by getting inside it and doing what it did: "When he wished for rain, he set up within his own consciousness the utmost intensity of realization of rain of which he was capable" (1930b, 35). Cushing had also identified a strong and pervasive "dramaturgic tendency" among Zunis and other primitive peoples: "That tendency to suppose that even the phenomena of nature can be controlled and made to act more or less by men, if symbolically they do first what they wish the elements to do, according to the ways in which, as taught by their mystic lore, they suppose these things were done or made to be done by the ancestral gods of creation time" (Cushing 1979, 215). Cushing, too, exhibited a strong dramaturgic tendency in playing Indian (Fig. 45).

Along similar lines, because Indian languages were not written (one of the defining features of the primitive), their only forms of verbal expression being the song and speech, they were imagined to be melodious, metaphoric, and mimetic. Reviewing the anthology of Indian poetry *Path on the Rainbow* in the *Nation* in 1919, Hartley Burr Alexander compared the oral and the literate:

> Indian songs and chants are songs and chants, and bereft of their melodies, their singing tones, they fall thin and fragmentary. As for all unlettered peoples, poetry is for the Indian purely vocal, and the vocal syllables are melodic notes. Furthermore, the mood and meaning of the poem is carried as much by the quality of the melody as by the verbal content. . . . This fact means an aural, and not a visual sense of form, and a poetic art less artificial, and therefore less capable of generalization than is the poetry of books and letters. (1919, 757)

Like dance, primitive languages were thought to "act out" expression, in a kind of mimesis, which made Indian languages seem naturally poetic (Chamberlain 1896, 43–47). Indian language was more authentic because it was more transparent; it seemed to have a direct representational relationship to the world.

Similarly, Indian art forms and decorative motifs were understood to have an iconic relationship between signifier and signified. Abstract shapes, meaningless to non-Indians, actually had referents in nature. The prevailing belief was that abstraction in Indian decorative arts was like a language. Franz Boas wrote in 1903: "The extended investigations on primitive decorative art which have been made during the last twenty years have clearly shown that almost everywhere the decorative designs used by primitive man do not serve purely esthetic ends, but that they suggest to his mind certain definite concepts. They are not only decorations, but symbols of definite ideas" (1903, 481). Boas argued that designs have their origins in real things but they become conventionalized through use and as they are transferred from one medium to another. He was interested in what designs revealed about the primitive mind, and in his *Primitive Art* (1927) he constructed a general theory of human artistic creativity based on primitive cultures. Reiterating Boas's views, the Native American poet Charles A. Eastman wrote in the *Craftsman* in 1914 that Indian people do not imitate or re-present nature: the forms depict an essence of the object represented; they are "decorative and emblematic rather than imitative" (180). And in *Harper's* in 1903 Natalie Curtis wrote: "The Hopis do not make a picture of cloud, water, bird, flower, or feather in the way that we would. They make a sign which stands for that thing. For instance, a wavy line, a symbol so common among Indians, is not intended to depict water; it simply *means* water" (627).

In paintings such as Hartley's *Indian Composition* (Fig. 49), one can see how the artist deployed this grammar of primitive design. Hartley borrowed "Indian" forms, like the repeated triangular tepee and the abstract blanketed and bonneted Indians, and assembled them into a collage. In addition to being a "composition" about form, the painting suggests a narrative. Hartley used a kind of pictographic communication. The blue curved band with white zigzags in the left half of the painting suggests a river, and there seem to be tepees pitched beside it. The representations of Indians also suggest a story, but the language is more like a Boy Scout exercise in playing Indian. This painting also recalls early ethnographic drawings such as the disassembled Snake dancer in Figure 4. Hartley appropriated a vocabulary of Indian decorative language and arranged it according to his own formal syntax.

Modernist representations of Indians displayed an overall lack of concern for the *meaning* of Native American expression. Austin's re-expression of the "Song of the Basket Dancers" in *The American*

Rhythm is a case in point. In a footnote to the poem in the 1923 edition (the note does not appear in the 1930 edition) she says her version is based on a song given to her by a young man at San Ildefonso Pueblo. She believed it might not be the actual song sung at the Basket dance, and she speculated that for "superstitious reasons" he may have given her the wrong song. She concludes: "However, the Basket Dance is undoubtedly a fertility rite and this is quite certainly a fertility song. Whether the dance and the song belong together is a matter in interest only to the ethnologists" (154).

Here is Austin's reexpression of the "Song of the Basket Dancers":

I.

We, the Rain Cloud callers,
Ancient mothers of the Rain Cloud clan,
Basket bearers;
We entreat you,
O ye Ancients,
By the full-shaped womb,
That the lightning and the thunder and the rain
Shall come upon the earth,
Shall fructify the earth;
That the great rain clouds shall come upon the earth
As the lover to the maid.

II.

Send your breath to blow the clouds,
O ye Ancients,
As the wind blows the plumes
Of our eagle-feathered prayer sticks,
Send, O ye Ancients,
To the Six Corn Maidens.
To the White Corn Maiden,
To the Yellow Corn Maiden,

To the Red Corn Maiden,
To the Blue Corn Maiden,
To the Many Colored Maiden,
To the Black Corn Maiden,
That their wombs bear fruit.

III.

Let the thunder be heard,
O ye Ancients!
Let the sky be covered with white blossom clouds,
That the earth, O ye Ancients,
Be covered with many colored flowers.
That the seeds come up,
That the stalks grow strong
That the people have corn,
That happily they eat.
Let the people have corn to complete the road of life. (100–101)

Austin's translation works much like Hartley's painting. The repetitive naming of the Corn Maidens seems particularly liturgical and "Indian," echoing what Hartley Burr Alexander said about the melodic nature of Indian poetry—that it could not be understood apart from its song origins. On the page the repetition reads more like a list, and one has to imagine the phrases uttered in conjunction with a melody and dance steps. However, the use of metaphors like "the road of life," "As the lover to the maid," "white blossom clouds," and "Send your breath to blow the clouds" are familiar poetic tropes. If repeating the names of the Corn Maidens seems strange and primitive, the very conventionality and familiarity of the metaphors showed how "poetic" Indian expression was.

The affinity of the Indian and the modern occupied the realm of form rather than content. Austin was quick to dismiss the concerns of ethnologists because she was looking for the universal structures of human expression. The formal qualities of Native American art, such as abstraction, meter, and dance gestures, were thought to be universally understandable, and their similarity to other forms of expression was "natural," but the meanings of rituals were beside the point (Foster 1985, 184–85).

The affining of the modern and the Indian had the effect of eliding differences between Native American groups and collapsing Native American expressions into a generalized primitive, Indian culture. Even though Austin claimed to have a lot of experience with Native American individuals and named the specific tribal origins of the translated poems in *The American Rhythm,* in the book's introduction she consistently generalized about the nature of the "aboriginal"; all her arguments assumed a generic primitive or "Amerind." Even the Japanese were the "cognate" of the Native American, and she found affinities as well between Native American rituals and ancient Greek, Hebrew, and Anglo Saxon poetry (56). Austin assumed that primitive people all over the world were the same, that everywhere the same myths prevailed dressed in different clothing.

THE SEMIOTICS OF PLAYING INDIAN

Ethnographic meaning got in the way of the usefulness of Native American expression to non-Indians, but at a formal level it was assumed that almost anyone could paint or write like an Indian. The very concept of the primitive as simple and universally understandable made appropriation possible, as did the modernist aestheticization of Indian expression. In claiming affinity between their work and Indian "art," modernists such as Austin and Hartley imagined themselves as speakers of an American dialect of a universal primitive aesthetic language. To understand how this playing Indian worked as a signifying strategy, Mary Austin's writings about her creative processes are illuminating.

Writing from an Indian point of view, as Mary Austin often did, was, of course, not a new idea. For example, Adolph Bandelier's novel *The Delight Makers* (1890) described ancient life among the Queres people of the Southwest from their point of view. And Frank Hamilton Cushing's "Commentary" to Edna Dean Proctor's long poem *The Song of the Ancient People* (1892) is a myth of creation narrated by a "Zuñi Familiar" (27). It is telling that these scientists turned to fiction to depict Native American subjectivity, which was largely elided from scientific discourse. Cushing's and Bandelier's fictional representations seem to suggest that the most appropriate way to depict Indian subjectivity was to *imagine* it.

Austin's writing was informed by this tradition, but she insisted on her ability to *become* an Indian and claimed that this ability was crucial to her creative process. In *The American Rhythm* she described the process of reexpressing Indian poetry as a "saturation":

> My method has been, by preference, to saturate myself in the poem, in the life that produced it and the environment that cradled that life, so that when the point of crystallization is reached, I myself give forth a poem which bears, I hope, a genetic resemblance to the Amerind song that was my point of contact. (38)

Farther along in the essay she described this saturation in more detail:

> I have naturally a mimetic temperament which drives me toward the understanding of life by living it. If I wished to know what went into the patterns of the basket makers, I gathered willows in the moon of white butterflies and fern stems when these were ripest. I soaked the fibers in running water, turning them as the light turned, and did my ineffectual best to sit on the ground scraping them flat with an obsidian blade, holding the extra fibers between my toes. I made singing medicine as I was taught, and surprised the Friend-of-the-Soul-of-Man between the rattles and the drums. Now and then in the midst of these processes I felt myself caught up in the collective mind, carried with it toward states of super-consciousness that escape the exactitudes of the ethnologist as the life of the flower escapes between the presses of the herbalist. So that when I say that I am not, have never been, nor offered myself, as an authority on things Amerindian, I do not wish to have it understood that I may not, at times, have succeeded in being an Indian. (40–41)[28]

What stands out in these passages is Austin's emphasis on mimesis as a source of her creativity and authority. By physically doing what Indians do—through "saturation" in making baskets—she "became" Indian and was able to achieve a state of mind conducive to producing poetry. Thus for Austin writing poetry, in its mimetic methods and cultural and spiritual powers, was analogous to performing Indian rituals.[29]

Part of the effectiveness of playing Indian for Austin lay in the power of mimesis to unite the assumed division between the body and language.[30] Through mimesis, Austin tried to "suture" them together. This is one of the functions of mimesis; it enacts a fantasy driven by the desire to forget the arbitrariness of the sign, the desire for signs to seem natural (Taussig 1993, xviii). Thus the process of poetic creation for Austin was one in which language was *born* out of saturation, and "super-consciousness" came out of the experience of weaving baskets. As she did for American literature, Austin here seems to have written an origin myth for a new kind of language, one that unites sense and sensuousness, nature and culture.

In addition to reconfiguring the processes of signification, Austin's saturation describes the process by which she became an *American* writer. Through playing Indian, she negotiated another duality, between achieved and ascribed identity. In her description of being an Indian, Austin laid claim to her Americanness through achievement and inheritance. As a race, *Indian* signified an ascribed, pure American identity, but Austin was able to *achieve* this identity through mimesis, and as an Indian, she became a bearer, literally, of American literature.

However, although her claim to Indian identity may have been intended to make her writing seem solidly authentic and American, by playing Indian, Austin became a kind of "third term" playing in the distance between the self and the other, between signifier and the signified, embodying and enacting the *instability* of signification and identity (Garber 1993, 12). Thus, even though playing Indian seemed to Austin to be a unifying strategy, it depended on and reified the boundaries it erected between American artists and Indians. The modernist artist or poet was able to "play" and transgress these boundaries in order to produce signification, but the power relationship between artists and Native Americans was still hegemonic. The artist, in the role of mutable, mobile maker of meaning, retained the power of signification and subjectivity; the Indian was reduced to a set of appropriable signifiers and was not expected to engage in mimesis of the civilized.

In the modernist embrace of the primitive, the Indian came to represent the subconscious of the national mind, the id to the modern artist's ego, a rich and undercultivated region of American culture awaiting the sensitive and yet powerfully transformative touch of the modern artist. In traversing the distance between self and other Austin achieved authenticity based—like travel writing and ethnography—on the experience of having "been there." But her authority relied on her mobility; her journeys into Indian territory always ended with a return to modernity. Austin always put down the basket and picked up a pen.

Although Austin's longing for authentic ways of being, for experience, was undoubtedly genuine, her identification of authenticity as other and primitive was problematic and ultimately precluded personal (and cultural) transformation. Playing Indian could never be a cure for personal or cultural inauthenticity. First of all, primitivism is posited on a dualism that maintains a distance that obviates meaningful contact and dialogue. The Indian, supposedly a model for authenticity, was conceived of as an oppositional other to the self, and so, paradoxically, authentic states of being were apparently only accessible through acting, impersonation, and/or acquisition. Because of this opposition, which placed the "real thing" outside the self, the achievement of authentic selfhood or expression was always just out of reach (Orvell 1989, 295). Second, even though modernists glorified the primitive, hegemonic relationships haunted all contact between Indians and the modernists who represented them. Finally, and this is related to the previous two points, primitivist understanding of Indians was emptied of any sense of historical context and agency. In Marxist terms, this is like commodity fetishism, in which the value of labor that goes into producing commodities is elided and the commodities become significant as value accrues to them in other ways. In the case of Native Americans, what is elided is history, and Indians emerge as free-floating signifiers available for all kinds of signification.

Primitivism will never transform modernity, because it reinforces the idea that modern culture is spurious and the primitive is genuine, and it doesn't allow people to grasp the actualities and complexities of history. To achieve cultural and political transformation, one must discover wholeness and authenticity "here"—wherever that is—and remake the relationship between "us" and "them" into something that does not rely on hegemony and dualism. Mimesis as a cultural practice isn't the problem; if we dispense with the notion that it is about imitation, which implies a spuriousness, we can see it in a more meaningful and useful way, as a powerful strategy in which identities are continually negotiated and renegotiated. But mimetic practices have to allow for all kinds boundary redrawings and crossings by all the parties involved. Realizing that identities and meanings are contingent may suggest a frightening instability, but it also frees people to find new ways of understanding one another and reality. Our understanding of the world needs to grow more complex, not simpler. The meanings we make should not be dependent on the "othering" of difference but on seeing clearly what is (and was) and recognizing that we are all at play in the fields of signification.

EPILOGUE

There is a moment in Victor Masayesva Jr.'s 1992 film *Imagining Indians* in which viewers see a painted photo-booth backdrop depicting life-sized cartoon renderings of a Navajo man and woman. The faces of these figures have been cut out so that customers standing behind the backdrop can put their own faces in the cutouts and have their pictures taken. Suddenly two customers' faces appear in the oval cutouts: they belong to a man and a woman, both of whom are Native American.

Pearlene is a character who has appeared in many of Nora Naranjo-Morse's poems and clay sculptures. In one of her poems, "Pearlene," a group of gossiping Pueblo women ask, "What kind of Pueblo girl is she? / Wearing tight-fitted skirts / high above her knees" (Naranjo-Morse 1992, 59). When confronted with the sculpture *Pearlene's Roots* (Fig. 53), I found myself asking the same question.

In these works, Masayesva and Naranjo-Morse are reworking the practices and politics of playing Indian. In *Imagining Indians,* the painted backdrop perfectly represents the absence of Indian subjec-

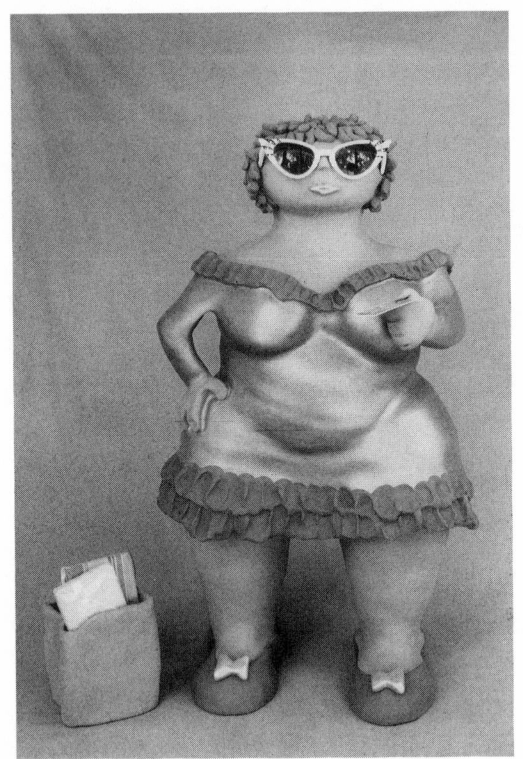

Figure 53. Pearlene's Roots, *by Nora Naranjo-Morse (1989); micaceous clay; 38 × 12 in. Naranjo-Morse has said of Pearlene that she represents "a Pueblo woman who has one foot in tradition and one foot in this other world . . . and she gets into all sorts of trouble. She is a little wild, but she has got a good heart, and she is, in a sense, centered" (Eaton 1989a, 11). (Photograph by Mary C. Fredenburgh)*

tivity and the availability of Indian signifiers; here is the vanished Indian rendered as a collection of attributes that anyone can try on. Well, almost anyone. When the Native American man and woman put their faces in the cutouts, the signifiers they are supposed to activate are rendered meaningless. The other occupying the subject position in this situation disrupts the chain of signification and shows how the Indian as other is only and always a "potential sign and symbol of the self" (Torgovnick 1990, 171). The viewer experiences a mild sense of shock as signification falls apart; assumptions fail; one is forced to *see* what's there: a man and a woman surrounded by the broken apparatus of signification.

Pearlene's Roots seems to be a reversal of playing Indian. With her tight, short dress, her cat-eye sunglasses and her American Express card in hand, Pearlene seems to be "playing civilized": the Pueblo woman as capitalist consumer. Naranjo-Morse has reversed the positions of self and other; the Pueblo woman is in the subject position deploying the signifiers of "white woman." In the history of white representations of Indians, this kind of reversal has "traditionally" been played for comic effect, but here Pearlene's erect head and resolute posture suggest that she is in control and is deploying the power these signifiers carry according to her own reasons and desires. Pearlene, in this and her other appearances, is fully a subject on her own terms.

Nora Naranjo-Morse and Victor Masayesva Jr., who are both Native Americans, create works that address the history and politics of representing Indians. They are both conscious of their situations within the "spectacle" of information about Indian people. Both are "appearing" in American culture in familiar ways—as Native American artists—and both artists are "subalterns" who use the language of their oppressors. Masayesva uses photography, film, and video to comment on how Indian people have been represented in these media but also as a means of telling Hopi narratives. And Naranjo-Morse uses the traditional medium of clay, in addition to poetry in English and Towa, to explore her relationships to her home and history and to the marketplace (Fig. 54). Perhaps as a consequence of their cultural positions, both show a wariness around the idea that the sign is a transparent window on the subject. Although their works may be "useful" ethnographically, Masayesva and Naranjo-Morse constantly elude and remake representational strategies; they do not simply speak about Indians but speak to the constitution of meaning and identities (Ashcroft, Griffiths, and Tiffin 1989, 59). Their works resist simplicity; instead they insist on the presence of history and the complexity of contexts and shifting meanings.[1]

The potter and poet Nora Naranjo-Morse has been described as a "nontraditional Indian artist" (Eaton 1989b, 46). What this description seems to indicate is that, although she is a potter from Santa Clara Pueblo, the works for which she is most widely recognized are figurative pieces rather than the carved and polished black vessels considered "traditional" Santa Clara pottery.[2] Naranjo-Morse's ce-

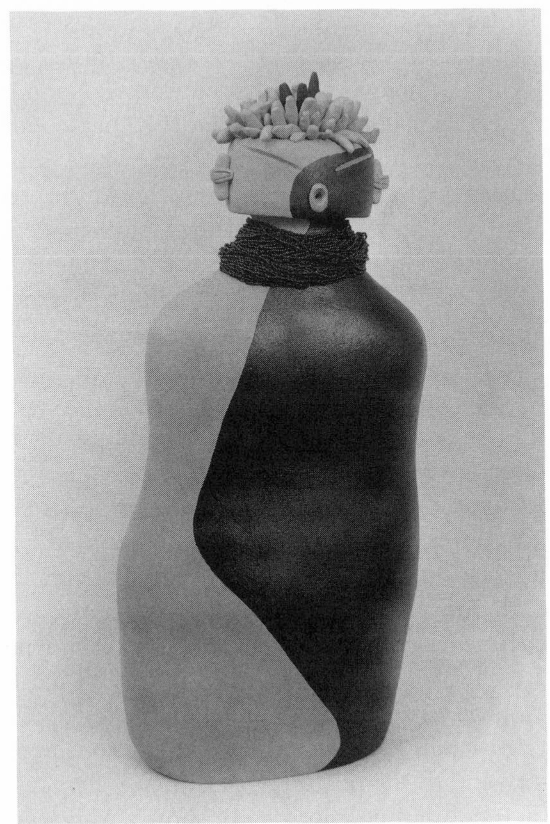

Figure 54. Black and White Fetish, *by Nora Naranjo-Morse (1990); micaceous clay; 34 × 18 in. Naranjo-Morse's poems and ceramics are often about the ways she moves between Pueblo and non-Indian worlds; this "fetish" seems to embody that division. (Photograph by Mary C. Fredenburgh)*

ramic works, as well as her poetry, speak directly to questions concerning what is traditional and what is not and how these questions come to bear on her own identity and work.

Pearlene is the focus of many of her meditations on identity. Pearlene, too, appears to be nontraditional. In the poem "Pearlene," other Pueblo women gossip that she doesn't know how to bake bread, so what kind of man would marry her? In "Pearlene's Aunts," Aunt Celestine laments, "Pearlene should be ashamed, / running wild into the night / toward a place called 'Vegas'" (Naranjo-Morse 1992, 64).

She flirts with men; she dances till dawn. Her aunts pray that "she will return to tradition," yet at the end of the poem, Aunt Virgie wishes to be Pearlene "for just one night" (66). Pearlene doesn't speak in these poems, but her actions are telling. We learn that she is a "no-nonsense, / hardworking Pueblo woman." When Pueblo men (some of whom are the husbands of the gossips) arrive at her door at night and invite her for rides in their pickups, she declines: "she will accept a ride / only on her own terms" (59).

Naranjo-Morse has said of Pearlene that she "is the antithesis of the characteristics of Pueblo women that anthropologists love to point out" (Babcock 1994, 180). Indeed, the sculpture *Pearlene's Roots* turns the stereotype of the olla maiden on its head, representing not the "eternal feminine," a vessel for others' desires, but a woman who is emphatically in the present, who embodies and, to some extent, resolves the opposition between the modern and the traditional. In the companion poem, also called "Pearlene's Roots," Naranjo-Morse insists that Pearlene's modern "veneer" does not hide her Towa "roots."

The sculpture *Pearlene's Roots* also comments on commodity fetishism and the aestheticization of the Indian woman. The figure of Pearlene refuses to be an object of desire; with her American Express card drawn, she is the one doing the desiring. But she is not an endorsement of female consumerism. Her cat-eye sunglasses render her expression opaque, and her stance issues a challenge. This is not an image of a woman in ecstasy brought on by a particular commodity; Pearlene has a much clearer relationship to the market. She knows what she wants and how to get it, but there is not a hint of coyness about her. There is no sense that her identity is dependent on possessing commodities. In addition, she offers a mirror image of the purchaser of Indian art, suggesting the tangled relationships between artist, consumer, and art object in the marketplace.

The production and marketing of her work is often the subject of Naranjo-Morse's poems.[3] She makes both the processes of working with clay and the exigencies of selling her work explicit in poems, such as "Mud Woman's First Encounter with the World of Money and Business," "The Living Exhibit under the Museum's Portal," and "Tradition and Change." In these poems Naranjo-Morse contemplates the meaning of her works as they circulate in the art market.

In "Mud Woman's First Encounter," after a gallery owner asks if she has a résumé and if her family is "known in the Indian art world," she says,

> The center of what Mud Woman knew to be real
> was shifting with each moment in the gallery.
> The format of this exchange was a new dimension
> from what was taken for granted at home,
> where the clay, moist and smooth,
> waited to be rounded and coiled
> into sensuous shapes, in a workroom
> Mud Woman and her man had built
> of earth too. (Naranjo-Morse 1992, 35–36)

The gallery owner is not sure the figures will sell because they aren't traditional. But she decides to buy them, because if Mud Woman makes it "big," she "can be the first to say, 'I discovered you.'" "Hesitantly, Mud Woman exchanges her work for the / unexpectedly smaller sum that wholesale prices dictated" (36). The exchange, like a version of the Columbian exchange, involves a negotiation across boundaries that alters the meanings and values of objects and people as they are crossed. The poem ends with Mud Woman returning home, her mind full of questions, her vision clouded "with a mist / of lost innocence" (37).

The notion of negotiations carries over into Naranjo-Morse's poems about identity. In "Two Worlds" the poet sits on a Hawaiian beach and contemplates her presence there:

> Damn, Indian women,
> especially Pueblo women,
> don't drink Pina Coladas
>   on Kauai beaches
>   in December and enjoy it! (1992, 47)

Then she muses:

> Unlike the characteristically
> homebound Towa,

> I now had grown comfortable
> in venturing out of Pueblo boundaries.
> I wondered if there was a balance for me. (48)

Her husband urges her to forget what is "crossing" her:

> I eased into thought,
> consoling myself,
> reassessing my place in these worlds.
> I am a brown woman,
> who will always be a Towa,
> even under a hot Pacific sun. (50)

It is significant that Naranjo-Morse sets this poem in the quintessential tourist spot of the late twentieth century, a place redolent of postcolonial politics. On a tropical beach, once the site of imperial expansion (as well as "discoveries") and now the site of white tourists getting suntans, the Pueblo woman, a subject from another colonial site, considers the boundaries she has crossed and her present cultural location.

The beach in the poem is an example of Mary Louise Pratt's "contact zone," a social space "where disparate cultures meet, clash, and grapple with each other, often in highly asymmetrical relations of domination and subordination—like colonialism, slavery, or their aftermaths as they are lived out across the globe today" (Pratt 1992, 4). In "Two Worlds" the poet's discomfort stems from the fact that she feels out of place, that she is engaging in "white" activities. In the end she "consoles" herself with the thought that she will always be a Towa, "even under a hot Pacific sun," suggesting a sense of essential identity that is firmly in place and that survives boundary crossings. Although Naranjo-Morse often returns to this note of essentialism as a way to resolve "contact zone" situations—in the gallery, under the portal at the Palace of the Governors in Santa Fe, or on the beach—she represents these situations as marked by breaches and slippages. She recognizes boundaries and differences between Towa and white, but unlike other boundary crossers, such as Mary Austin, she also recognizes the politics that inhabit their relationships.

Like Nora Naranjo-Morse, the filmmaker and photographer Victor Masayesva Jr. is acutely aware of how Native Americans have been represented by whites. He is also aware of how he, as a Hopi photographer and filmmaker, is situated within the "spectacle" of representations about Indian people. But his work goes beyond simply subverting or resisting the structures of hegemony; he remakes these structures continually in every one of his works. He is clearly committed to remaking the terms of representation in ways that serve Hopi interests. Masayesva's videos, especially, are didactic and polemical works. He has chosen each of his subjects well and has brought to each one appropriate, distinctive approaches.

To begin with, behind what Masayesva has chosen to photograph or film are decisions about what *not* to represent. He knows the importance of secrecy and silence in the Hopi world view and has written that Hopi photographers are in a "delicate place" and "dangerous time." He admits that Hopi photographers may desire to photograph sacred ceremonials and dancers, but "when we arrive at the place and time when we do carry out those desires, when we have a disregard for everyone, everything, we will have arrived at the dangerous time prophesied by the old people. Refraining from photographing certain subjects has become a kind of worship" (Masayesva 1984a, 10).

Many of Masayesva's works speak directly to stereotypes that have dogged Hopis and other Pueblos. For example, his short videotape *Pott Starr* (1990) opens with a shot of a Pueblo woman by a pond balancing an olla on her head. Soon, however, this classic olla maiden is replaced by a computer-animated olla with arms and legs, which goes on to walk the streets of Santa Fe, encountering a white woman tourist interested in buying it. I take this sequence, in its literalization of the olla maiden as vessel, to be a comment on the objectification of Pueblo women and the commodity fetishism of the marketplace. Similarly, in one of his still photographs, of a Hopi weaver at work, Masayesva speaks to the long tradition of representing Indian artisanal labor (Masayesva and Younger 1984, 96). But whereas Indian artisans represented by whites have traditionally appeared as timeless and natural, Masayesva has included in the foreground of this photograph a 1982 picture calendar from a Gallup, New Mexico, car dealership. The picture on the calendar is a rendering of the Alamo, which suggests the history of U.S. imperialism. By reinserting history—and the history of representation—into this photograph, the Hopi man at work cannot stand as a timeless icon of primitive labor.

In *Siskyavi: The Place of Chasms* (1990), Masayesva takes on the discourse of science. A group of Hopi high school students prepare for a visit to the Smithsonian Institution, where they will study ancient Anasazi pottery. One girl won't be going, because her grandmother has asked her to stay and help her make clay pots. The video alternates between the class's experiences in Washington, hearing museum scientists discuss electron microscopy, and scenes of the girl helping her grandmother and listening to her lessons about the significance of the objects she is making. The film was funded in part by the Smithsonian, and all the scientists and teachers seem earnest and well intentioned. The class returns home and delivers reports at school. The film ends with scenes of the girl and her grandmother, who seems disturbed. When her granddaughter tells her some of what the class learned, she responds, "There's no respect now," and says she doesn't feel good about her painting today. Through the juxtapositions of the class's experience and the girl's, Masayesva comments on the scientists' and grandmother's different understandings of nature and history. Furthermore, he shows the girl's relationship to these different authorities. In the end, the girl seems to come closer to her grandmother's understanding of the significance of pottery making, but her understanding is informed also by ethnographic knowledge. The video leaves the viewer not with the idea that one approach is more correct than the other, but that knowledge and knowing exist in different ways.

Another of Masayesva's videos that addresses the subject of history is *Itam Hakim, Hopiit* (1984), an educational video, part of a series made through a grant from the Ethnic Heritage Program of the Department of Education (Younger 1984, 39). It was made in recognition of the Tricentennial of the Pueblo Revolt of 1680. The video was intended for a Hopi audience; later Masayesva added a voiceover in English. The video begins with the Hopi storyteller Ross Macaya telling a series of origin and migration stories to a group of young Hopi boys. He goes on to tell about the Pueblo Revolt. After this, there is a sequence depicting rituals and activities having to do with planting, harvesting, and preparing corn. The last section, called "Prophecy," asserts that Hopi rituals and history and their power will continue. The video ends with Ross Macaya's words, "This will not end anywhere."

Traditionally, Hopi beliefs and practices have been transmitted through oral narrative. In *Itam Hakim, Hopiit,* which translates roughly as "We, someone, the Hopi," Masayesva brings video into the mix of cultural transmission. That he has attempted this indicates that he is not advocating a simple "return to tradition." Unlike Naranjo-Morse, he doesn't assert any notions of "timeless tradition." Tradition in his work is always bound up with history, but "history" appears in these works as multivalent and complex and in dialogue with the present and the future; Hopi and non-Hopi versions and representations converge and diverge, reflect and refract, enrich and impoverish one another.

In his feature-length film *Imagining Indians* (1992), Masayesva addresses Hollywood's relationship with Native Americans. For this project Masayesva chose to use film (as well as some video) to discuss filmmakers' exploitation of Native Americans. Interviews with actors, extras, and other Native Americans who have worked on Hollywood movies, especially *Dances With Wolves* (1990) and *Thunderheart* (1992), form the core of the film. There are also interviews with men who acted in films in the 1950s. Interspersed with these interviews is a staged sequence depicting a Native American woman's visit to a dentist. The woman also appears in many of the interviews, listening or asking questions. In addition, a section of the film deals with the Indian art market; collectors and buyers of Indian art are interviewed. In *Imagining Indians,* Masayesva is concerned not with the inauthenticity of Hollywood representations of Indians but with the exploitation of Indian "authenticity" and labor. Interviewees tell stories about how they were treated on the set of *Dances With Wolves,* and several people discuss the recreation of a Ghost Dance in *Thunderheart,* which many interviewees felt should not have been depicted. At one point Masayesva filmed a meeting of the Hopi tribal council discussing whether to give Robert Redford the right to film *Dark Wind* on the Hopi Mesas, and there is another section about a comic book published by Marvel Comics that depicted the unmasking of a group of kachinas. In all of these incidents what is at stake is Native Americans' control over knowledge about themselves. The movie depicts the complexity of responses and interests involved in these situations. More often than not, the interests of Hollywood (and the art market) have won out, but Masayesva doesn't just paint a picture of victimized, exploited Indians; rather, he shows how individuals and communities are situated in a complex web of money and power, refusal and capitulation.

The scenes in the dentist's office link the other parts of the film together. Masayesva loads the situation with irony and symbolic significance. The dentist is a white man whose office is decorated with travel posters depicting the attractions of the Southwest. Masayesva inserts ethnographic discourse into the encounter through a radio that is broadcasting a documentary history of U.S. government–Native American relations. While someone on the radio is reading a historical justification for the policy of Manifest Destiny, the woman gets a shot of novocaine. The dentist says she is "very brave" and then goes on to say that he saw *Dances With Wolves* four times and that he identifies with Kevin Costner. He also talks about how he is involved in developing a "higher consciousness resort" near Phoenix, which should be "beneficial" and "lucrative." Masayesva's dentist is a comic figure embodying the oppressive presence of the U.S. government and well meaning non-Indians in Native Americans' lives. As he drills away and extracts a tooth, he effectively silences his patient. The scene strongly suggests a rape.

In the final scene of *Imagining Indians,* the patient, her mouth stuffed with cotton, rises from the dentist's chair, takes the drill in her hand, and begins to use it to mark the lens of the camera, gradually obliterating her image (Fig. 55). As she does this, a series of the famous Indian portraits by the painter George Catlin fade in and out over her face. She seems to be effacing a history of romanticized representations of Indians as well as the present filmic one. The movie ends when she pushes Masayesva's camera over with her hand. Masayesva has explicitly implicated himself in the history and processes of these representations. In an interview he commented on *Imagining Indians:* "It really was a composite process to let people know that there were a lot of cracks in the seams. It was *about* imagining Indians, and *I* was part of that imagining. And I wasn't trying to absolve myself. . . . I was implicating myself by having, by showing

Figure 55. Still photograph from Imagining Indians, *a film by Victor Masayesva Jr. (1992). The dental patient (played by Patty Runs With Swallows) obscures the camera lens with the dentist's drill, thereby removing herself from the spectacle of imagined Indians. (Courtesy of Electronic Arts Intermix, New York)*

the technology, the filmmaking, the transparency *behind* the scenes" (Rony 1994–95, 31).

That Masayesva comments about his film's being a "composite" and there being "cracks in the seams" illuminates his methodology. Whereas Nora Naranjo-Morse tends to cast her position in terms of dualities, Masayesva's approach is more multivalent and dialogic. In writing about Native American and postcolonial literature, David Moore has contrasted dialectics, which relies on binary oppositions, to dialogics:

> Dialogics . . . is a multiple, four-dimensional, relatively dynamic system, seeking not certainty, but relationality. It converges a field of binaries into a fluid sphere, so that the pragmatic center and cir-

> cumference of their intersections and extremities are in constant motion. Here not only the binaries pull on their own polarities, but they pull and are pulled by all the other lines and points of power in the moving field. (1994, 3)

I find this model helpful in understanding Masayesva's films. For example, in *Siskyavi,* which relies on a fairly binary juxtaposition between science and tradition, knowledge about the significance of pottery is rendered not in terms of a synthesis but in terms of a situation; the film does not negate any of the understandings of ancient pottery but makes clear how knowledge is informed by context. Similarly, *Imagining Indians* allows for a multitude of voices, but by not identifying any of the interviewees on screen, Masayesva does not achieve a sense of documentary objectivity. And indeed that is not his aim. This work is certainly polemical, but as each person speaks and develops stories and points of view, what emerges is a picture of complex relationships rather than simply a condemnation of Hollywood.

Imagining Indians is about representations. Because the film's representational strategies call attention to themselves, viewers become aware of how they—as well as the filmmaker—are situated in this web of representations. The form of this and Masayesva's other movies is somewhat disjointed; he uses juxtapositions that involve more than two terms, layerings, and lapses to convey his meaning. He plays with film and video technology, using computer animation techniques as well as split screen and inset images. He toys with the conventions of nature and history documentaries. For example, in translating *Itam Hakim, Hopiit* for non-Hopi audiences, Masayesva chose to use a voiceover in English rather than subtitles, a decision that helps the film convey the primacy of orality in this telling of history. But it also avoids allowing the viewer to have any sense of transparency; Ross Macaya's voice can be heard throughout, and often it is hard to make out the words in the English voiceover. This strategy calls attention to the mediation involved in this representation of history.

Masayesva's film and video works do not lend themselves to a simple aesthetic appreciation: they are not seamless; they do not try to seduce the viewer. They are more likely to induce a state of discomfort in non-Hopi viewers. I have shown *Itam Hakim, Hopiit* to two of my classes at Long Island University in Brooklyn: one a basic writing class and the other a graduate course in regional American literature. Students' initial responses to the video ranged from utter boredom to mild curiosity; this was not a work aimed at them, and it didn't seem like a familiar documentary about Indians. Both courses had addressed issues of representation and ethnicity, so the video was relevant to what we had been talking about, but even so, most of the students were completely flummoxed by it. In retrospect, *Imagining Indians* would have been more accessible to these students, but what happened in those classrooms continues to intrigue me. It seems that what we experienced was a distant echo of the Columbian encounter, as many textual encounters with Native Americans are, but our assumptions about what we thought we knew about "Indians" were not reaffirmed, and our expectations about what a video was supposed to be were not met. Now that I look back on it, those events were opportunities for dialogic encounters. Without the actual participation of Masayesva or Ross Macaya, the dialogue would remain incomplete and distanced, but I believe that Masayesva's films, as they continue to circulate in various contexts, present opportunities for what David Moore has called "radical understanding":

> Radical understanding is not "esthetic universalism," but a humane yet tough recognition of difference, of fragmentation, an understanding that I cannot understand, a knowledge that the other has a right to not be known, and that such a right fits with an epistemology of process and discovery rather than of product and commodity. Radical understanding accepts change; its telos is not truth but relationality. (1994, 4)

Because Masayesva's films and videos and Naranjo-Morse's poems and sculptures point to their own textual situations—their production and circulation—they reveal how these situations set the scene for the constitution of meaning. They disrupt primitivist discourse by calling attention to and reworking the relationships between all the terms of signification: viewer and reader, writer and filmmaker, language and image, and the subjects of the representations. Trying to make meaning out of encounters with these works becomes a self-conscious act, and the model of exchange, which tends to commoditize and universalize knowledge, falls apart. What's left may, at times, be a "totally ambivalent site for communication" (Ashcroft, Griffiths, and Tiffin 1989, 186), but within this site there is the opportunity to see the social relations that inform knowledge and meaning. This insight may in turn lead to new interpretive practices and understanding, which might even, eventually, transform social relations.

NOTES

INTRODUCTION

1. The "triculturality" of the Southwest is a problematic schematization of the people who inhabit the region. Nevertheless, because its construction is part of the history I am interested in telling, I will rely on the concept in using the terms *Anglo, Hispano,* and *Native American* to describe the people in this study. I use *Native American*—although it has troubling nativist, hierarchical connotations—and occasionally *Indian people* to refer to actual people who are subjects and agents in this book, and *Indian* to refer to the represented, or imagined, "other."
2. For more on constructions of the primitive, see Diamond (1960, ix–x; 1981) and Miller (1991, 67). See also Fabian (1983) on the primitive as a temporal concept.
3. The first two chapters of Edward Said's *Beginnings* (1975) have been helpful to me in understanding the conception of the primitive as "primal." See also Handler (1986a).
4. For more on conceptions of folk cultures, see Ames (1977) and Graburn (1976). Marianna Torgovnick has written that "primitives, as often as not, do not vanish but change into the urban poor, and thus can no

longer serve as a locus for our powerful longings precisely because they have entered our own normative conditions of urban life" (1990, 192).

5. See Green (1988b) and Deloria (1994) for full, historical discussions of playing Indian in the United States.
6. See Hoxie (1977, 1984) and Bolt (1987) for more on government Indian policies during the late nineteenth century.
7. Charles Lummis was also an early activist in Indian affairs. See his *Bullying the Moqui* (1968).
8. Some of these works continue to circulate in reprint editions without any editorial comment or introduction. See, for example, George Dorsey's *Indians of the Southwest* (1903), which was reprinted in 1976.
9. There are many books about the Santa Fe and Taos art colonies, but some of the best are by Gibson (1983); Eldredge, Schimmel, and Truettner (1986); and Coke (1963). See also Broder (1984); Bryant (1978); and Udall (1984).

CHAPTER 1. REPRESENTING THE HOPI SNAKE DANCE

1. See newspaper references cited in Fewkes ([1897] 1986, 312); see also Baxter (1895), Edwardy (1889), James (1900c), Long (1896), Oliver (1911), Rust (1896), and Schultz (1908). The date of the first account of the Snake dance in the American press is uncertain, but accounts began appearing in newspapers by 1879 (Harrison 1964).
2. At the end of the nineteenth century, the Snake and Antelope ceremony was performed in even years at the pueblos of Oraibi, Shongopavi, and Sipaulovi. In odd years it took place at Walpi and Mishongnovi. Sichomovi apparently did not have the ceremony. The Flute dance occurred at each pueblo in years when the Snake dance did not. In the mid-1980s, the Snake dance continued to be performed only at Mishongnovi and Shongopavi. It was last performed at Oraibi in 1916, at Walpi in 1969, at Sipaulovi in the 1970s, and at Hotevilla in 1980 (Lyon 1988, 263).
3. For good summaries and discussions of the theory of cultural evolution, see Hinsley (1981, 133–37) and Stocking (1968, 110–32).
4. "Moqui" or "Moki" is what Hopi people were called by early Anglo observers.
5. Hinsley (1983, 68) argues that the tension in the disparity between Cushing's and Fewkes's approaches to ethnography continued to be embodied in Boasian anthropology. For more on Cushing and ethnographic patronage, see Hinsley (1989).

6. This is not to say that Bourke was less of a scientist than Fewkes; Bourke went on to write several well-regarded monographs for the Bureau of American Ethnology, and it was actually Fewkes whose reputation was not very good. Other ethnographers, including Bourke, Washington Matthews, and Frank Cushing, claimed Fewkes plagiarized others' work, especially that of Alexander M. Stephen. For more on Fewkes's reputation, see Hinsley (1983, 64) and Porter (1986, 277–78).
7. Whites who signed included trader Thomas Keam, Alexander Stephen, missionary H. R. Voth, Frank Hamilton Cushing, John Wesley Powell, and ethnologist James Mooney (Whiteley 1988, 81).
8. For an excellent account of the "Oraibi split," see Whiteley (1988). See also Rushforth and Upham (1992, Chap. 6).
9. For example, a pamphlet advertising the Tertio-Millennial Celebration of Santa Fe in 1883 (supposedly one-third of a thousand years, to the day and hour, since the arrival of Europeans in the area) described the local Indians as "the direct descendants of the Aztecs, who were found here in 1534 by Cabeza de Vaca—tilling the soil and living under wholesome laws" (*Santa Fe Tertio-Millennial Celebration* 1883, n.p.). See Mauzy (1936) for more about this exposition.
10. Alexander M. Stephen (d. 1894), a friend of the trader Thomas Keam, had lived at Keam's Canyon, near the Hopi mesas, since 1881 and had recorded his observations of the Hopis and the Navajos since 1882. Fewkes enlisted Stephen's help in observing the Hopis beginning in 1890 and published accounts based on Stephen's recorded observations. These publications (notably "The Snake Ceremonials at Walpi") appeared under Fewkes's name, with Stephen acknowledged in the introduction. Stephen's writings went largely unpublished until his journals, edited by Elsie Clews Parsons, appeared in 1936. See Stephen (1936, 577–767) for accounts of various performances of the Snake dance in the 1880s and 1890s. See also his *Hopi Indians of Arizona* (1940).
11. One of Bourke's companions during his visit to the Hopi villages was the artist Peter Moran, brother of the painter Thomas Moran. Moran was not affiliated with the Bureau of Ethnology, and his task was distinct from Bourke's: the painter was "obtaining material which will one day be serviceable in placing upon canvas the scenes of this wonderful drama" (Bourke [1884] 1984, 141). In other words, Moran was making sketches that he would later develop into oil paintings of artistic value. Unfortunately, his sketchbooks are not known to have survived (Porter 1986, 320). It would be useful to compare his depictions of Hopi life to Harmer's. A description of the Snake dance written by Peter Moran

appears in the *Extra Census Bulletin* on the *Moqui Pueblo Indians of Arizona* (1893) by Thomas Donaldson.

12. Walter Benjamin cited in Clifford (1986, 119). See also Clifford's "On Ethnographic Authority" (1983).
13. Paintings and drawings of the Snake dance by Scott also figured prominently in the 1893 *Extra Census Bulletin* on the Hopis, by Thomas Donaldson.
14. For more on the history of ethnographic photography, see Banta and Hinsley (1986); Blackman (1980); Edwards (1992); Lyman (1982); and Scherer (1975).
15. When it became possible to do so, ethnographers and others began making films of the Snake dance. Edward Curtis filmed the Snake dance in 1904 at Oraibi; apparently this film became part of Curtis's "musicale" delivered in 1911 and 1912 (Gidley 1982, 71–72). William E. Kopplin, an advertising executive with the Santa Fe Railway, made a film of the Walpi dance in 1911 (Lyon 1988, 262; McLuhan 1985, 131–42). The Library of Congress has a paper print of a film of the Snake dance at Walpi copyrighted in 1901 by Thomas Edison.
16. As anthropologist Peter Whiteley has observed of Hopi cosmology, "Secrecy and the attendant social care and respect accorded to esoteric knowledge guarantees both authority conferred by initiation and instrumental efficacy when the power and knowledge is activated." Therefore, making this knowledge public destroyed its effectiveness and could "damage the spiritual health of the community" (1993, 139).
17. *Sun Chief* was edited by anthropologist Leo Simmons from interviews with and diaries kept by Talayesva at Simmons's request.
18. This approximate date for the Snake dance life group comes from "Brief Illustrated History of the Manikins," by Thomas Kavanagh (1990). In a conversation with Dr. Kavanagh at the National Museum of Natural History in the summer of 1990, I learned that this same Snake dance life group was on display in the museum until a couple of years before, when it was put into storage because of continuing sensitivities on the part of Hopis.
19. See also Boas (1893); Braun (1975); Jacknis (1985); Rydell (1984); Starr (1893); and Trennert (1987) for information about ethnographic exhibits at the Chicago World's Columbian Exposition. For thoughtful analyses of ethnographic exhibits, see Hinsley (1991) and Fowler and Fowler (1991).
20. There was a very popular Cliff Dwellers exhibit on the Midway at Chicago, but it exhibited artifacts and ruins of the Southwest, not living Native Americans (*Cliff Dwellers* 1893).

21. Although his photographs of the Snake dance represented his greatest success, the ceremony was also the cause of his demise: Wittick died in 1903 from a snake bite he received at Fort Wingate while he was packing some snakes to take to the Snake dance (Packard and Packard 1970, 46).
22. I am indebted to Mrs. Mary Jean Cook of Santa Fe for this observation.
23. The Smokis (pronounced "smoke-eyes") is an elite organization that has claimed President Coolidge and Barry Goldwater as initiates. It also has an auxiliary "Squaw" organization. A Smoki museum in Prescott opened in 1935 and has a collection of Southwest Indian material culture and art. Two anonymous articles in the *Santa Fe Magazine,* "Weird Snake Dance of the Smoki People" (1923) and "Arizona Will Be Host to Thousands of Visitors in June" (1929), indicate that the Smoki ceremonials were important tourist attractions. For a fuller discussion of the Smokis and other "Indian hobbyists," see Deloria (1994, 335–95).
24. The Smokis were probably not the first Anglos to perform the Snake dance. In 1906 Edward S. Curtis apparently participated in the ceremony, but not the public dance (Gidley 1982, 72). Years later, however, Curtis described his role thus: "Dressed in a G-string and snake dance costume and with the regulation snake in my mouth I went through [the ceremony] while spectators witnessed the dance and did not know that a white man was one of the wild dancers" (Boesen and Graybill 1977, 136). Gidley suggests that Curtis may have embroidered on the story of his participation, and his claim to have been initiated into the Snake clan and to have danced in the public ceremony may have been exaggerated or untrue (72).

CHAPTER 2. DISCOVERING INDIANS IN FRED HARVEY'S SOUTHWEST

1. For mythologies of Fred Harvey, see Bryant (1974, 106–22); Poling-Kempes (1989); Spence (1987); and Thomas (1978). See also *The Harvey Girls,* MGM, dir. George Sidney, 1946.
2. Schweizer eventually capitulated and sent the coveted objects to Hearst, because, well, he was William Randolph Hearst and he was a regular traveler on the Santa Fe (Schweizer 1906).
3. The development of a "Santa Fe style" in architecture and interior design has been well documented (Whiffen and Breeze 1984; Sheppard 1988), and Colter is recognized as one of its main promoters. The Santa

Fe Railway's architects and engineers drew up the plans after Colter's designs and hired contractors to build the buildings. Colter was paid by Fred Harvey and the ATSF. She worked for the Harvey Company from 1902 to 1948 and designed Hopi House, the Watchtower, and the Lookout at the Grand Canyon, as well as Bright Angel Lodge, La Posada at Winslow, and El Navajo in Gallup (Grattan 1980; Weigle 1991, 120–30).

4. Between 1902 and 1912 Voth collected for both the Field Museum and for Fred Harvey (Eggan 1971, 1–2). Voth oversaw the construction of Hopi House and built at least two Hopi altars for the Harvey Company, one of which was in the Indian Building and the other at Hopi House in 1913 (Harvey 1963, 39).
5. Nampeyo and her family made a similar stay at Hopi House in 1907 (Kramer 1988, 48–49).
6. The display of the domestic life of the Indians of the Southwest was very persistent in Harvey attractions. In Gallup in 1923 the Harvey Company held an "authentic" "Blessing-of-the-House" ceremony at the new El Navajo Hotel. Colter had installed replicas of Navajo sand paintings on the walls. Several Navajos objected that their religious symbols were being used in this way, and "the management ordered the paintings removed immediately in compliance with their wishes. When the Indians learned of this considerate response, they asked that the paintings be left intact but that they be dedicated to the gods with appropriate ceremony. After a day of dancing and feasting the hotel received truly authentic decoration that was acceptable to the Navajos and to their gods" (Henderson 1969, 31). See also Grattan (1980, 42–44) and "Remarkable Indian Ceremony" (1923, 17–22).
7. For more information on the Santa Fe Railway's and Harvey's involvement in these expositions, see "Grand Canyon of Arizona" (1914); Kropp (1996); Miller (1985); "Museum and School" (1914); Sheppard (1988); and "Sidelights" (1915).
8. The job of courier was considered quite glamorous; all the couriers were required to be college educated, and they attended a special school to be trained by members of the Anglo New Mexican intelligentsia, such as Charles Lummis, F. W. Hodge, and Edgar Hewett (*Harveycar Motor Cruises* n.d., 11; Thomas 1978, 75–94).
9. William Henry Jackson, the expedition photographer, worked for the Detroit Publishing Company from 1898 to 1924 in a number of capacities, including photographer, plant manager, and member of the board of directors (Ryan 1982, 150). Many of his photographs were reproduced as Detroit postcards.
10. My sample of postcards is based mainly on a collection sent to the New

York Public Library in 1910 by John Huckel. There are 299 postcards in this collection, most of which bear the Fred Harvey imprint, but some bear only the Detroit Publishing Company's mark. I draw on this collection, because the cards can be dated and it appears to be more or less representative of Harvey output in the first decade of the century. The copyrights on most of the images date from 1900 to 1907. I have also examined postcards in the following archives and libraries: the Museum of New Mexico History Library, Santa Fe; the Heard Museum Library, Phoenix; the University of Arizona Library Special Collections, Tucson; the Arizona Historical Society, Tucson; and the National Museum of American History, Archives Center, Blenkle Collection, Washington, D.C.

11. In 1990 a new facsimile edition of "The Great Southwest Souvenir Playing Cards" was for sale at souvenir shops in the Grand Canyon. My thanks to Kathleen Howard of Phoenix, Arizona, for this information. My observations are based on a deck I examined in the University of Arizona Library Special Collections in Tucson.
12. I base the date for the first edition of *First Families* on a 1913 letter from Huckel to F. W. Hodge, director of the Southwest Museum in Los Angeles. Thanks to Kathleen Howard for dating the first edition of *The Great Southwest.*
13. Herman Schweizer bought and sold objects of Hispanic manufacture for Harvey shops and displays, and there was some demand locally for Hispanic crafts, but it was not until the 1930s that there was a national market for them (Dutton 1983, 98). For more information on the preservation of Hispanic culture in New Mexico, see Rodríguez (1990) and Forrest (1989).

    As the Indian Southwest was being invented in New Mexico and Arizona, Anglo cultural elites in southern California, such as Charles Lummis and Helen Hunt Jackson, were promoting a romanticized Spanish past. This California regionalism focused on the preservation of the Spanish missions. The California preservationist movement managed to preserve the buildings and promote a "style," but Catholicism itself was more or less erased from the romance.
14. Thanks to Jeanne Lawrence for calling Emily Post's account to my attention.
15. Karen Seger and Joseph Wilder have discovered that a later version of Figure 27 was radically altered. In the later version, the two trainmen in the center have been transformed into Pueblo women, one of whom carries a child on her back. (These two women were lifted from another Harvey postcard.) In addition, two of the Pueblo women have had their

black stockings and leather shoes painted over to appear as moccasins and leggings (Seger and Wilder 1990, 378).

16. In Harvey publications there were almost no representations of tourists taking photographs—much less paying Native Americans for the privilege, which was the common practice. This omission was perhaps because the Harvey Company wanted tourists to buy the souvenir publications it produced rather than to take their own snapshots.
17. Thanks to Sally Stein for suggesting this identification of the doll and for her helpful interpretation of this image.

CHAPTER 3. THE SPECTACLE OF INDIAN ARTISANAL LABOR

1. Nampeyo was born in about 1860 to a Hopi father and a Tewa mother in the village of Hano, the Tewa village on First Mesa. She died in Polacca, the village at the base of the mesa, on July 20, 1942. She did not speak English or read or write (Kramer 1988, 47; Nequatewa 1943). She was named Tcu-mana (Snake Girl) by her paternal Hopi grandmother, but her name was translated into Tewa: Nampeyo. She married Lesso, a Hopi man from Walpi, in 1881, and they had five children together. Lesso died in 1932 (Frisbie 1973, 232).

   Nampeyo learned to make pottery from her paternal grandmother, who lived at Walpi. Potters at Hano were making undecorated utility ware, but Nampeyo learned to make the decorated pottery of the Hopi. This had a crackled surface and was considered inferior to ancient pots by the scientists who were digging in the area in the 1890s (Frisbie 1973, 232). From the beginning Nampeyo was considered a talented potter. Probably with trader Thomas Keam's encouragement, she began trying to replicate ancient designs and techniques in her pottery in about 1895 (McChesney 1994, 6). These efforts coincided with the arrival of archaeologists and ethnologists in the area and the beginning of an art market in Pueblo pottery. In her lifetime she was credited with starting the so-called Sikyatki revival style of pottery, which other potters quickly imitated. Generally Nampeyo molded and painted the pots, but often Lesso helped her paint them. By 1920, though, she was probably almost totally blind; she continued to mold pottery, but Lesso and other family members did the painting. Her children continued the revival style, and as of this writing, four generations of her descendants have continued to make pottery (Ashton 1976; Monthan and Monthan 1977; Traugott 1983).

2. See Melanie Herzog's forthcoming "Aesthetics and Meanings: the Arts and Crafts Movement and the Revival of American Indian Basketry" (Winterthur, Del.: Winterthur Museum) for an excellent discussion of the arts and crafts interest in Indian baskets and another interpretation of James's Indian corner.
3. See, for example, Connor's "Confessions of a Basket Collector" (1896, 4–5) and Mary Austin's short story, "The Basket Maker" ([1903] 1988, 65).

   There is also, of course, a history of shady dealings between collectors and Native Americans. Accounts of them were rarely published, but they do occasionally appear in records of correspondence. For example, in 1911 William Randolph Hearst wrote to Herman Schweizer inquiring about some "buffalo shields" in the Harvey collection. Schweizer replied: "We have never sold a one since we have been in business, and would not sell any one of them only to you. Not a single one of these shields could ever have been bought openly from the Indians. All of them were obtained through some relegate who stole them and got them out of the village at night" (Schweizer 1911a). As in the case of the "exhibit rugs" in the Harvey collection, Hearst got the desired shields anyway (Schweizer 1911b).
4. See Fane (1991, 23–25) for an excellent discussion of how Stewart Culin, a contemporary of James's and curator of the Brooklyn Museum's ethnographic collections, understood ethnographic objects as embodying narratives.
5. See Trachtenberg (1982, 145–47) for more on the problem of "feminized" culture at the turn of the century.
6. See also Handler (1986a, 4) on individualism and Agnew (1989) for a discussion of the "commodity aesthetic" and the self as consumer in literary representations of domestic interiors at the turn of the century.
7. A partial list of photographers who made images of Nampeyo would include William Henry Jackson, Adam Clark Vroman, Edward Curtis, Homer Earle Sargent, S. W. Matteson, and H. F. Robinson.
8. This photograph is sometimes attributed to Ben Wittick, but prints of this image in the National Anthropological Archives of the Smithsonian Institution suggest that Wittick printed Randall's image on his own cardboard mounts.
9. The photographer Karl Moon, in photographs such as *A Tale of the Tribe,* also made generational continuity his subject (Moon 1910). Moon

contracted with the Harvey Company to sell his photographs at the El Tovar Hotel at the Grand Canyon.

10. Magazines such as the *Craftsman* often included articles about Indian crafts. See, for example, Akin (1906); Burbank (1900); Du Bois (1904); Lang (1882); and Sargent (1904). For more on the significance of the arts and crafts movement in the United States, see Lears (1981, 60–96); Boris (1986); and Gilbert (1977, 83–96).
11. See Deloria for a discussion of Ernest Thompson Seton's Woodcraft Indians and Camp Fire Girls (1994, 261–334). See also Mechling (1980) on the Koshare Boy Scouts.
12. In 1893 at the World's Columbian Exposition in Chicago, Native American students from the Carlisle Indian School participated in a slightly different spectacle of artisanal labor. In a parade on the first day of the fair, Carlisle students marched in ten platoons, "each representing one of the industries taught at the school. The front row of students in each group carried the tools of the trade, while those in the rear held high samples of the finished products" (Hoxie 1977, 284–85).
13. The quote is from Curtis (1913b, 401). For a transcript of a corn-grinding song, see Curtis (1904). Hinsley (forthcoming) has also written on the subject.

CHAPTER 4. MODERNISM, PRIMITIVISM, AND *THE AMERICAN RHYTHM*

1. These are, of course, perennial modern problems. Since Rousseau at least, each generation of European and American intellectuals has experienced some kind of "crisis of cultural authority," but this chapter is concerned with modernist primitivism as an aesthetic response to these dilemmas in the United States in the 1910s and 1920s. The modernists I refer to are artists and writers working during this period who incorporated such methods as formal abstraction and "imagism" in their work as a way to break with tradition and find aesthetic authenticity. By *modernist primitivists* I mean those who located aesthetic authenticity in the aesthetic expressions of "primitive" societies. For more on the cultural criticism of the time, see Wertheim (1976) and Blake (1990).
2. In addition to *The American Rhythm,* see Bynner (1929); Cronyn (1918); Henderson (1928).
3. For a good compendium of paintings of Pueblo dance rituals, see Truettner (1986). For poetic renderings, see Henderson's "Green Corn Dance,

San Ildefonso" and "Buffalo Dance" in *Red Earth.* See also Lowell, "Songs of the Pueblo Indians." In *The American Rhythm* Austin "reëxpressed" the chants from two communal dances, "Song of the Basket Dancers" and "Rain Songs from the Rio Grande Pueblos." The 1928 anthology of Southwestern poetry edited by Alice Henderson, *Turquoise Trail,* includes Marsden Hartley's poem "The Festival of the Corn" and Vachel Lindsay's "Babbitt Jamboree," in which the poet complains about the touristic consumption of Indian dances (88–89). In his 1929 *Indian Earth* Witter Bynner published a cycle of "Pueblo Dances (New Mexico and Arizona)," including one called "Snake Dance (Hotevilla)."

4. A sampling of this literature includes: Alexander (1919); Chamberlain (1896); Curtis (1903, 1904, [1907] 1950, 1922); Densmore (1905); Fillmore (1895); Fletcher (1894); Gilman (1908); Lummis (1905); and Matthews (1896).
5. For a good description of popular "Indian" songs that appeared as sheet music, see Matz (1988, 242–70). See also a sheet music interpretation of the Hopi Snake dance (Smith 1926).

   Many books and articles instructed Americans on how to make Indian costumes and crafts or perform Indian dances. See, for example, Buttree (1930); Natalie Curtis ([1907] 1950); Evans and Evans (1931); and Salomon (1928).
6. The poems were by Frank S. Gordon, Alice Corbin Henderson, Mary Austin, Constance Lindsay Skinner, and Edward Eastaway, with editorial comments by Monroe and Carl Sandburg. This issue of *Poetry* supposedly inspired the anthology *The Path on the Rainbow: An Anthology of Songs and Chants from the Indians of North America* (1918), edited by George W. Cronyn, with an introduction by Mary Austin (Henderson 1923b, 92).
7. The claim that the Exposition of Indian Tribal Arts was the first time American Indian artifacts were exhibited as art in New York was made by the organizers of the exhibition and is therefore probably open to question. But it was certainly the first major exhibition of its kind in New York. See Mullin (1993, Chap. 3) for an excellent analysis of the exposition.

   For a study of the American modernist interest in African art, see Levin (1984b). Some other examples of American modernist writers' interest in African and African American art are Vachel Lindsay's poem "The Congo" (1914); Hart Crane's poem "Black Tambourine" (1921); Waldo Frank's novel *Holiday* (1923); and Carl Van Vechten's novel *Nigger Heaven* (1926). For a contemporary aesthetic appreciation of African sculpture, see Fry (1920).

8. Apparently playing Indian extended to Austin's personal life. She was known to have lived from time to time in a tree house she called a "wickiup" in Carmel, California. And in 1922 at a dinner in her honor at the National Arts Club in New York, Austin was escorted by an artist friend dressed in an Indian costume (Stineman 1989, 123–25).
9. The revised edition of *The American Rhythm* included an "Addenda for the Second Edition" after the introductory essay and fifteen new poems translated from various Native American groups. It excluded all of the "Songs in the American Manner" as well as four reexpressed songs. The 1930 edition also included at the end translations of "Magic Formulas from the Cherokee" and "Tribal Lays." Because it included none of Austin's own poems, the second edition has a more ethnographic air about it. The poems I discuss in this chapter were all included in the 1923 edition, but the page references are from the 1930 edition, unless otherwise noted.
10. For more on "achieved" and "ascribed" identities, see Sollors (1986) and Gardner (1992).
11. In addition to Mary Austin, some of the writers who argued that the Indian was an appropriate source for American arts and letters were Brooks (1915); Curtis (1913b); Hartley (1918c); Henderson (1923b); Lummis (1905); and Walton and Waterman (1925).
12. Many ethnographers at the turn of the century believed that cultural differences were in large part the result of environmental factors, for example, Fynn (1907). But Austin took the theory much further and argued that almost all American institutions, including political democracy and the public library, could be traced to environmental influences. In the *Cambridge History of American Literature* (1921), she wrote: "These early Amerinds had been subjected to the American environment for from five to ten thousand years. This had given them time to develop certain characteristic Americanisms. They had become intensely democratic, deeply religious, idealistic, communistic in their control of public utilities, and with a strong bias toward representative government" (610). See also Austin, "Where We Get Tammany Hall and Carnegie Libraries" (1918), in which she claims that the potlatch is the original Carnegie Library.
13. For more on the perceived oppressive influence of European culture, see Austin (1926a). Hartley Burr Alexander, a University of Nebraska philosopher and promoter of cultural regionalism, called the United States' relationship to European arts "colonial" and noted that "we have not as yet become spiritually acclimated to our new home. We live

in America, but we still think European thoughts" (1926, 127–28). See also Dorman (1993, 55–57).

14. For more on "print-languages" and nationalism, see Anderson (1991, 133–35).
15. There were, however, some contemporary attempts to treat Native American oral expression as a literature in Western, scholarly terms. See, for example, Barnes (1921).
16. Yet another example of the nationalist evocation of the Indian, the song "Indianola" is about an Indian brave who leaves his loved one to go "tomahawk Kaiser Bill" (Matz 1988, 266).
17. For a discussion of Austin's embattled relationship with her East Coast publishers, see Langlois (1988a).
18. My understanding of Austin's regionalist authority is deeply informed by Richard Brodhead's thoughts on regionalist writing of the late nineteenth century. See his *Cultures of Letters* (1993, 107–41). However, the modernist regionalism of Austin is different from the regionalist writing of the post–Civil War period in its valorization of the primitive; unlike regionalist writers such as Murphree, Freeman, and Jewett, who valued the regional other as fitting subject matter but not as a representative American literary voice, Austin tried to relocate the center of literary authority to the regions and not only to speak for the Indian but also to speak *as* an Indian.
19. For more on the cultural criticism of Bourne, Brooks, Mumford, and Frank, see Blake (1990). See also Shannon (1992) for a discussion of Ruth Benedict and the culture concept.
20. For a study of modernist American poetry in relation to science and technology, see Steinman (1987). Steinman notes that Duchamp's *Nude Descending a Staircase* also evinces a machine aesthetic in the way it suggests mechanized motion (39). That Theodore Roosevelt thought the painting resembled a Navajo rug suggests that it is an image that points in both modernist primitivist directions—to the past and the future.

    See also Seltzer (1992) for an analysis of how nature and technology figured in American literature the turn of the century.
21. The therapeutic value of Native American rituals was a notion Austin expressed many times (1924b, 252; 1928b, 49–59; 1929b, 267; 1930a, 732).
22. For similar views, see Pach (1920, 59) and Henderson (1923b, 92).
23. The last two song titles are from *The American Rhythm* (90, 96).
24. The first quote is from Hartley (1922a, 117); the second is from Oppenheim (1923, 612).

25. Ezra Pound quoted in Coffman (1951, 28–29).
26. In his study of the poetry of the anthropologists Ruth Benedict and Edward Sapir, Richard Handler (1986b) argues that Sapir formulated his ideas about genuine and spurious cultures along aesthetic lines: genuine cultures were hard; spurious cultures were soft. Furthermore, these characterizations implied a gendered construction of authenticity: Victorian cultural tradition was viewed by modernists as soft and inauthentic (read: feminine); modernism was hard and authentic (read: masculine). Handler argues that for Benedict writing modernist poetry and practicing anthropology put her in a dilemma of gender identity. Austin may have found herself in a similar dilemma. Although she was very aware of the difficulties she had as a woman trying to make a career as a writer, in *The American Rhythm* she argued that "poetry is a man's game. Women are only good at it by a special dispensation as men are occasionally good at millinery. If you look for the determinant of poetic form in a given period, look for the gesture by which maleness is in that age expressed. In Europe for a thousand years before American settlement began, the sword had been the extended flourish of man's personality, as the cloisteral pace was the measure of his profoundest meditation" (12). Given this argument, Austin herself is practicing a gendered cross-dressing by making poetry her game, too.
27. For more on the gestural origins of language, see Austin's "Gesture in Primitive Drama" (1927).
28. Austin also explained her "mimetic" nature in a 1919 letter to "Lady" (possibly Alice Corbin Henderson). She claimed to have always had a keen interest in rhythm: "In those days the most absorbing occupation of literary life was the search for the subtle rhythms that lay hidden under all nature and the activities of man. I would persuade the drivers to let me handle the twenty mule teams in order that the rhythm of their movement might be transmitted to me through the reins. I would follow flocks of quail for miles across the mesa, and nearly caught my death sitting in at Indian dances."
29. Austin believed that all kinds of playing Indian could lead to enlightenment. In *The Land of Journey's Ending* she suggested that when the Smokis of Prescott, Arizona, enacted their yearly imitation of the Hopi Snake dance, they "were pierced through with understanding. The earth spirit took them, and what was begun as a light adventure became a serious pursuit" (444).
30. This notion of an essential gap between the body and language (i.e., culture) persists in psychological and semiotic discourse. See Eagleton (1990, 265) for elaboration on the idea in relation to the idea of the aesthetic.

EPILOGUE

1. Nora Naranjo-Morse was born in 1953 to parents from Santa Clara Pueblo. She spent much of her youth in Taos Pueblo, where her father was a Baptist missionary. She began to work with clay in 1976 at Santa Clara, and her work gained recognition by the late 1970s. In 1980 she married Greg Morse and graduated from the College of Santa Fe with a major in social welfare. With her family, she built an adobe house in Santa Clara, where she lives and works. She has won many awards for her pottery, and she has published her poems in a number of books, periodicals, and journals. In 1992 the University of Arizona Press published *Mud Woman: Poems from the Clay,* a collection of her poems and photographs of her ceramic works, from which the poems and works discussed here are drawn. For more on Naranjo-Morse and her work, see Eaton (1989a, 1989b); Pardue and Coe (1989); and Trimble (1987).

   Victor Masayesva Jr. was born in 1951 in Hotevilla, Arizona. He attended the Horace Mann School in New York and went on to Princeton as a University Scholar. He completed his studies in literature and photography there in 1976 and in 1978 pursued graduate work in the same fields at the University of Arizona. In 1980 he became director of the Ethnic Heritage Program at Hotevilla. In 1982 he formed his own video production company in Hotevilla (Masayesva and Younger 1984, 90). In addition to his photographic work, his videos include *Hopiit* (1982), *Itam Hakim, Hopiit* (1985), *Ritual Clowns* (1988), *Pot Starr* (1990), and *Siskyavi—the Place of Chasms* (1991). His film *Imagining Indians* was released in 1992. For more on Masayesva's work, see Marks (1992); Rony (1994–95); and Silko (1990).
2. Barbara Babcock has studied the "invention" of Pueblo pottery traditions and has noted that ollas are overrepresented in most collections, whereas figurative ceramics—even though they were produced in many pueblos at the turn of the century—have been dismissed by collectors and scholars as inauthentic (Babcock 1994, 188–89).
3. Naranjo-Morse has also discussed the subject in interviews (Eaton 1989b, 53; Trimble 1987, 64–65).

REFERENCES

Adair, John. 1944. *The Navajo and Pueblo Silversmiths.* Norman: University of Oklahoma Press.

"The Age of Nampeyo the Potter." 1942. *Masterkey* 16:223.

Agnew, Jean-Christophe. 1986. *Worlds Apart: The Market and the Theater in Anglo-American Thought, 1550–1750.* Cambridge: Cambridge University Press.

———. 1989. "A House of Fiction: Domestic Interiors and the Commodity Aesthetic." In *Consuming Visions: Accumulation and Display of Goods in America 1880–1920,* edited by Simon J. Bronner, 133–55. New York: W. W. Norton.

Akin, Louis. 1906. "Hopi Indians—Gentle Folk: A People without Need of Courts, Jails or Asylums." *Craftsman* 10 (June): 314–29.

———. 1907. "Frederick Monsen of the Desert—The Man Who Began Eighteen Years Ago to Live and Record the Life of Hopi-Land." *Craftsman* 11 (March): 678–82.

Albers, Patricia C., and William R. James. 1987. "Illusion and Illumination: Visual Images of American Indian Women in the West." In *The Women's West,* edited by S. Armitage and E. Jameson, 35–50. Norman: University of Oklahoma.

Alexander, Hartley Burr. 1919. "The Poetry of the American Indian." *Nation* 109 (December): 757–59.

———. 1926. "For an American Indian Theatre." *Palacio* 20 (April 1): 123–43.

Altieri, Charles. 1989. *Painterly Abstraction in Modernist American Poetry: The Contemporaneity of Modernism.* New York: Cambridge University Press.

Ames, Kenneth. 1977. *Beyond Necessity: Art in the Folk Tradition.* Winterthur, Del.: Winterthur Museum.

Amsden, Charles Avery. 1934. *Navaho Weaving: Its Technic and Its History.* Chicago: Rio Grande Press.

Anderson, Benedict. 1991. *Imagined Communities: Reflections on the Origin and Spread of Nationalism.* London: Verso Editions.

"Arizona Will Be Host to Thousands of Visitors in June." 1929. *Santa Fe Magazine* 23 (May): 45–48.

Armfield, Maxwell. 1925. *An Artist in America.* London: Methuen.

Armitage, Merle. 1948. *Operations Santa Fé.* New York: Duell, Sloan, and Pearce.

Arreola, Paul R. 1986. "George Wharton James and the Indians." *Masterkey* 60:11–18.

"Art in a Natural History Museum." 1913. *American Museum Journal* 13 (March): 99–102.

"Art of the American Indian." 1905. *Brush and Pencil* 15:84–93.

Ashcroft, Bill, Gareth Griffiths, and Helen Tiffin. 1989. *The Empire Writes Back: Theory and Practice in Post-Colonial Literatures.* London: Routledge.

Ashton, Robert, Jr. 1976. "Nampeyo and Lesou." *American Indian Art Magazine* 1 (3): 24–33.

Austin, Mary. [1903] 1988. *The Land of Little Rain.* New York: Penguin.

———. 1904. *The Basket Woman.* Boston: Houghton Mifflin.

———. 1911. *The Arrow Maker.* New York: Duffield.

———. 1918. "Where We Get Tammany Hall and Carnegie Libraries." *World Outlook* (January): n.p.

———. 1919. Letter to "Lady," 7 July. Mary Austin Papers. Special Collections. University of Arizona Library, Tucson.

———. 1920. "New York: Dictator of American Criticism." *Nation* 31 (July): 129–30.

———. 1921. "Non-English Writing II." In *The Cambridge History of American Literature,* edited by William Peterfield Trent. 4 vols. New York: Putnam's.

———. 1923. *The American Rhythm.* New York: Harcourt, Brace.

———. 1924a. "Cults of the Pueblos: An Interpretation of Some Native Ceremonials." *Century Magazine* (November): 28–35.

———. 1924b. *The Land of Journeys' Ending.* New York: Century Co.

———. 1926a. "The Indivisible Utility." *Survey* (December): 301–6, 327.

———. 1926b. "The Town that Doesn't Want a Chautauqua." *New Republic* 47 (July 7): n.p.

———. 1927a. "Gesture in Primitive Drama." *Theatre Arts Monthly* (August): 594–605.

———. 1927b. "Primitive Man: Anarchist or Communist?" *Forum* (November): 744–752.

———. 1928a. "Indian Arts for Indians." *Survey* (July): 381–88.

———. 1928b. "Primitive Stage Setting." *Theatre Arts Monthly* 12 (January): 49–59.

———. 1929a. "Regional Culture in the Southwest." *Southwest Review* (July): 474–77.

———. 1929b. "Sekala Ka'ajma: An Interpretive Dance-Drama of the Southwest." *Theatre Arts Monthly* 13 (April): 267–78.

———. 1929c. "Why Americanize the Indian?" *Forum* (September): 167–73.

———. 1930a. "American Indian Dance Drama." *Yale Review* 19 (June): 732–45.

———. 1930b. *The American Rhythm.* 2d ed. New York: Houghton Mifflin.

———. [1932] 1991. *Earth Horizon.* Reprint, with an afterword by Melody Graulich. Albuquerque: University of New Mexico.

———. 1932. "Regionalism in American Fiction." *English Journal* 21 (February): 97–107.

———. 1933. "Folk Plays of the Southwest." *Theatre Arts Monthly* 17 (August): 599–606.

Babbitt, Bruce. 1973. *Color and Light: The Southwest Canvases of Louis Akin.* Flagstaff, Ariz.: Northland Press.

Babcock, Barbara A. 1990. "'A New Mexican Rebecca': Imaging Pueblo Women." *Journal of the Southwest* 32:400–437.

———. 1994. "Mudwomen and Whitemen: A Meditation on Pueblo Potteries and the Politics of Representation." In *Discovered Country: Tourism and Survival in the American West,* edited by S. Norris, 180–95. Albuquerque: Stone Ladder Press.

Babcock, Barbara A., Guy Monthan, and Doris Monthan. 1988. *The Pueblo Storyteller: Development of a Figurative Ceramic Tradition.* Tucson: University of Arizona Press.

Bach, Cile M., and Marlene Chambers, eds. 1974. *Picturesque Images from Taos and Santa Fe.* Denver: Denver Art Museum.

Bandelier, Adolph. [1890] 1971. *The Delight Makers.* Reprint, with an introduction by Stefan Jovanovich. New York: Harcourt Brace Jovanovich.

Banta, Melissa, and Curtis M. Hinsley. 1986. *From Site to Sight: Anthropology, Photography, and the Power of Imagery.* Cambridge: Peabody Museum Press.

Barnes, Nellie. 1921. "American Indian Verse: Characteristics of Style." *Bulletin of the University of Kansas Humanistic Studies* 2:9–56.

Bartlett, Charles H. 1900. "The Art of the American Indian." *Chautauquan* 31:595–603.

Batkin, Jonathan. 1987. *Pottery of the Pueblos of New Mexico 1700–1940.* Colorado Springs: Taylor Museum of the Colorado Springs Fine Arts Center.

Baxter, Rupert H. 1895. "The Moqui Snake Dance." *American Antiquarian* 17:205–7.

Bechdolt, Frederick R. 1921. "Another White Man's Trick." *Santa Fe Magazine* 15 (2): 17–23.

Bedinger, Margery. 1973. *Indian Silver: Navajo and Pueblo Jewelers.* Albuquerque: University of New Mexico Press.

Bell, Michael. 1972. *Primitivism.* London: Methuen.

Berger, John. 1980. "Why Look at Animals?" In *About Looking.* New York: Pantheon Books.

Berkhofer, Robert F., Jr. 1988. "White Conceptions of Indians." In *History of Indian-White Relations.* Vol. 4 of *Handbook of North American Indians,* edited by William C. Sturtevant, 522–47. Washington, D.C.: Smithsonian Institution Press.

Berman, Marshall. 1982. *All That Is Solid Melts into Air: The Experience of Modernity.* New York: Simon and Schuster.

Blackman, Margaret. 1980. "Posing the American Indian." *Natural History* 87 (October): 69–74.

Blake, Casey Nelson. 1990. *Beloved Community: The Cultural Criticism of Randolph Bourne, Van Wyck Brooks, Waldo Frank, and Lewis Mumford.* Chapel Hill: University of North Carolina Press.

Boas, Franz. 1893. "Ethnology at the Exposition." *Cosmopolitan* 15:607–9.

———. 1903. "The Decorative Art of the North American Indians." *Popular Science Monthly* 63 (October): 481–98.

———. [1927] 1955. *Primitive Art.* New York: Dover.

Boesen, Victor, and Florence Curtis Graybill. 1977. *Edward S. Curtis, Photographer of the North American Indian.* New York: Dodd, Mead.

Bolt, Christine. 1987. *American Indian Policy and American Reform: Case Studies of the Campaign to Assimilate the American Indians.* London: Allen and Unwin.

Boris, Eileen. 1986. *Art and Labor: Ruskin, Morris, and the Craftsman Ideal in America.* Philadelphia: Temple University Press.

Bourke, John G. [1884] 1984. *The Snake-Dance of the Moquis of Arizona: Being a Narrative of a Journey from Santa Fe, New Mexico, to the Villages of the Moqui Indians of Arizona.* Reprint, with a foreword by Emory Sekaquaptewa. Tucson: University of Arizona Press.

———. 1892. *The Medicine Men of the Apache.* Extract from the 9th Annual Report of the Bureau of Ethnology. Washington, D.C.: Government Printing Office.

Bourne, Randolph S. 1977. *The Radical Will: Randolph Bourne—Selected Writings, 1911–1918.* Edited by Olaf Hansen. New York: Urizen.

Braun, Judy. 1975. "The North American Indian Exhibits at the 1876 and 1893 World Expositions: The Influence of Scientific Thought on Popular Attitudes." Master's thesis, George Washington University.

Broder, Patricia Janis. 1984. *The American West: The Modern Vision.* Boston: Little, Brown.

Brodhead, Richard H. 1993. *Cultures of Letters: Scenes of Reading and Writing in Nineteenth-Century America.* Chicago: University of Chicago Press.

Brody, J. J. 1976. "The Creative Consumer: Survival, Revival and Invention in Southwest Indian Arts." In *Ethnic and Tourist Arts: Cultural Expressions from the Fourth World,* edited by Nelson H. H. Graburn, 70–83. Berkeley and Los Angeles: University of California Press.

Bronner, Simon J. 1989. "Object Lessons: The Work of Ethnological Museums and Collections." In *Consuming Visions: Accumulation and Display of Goods in America 1880–1920,* edited by Simon J. Bronner, 217–54. New York: W. W. Norton.

Brooks, Van Wyck. 1915. "Our Poets." In *America's Coming of Age.* New York: Huebsch.

Bryant, Keith L., Jr. 1974. *History of the Atchison, Topeka and Santa Fe Railway.* New York: Macmillan.

———. 1978. "The Atchison, Topeka and Santa Fe Railway and the Development of the Taos and Santa Fe Art Colonies." *Western Historical Quarterly* (October): 347–453.

Bunzel, Ruth. 1929. *The Pueblo Potter: A Study of Creative Imagination in Primitive Art.* New York: Columbia University Press.

Burbank, E. A. 1900. "Studies of Art in American Life III: In Indian Tepees." *Brush and Pencil* 7:75–91.

Buttree, Julia. 1930. *The Rhythm of the Redman.* New York: A. S. Barnes.

Bynner, Witter. 1929. *Indian Earth.* New York: Alfred A. Knopf.

The Camera in the Southwest. 1904. 2d ed. Kansas City: Fred Harvey.

Castro, Michael. 1983. *Interpreting the Indian: Twentieth-Century Poets and the Native American.* Albuquerque: University of New Mexico Press.

Chamberlain, A. F. 1896. "The Poetry of American Aboriginal Speech." *Journal of American Folk-Lore* 9 (January–March): 43–47.

———. 1903. "Primitive Woman as Poet." *Journal of American Folk-Lore* 16 (October–December): 205–21.

Chrisman, Laura, and Patrick Williams. 1994. "Colonial Discourse and Post-Colonial Theory: An Introduction." In *Colonial Discourse and Post-Colonial Theory: A Reader,* edited by Patrick Williams and Laura Chrisman, 1–20. New York: Columbia University Press.

The Cliff Dwellers. 1893. Chicago: M. Jay Smith Exploring.

Clifford, James. 1983. "On Ethnographic Authority." *Representations* 1 (2): 118–46.

———. 1985. "Objects and Selves: An Afterword." In *Objects and Others: Essays on Museums and Material Culture,* edited by George W. Stocking Jr., 236–46. Madison: University of Wisconsin Press.

———. 1986. "On Ethnographic Allegory." In *Writing Culture: The Poetics and Politics of Ethnography,* edited by James Clifford and George E. Marcus, 98–121. Berkeley and Los Angeles: University of California Press.

Coffman, Stanley K., Jr. 1951. *Imagism: A Chapter for the History of Modern Poetry.* Norman: University of Oklahoma Press.

Coke, Van Deren. 1963. *Taos and Santa Fe: The Artist's Environment 1882–1942.* Albuquerque: University of New Mexico Press.

Colton, Amy Richards. 1926. "The Red Man's Contribution to Our Household Art." *Garden and Home Builder* 44:31–32.

Colton, Mary-Russell F., and Harold S. Colton. 1943. "An Appreciation of the Art of Nampeyo and Her Influence on Hopi Pottery." *Plateau* 15 (3): 43–45.

The Complete Portfolio of Photographs of the World's Fair, St. Louis, 1904. 1904. Chicago: Educational Company.

Connor, J. Torrey. 1896. "Confessions of a Basket Collector." *Land of Sunshine* 5:3–10.

Coombes, Annie E. 1991. "Ethnography and the Formation of National and Cultural Identities." In *The Myth of Primitivism: Perspectives on Art,* edited by Susan Hiller, 189–214. London: Routledge.

Cowan, John L. 1912. "Bedouins of the Southwest." *Out West* 3:107–16.

Crane, Leo. 1925. *Indians of the Enchanted Desert.* Boston: Little, Brown.

Cronyn, George, ed. 1918. *The Path on the Rainbow: An Anthology of*

Songs and Chants from the Indians of North America. New York: Boni and Liveright.

Curtis, Edward S. 1906. "Vanishing Indian Types: The Tribes of the Southwest." *Scribner's Magazine* 39 (May): 513–29.

Curtis, Natalie. 1903. "An American-Indian Composer." *Harper's* 107:626–32.

———. 1904. "A Bit of American Folk-Music: Two Pueblo Indian Grinding Songs." *Craftsman* 7:35–41.

———. [1907] 1950. *The Indians' Book: An Offering by the American Indians of Indian Lore, Musical and Narrative, to Form a Record of the Songs and Legends of Their Race.* New York: Dover Publications.

———. 1913a. "The Perpetuating of Indian Art." *Outlook* 12:623–31.

———. 1913b. "The Pueblo Singer: A Bit of Native American History." *Craftsman* 24:400–401.

———. 1922. "Pueblo Poetry." *Freeman* 25 (January): 467–68.

———. 1892. "Manual Concepts: A Study of the Influence of Hand-Usage on Culture Growth." *American Anthropologist* 5:289–325.

Cushing, Frank Hamilton. 1886. "A Study of Pueblo Pottery as Illustrative of Zuñi Culture-Growth." In *Fourth Annual Report of the Bureau of American Ethnology 1882–83,* 467–521. Washington, D.C.: General Printing Office.

———. 1979. "Form and the Dance-Drama." In *Zuñi: Selected Writings of Frank Hamilton Cushing,* edited by Jesse Green, 215–18. Lincoln: University of Nebraska.

Damon, S. Foster. 1935. *Amy Lowell: A Chronicle.* Boston: Houghton Mifflin.

Dauber, Kenneth. 1990. "Pueblo Pottery and the Politics of Regional Identity." *Journal of the Southwest* 32:576–96.

"Death of Nampeyo." 1942. *Masterkey* 16:164.

Debord, Guy. 1983. *Society of the Spectacle.* Detroit: Black and Red.

DeHuff, Elizabeth. 1927. "Couriers' Instructional Bulletin No. 5," 9 December. Elizabeth DeHuff Collection. University of New Mexico Library Special Collections, Albuquerque.

Deloria, Philip Joseph. 1994. "Playing Indian: Otherness and Authenticity in the Assumption of American Indian Identity." Ph.D. diss., Yale University.

Densmore, Frances. 1905. "The Music of the American Indians." *Overland Monthly* 45:230–34.

Diamond, Stanley, ed. 1960. *Primitive Views of the World.* New York: Columbia University Press.

———. 1981. *In Search of the Primitive: A Critique of Civilization.* New Brunswick, N.J.: Transaction Books.

Dittert, Alfred E., Jr., and Fred Plog. 1980. *Generations in Clay: Pueblo Pottery of the American Southwest.* Flagstaff, Ariz.: Northland Press.

Dixon, Joseph K. 1914. *The Vanishing Race: The Last Great Indian Council.* Garden City, N.Y.: Doubleday, Pace.

Donaldson, Thomas. 1893. *Moqui Pueblo Indians of Arizona and Pueblo Indians of New Mexico.* Eleventh Census of the United States. Extra Census Bulletin. Washington, D.C.: U.S. Census Printing Office.

Dorman, Robert L. 1993. *Revolt of the Provinces: The Regionalist Movement in America, 1920–1945.* Chapel Hill: University of North Carolina.

Dorsey, George A. 1903. *Indians of the Southwest.* N.p.: Passenger Department, Atchison, Topeka and Santa Fe Railway System.

Dorsey, George A., and H. R. Voth. 1901. *The Oraibi Soyal Ceremony.* Chicago: Field Columbian Museum.

———. [1902] 1968. "The Mishongnovi Ceremonies of the Snake and Antelope Fraternities." In *Publications of the Field Columbian Museum Anthropological Series,* 159–262. New York: Kraus Reprint.

Drinnon, Richard. 1980. *Facing West: The Metaphysics of Indian-Hating and Empire Building.* Minneapolis: University of Minnesota Press.

Du Bois, Constance Goddard. 1904. "The Indian Woman as a Craftsman." *Craftsman* 6:391–93.

Dutton, Bertha P. 1983. "Commerce on a New Frontier: The Fred Harvey Company and the Fred Harvey Fine Arts Collection." In *Colonial Frontiers: Art and Life in Spanish New Mexico, the Fred Harvey Collection,* edited by Christine Mather, 91–104. Santa Fe, N.M.: Ancient City Press.

Eagleton, Terry. 1990. *The Ideology of the Aesthetic.* Oxford: Basil Blackwell.

Eastman, Charles A. 1914. "'My People': The Indians' Contribution to the Art of America." *Craftsman* 27 (November): 179–86.

Eaton, Linda B. 1989a. "Nora Naranjo-Morse, Santa Clara Sculptor." *Plateau* 60 (1): 10–17.

———. 1989b. "The Only One Who Knows: A Separate Vision." *American Indian Art* 14 (Summer): 46–53.

Edwards, Elizabeth, ed. 1992. *Anthropology and Photography 1860–1920.* New Haven, Conn.: Yale University Press.

Edwardy, William M. 1889. "Snake Dance of the Moqui Indians." *Harper's Weekly,* 2 November, 871.

Eggan, Fred. 1971. "H. R. Voth, Ethnologist." In *Hopi Material Culture:*

Artifacts Gathered by H. R. Voth in the Fred Harvey Collection, edited by Barton Wright, 1–7. Flagstaff, Ariz.: Northland Press.

Eldredge, Charles C., Julie Schimmel, and William Truettner, eds. 1986. *Art in New Mexico, 1900–1945: Paths to Taos and Santa Fe.* Washington, D.C.: Smithsonian Institution Press.

Evans, Bessie, and May G. Evans. 1931. *American Indian Dance Steps.* New York: A. S. Barnes.

Evans-Pritchard, Deirdre. 1989. "How 'They' See 'Us': Native American Images of Tourists." *Annals of Tourism Research* 16:89–105.

Fabian, Johannes. 1983. *Time and the Other: How Anthropology Makes Its Object.* New York: Columbia University Press.

———. 1990. "Presence and Representation: The Other and Anthropological Writing." *Critical Inquiry* 16 (Summer): 753–72.

Fane, Diana. 1991. "The Language of Things: Stewart Culin as Collector." In *Objects of Myth and Memory: American Indian Art at the Brooklyn Museum,* edited by Diana Fane, Ira Jacknis, and Lise M. Breen, 13–27. Brooklyn: Brooklyn Museum.

Fergusson, Erna. 1931. *Dancing Gods: Indian Ceremonials of New Mexico and Arizona.* New York: Alfred Knopf.

Fewkes, Jesse Walter. [1894] 1977. "The Snake Ceremonials at Walpi." *A Journal of American Ethnology and Archaeology,* vol. 4. Boston: Houghton Mifflin; Cambridge, Mass.: Riverside Press.

———. [1897] 1986. "Tusayan Snake Ceremonies." In *Hopi Snake Ceremonies Selections from Bureau of American Ethnology Annual Reports Nos. 16 and 19 for the Years 1894–95 and 1897–98.* Albuquerque: Avanyu Publishing.

———. 1898. "Expedition to Arizona in 1895." In *17th Annual Report of the Bureau of American Ethnology,* 660. Washington, D.C.: General Printing Office, 1898.

———. [1900] 1986. "Tusayan Flute and Snake Ceremonies." In *Hopi Snake Ceremonies Selections from Bureau of American Ethnology Annual Reports Nos. 16 and 19 for the Years 1894–95 and 1897–98.* Albuquerque: Avanyu Publishing.

———. N.d. Diary. J. Walter Fewkes Papers. Vol. 19. National Anthropological Archives, Smithsonian Institution, Washington, D.C.

Fillmore, John Comfort. 1893. "The Zuni Music as Translated by Mr. Benjamin Ives Gilman." *Music* 5:39–46.

———. 1895. "What Do Indians Mean to Do When They Sing, and How Far Do They Succeed?" *Journal of American Folk-Lore* 8:138–42.

———. 1900. "The Scientific Importance of the Folk-Music of our Aborigines." *Land of Sunshine* 7 (22): 22–25.

Fleisher's Knitting and Crocheting Manual. 1912. Philadelphia: S. B. and B. W. Fleisher.

Fletcher, Alice C. 1894. "Indian Music." *Music* 6: 188–99.

Forrest, Earle R. 1961. *The Snake Dance of the Hopi Indians.* Los Angeles: Westernlore Press.

Forrest, Suzanne. 1989. *The Preservation of the Village: New Mexico's Hispanics and the New Deal.* Albuquerque: University of New Mexico Press.

Foster, Hal. 1985. "The 'Primitive' Unconscious of Modern Art, or White Skin Black Masks." In *Recodings: Art, Spectacle, Cultural Politics,* 181–208. Seattle: Bay Press.

Foucault, Michel. 1977. *Discipline and Punish: The Birth of the Prison.* New York: Pantheon.

Fowler, Don D., and Catherine S. Fowler. 1991. "The Uses of Natural Man in Natural History." In *The Spanish Borderlands in Pan-American Perspective,* edited by David H. Thomas, 37–71. Columbian Consequences, vol. 3. Washington, D.C.: Smithsonian Institution Press.

Fox, Nancy. 1984. "Margaret Moses: Collector and Courier." *Palacio* 90 (3): 29–31.

Frank, Waldo. 1919. *Our America.* New York: Boni & Liveright.

Fried, Michael. 1985. "Realism, Writing, and Disfiguration in Thomas Eakins's *Gross Clinic,* with a Postscript on Stephen Crane's Upturned Faces." *Representations* 9:33–104.

Frisbie, Theodore R. 1973. "The Influence of J. Walter Fewkes on Nampeyo: Fact or Fancy?" In *The Changing Ways of Southwestern Indians: A Historic Perspective,* edited by Albert H. Schroeder, 231–43. Glorieta, N.M.: Rio Grande Press.

Frost, Richard H. 1980. "The Romantic Inflation of Pueblo Culture." *American West* 17:5–9, 56–60.

Fry, Roger. 1920. "Ancient American Art." In *Vision and Design,* 69–75. London: Chatto and Windus.

Fynn, A. J. 1907. *The American Indian as a Product of Environment, with Special Reference to the Pueblos.* Boston: Little, Brown.

Gans, Julius. 1920. *The Indian as an Artist.* Santa Fe, N.M.: Southwest Arts and Crafts.

Garber, Marjorie. 1993. *Vested Interests: Cross Dressing and Cultural Anxiety.* New York: Harper Perennial.

Gardner, Jared. 1992. "'Our Native Clay': Racial and Sexual Identity and the Making of Americans in *The Bridge.*" *American Quarterly* 44:24–50.

Garland, Hamlin. [1894] 1952. *Crumbling Idols.* Ann Arbor, Mich.: Edwards Brothers.

———. 1896. "Among the Moki Indians." *Harper's Weekly,* 15 August, 801–7.

Gates, Henry Louis, Jr. 1991. "'Authenticity,' or the Lesson of Little Tree." *New York Times Book Review* 141 (24 November): 1, 26–30.

Gibson, Arrell Morgan. 1983. *The Santa Fe and Taos Colonies: Age of the Muses, 1890–1942.* Norman: University of Oklahoma Press.

Gidley, Mick. 1982. "From the Hopi Snake Dance to 'The Ten Commandments': Edward S. Curtis as Filmmaker." *Studies in Visual Communication* 8 (3): 70–79.

Gilbert, James B. 1977. *Work without Salvation: America's Intellectuals and Industrial Alienation, 1880–1910.* Baltimore: Johns Hopkins.

Gilman, Benjamin Ives. 1908. *Hopi Songs.* Boston: Houghton Mifflin.

Gilpin, William. 1792. *Three Essays: On Picturesque Beauty; on Picturesque Travel; and on Sketching Landscape.* London.

Graburn, Nelson H. H. 1976. "Introduction: Arts of the Fourth World." In *Ethnic and Tourist Arts: Cultural Expressions from the Fourth World,* edited by Nelson H. H. Graburn, 1–32. Berkeley and Los Angeles: University of California Press.

———. 1977. "Tourism: The Sacred Journey." In *Hosts and Guests: The Anthropology of Tourism,* edited by Valene Smith, 17–31. Philadelphia: University of Pennsylvania Press.

"The Grand Canyon of Arizona at Panama-Pacific Exposition." 1914. *Santa Fe Magazine* 8 (8): 49–50.

Grattan, Virginia L. 1980. *Mary Colter: Builder Upon the Red Earth.* Flagstaff, Ariz.: Northland Press.

The Great Southwest Along the Santa Fe. [1911] 1921. 6th ed. Kansas City: Fred Harvey.

Green, Rayna. 1975. "The Pocahontas Perplex: The Image of Indian Women in American Culture." *Massachusetts Review* 16:698–714.

———. 1988a. "The Indian in Popular American Culture." In *History of Indian-White Relations,* 587–606. Vol. 4 of *Handbook of North American Indians,* edited by William C. Sturtevant. Washington, D.C.: Smithsonian Institution Press.

———. 1988b. "The Tribe Called Wannabee: Playing Indian in America and Europe." *Folklore* 99:30–55.

Greenblatt, Stephen. 1991. *Marvelous Possessions: The Wonder of the New World.* Chicago: University of Chicago Press.

Hall, Sharlot M. 1922. *The Story of the Smoki People.* Prescott, Ariz.: Way Out West.

Halseth, Odd S. 1926. "The Revival of Pueblo Pottery Making." *Palacio* 21:135–54.

Handler, Richard. 1986a. "Authenticity." *Anthropology Today* 2 (February): 2–4.

———. 1986b. "Vigorous Male and Aspiring Female: Poetry, Personality, and Culture in Edward Sapir and Ruth Benedict." In *Malinowski, Rivers, Benedict and Others: Essays on Culture and Personality,* edited by George W. Stocking Jr., 127–55. Madison: University of Wisconsin Press.

———. 1989. "Consuming Culture (Genuine and Spurious) as Style." *Cultural Anthropology* 4:346–57.

Handler, Richard, and William Saxton. 1988. "Dyssimulation: Reflexivity, Narrative, and the Quest for Authenticity in 'Living History.'" *Cultural Anthropology* 3 (3): 242–60.

Haraway, Donna. 1986. "Teddy Bear Patriarchy: Taxidermy in the Garden of Eden, New York City, 1908–1936." *Social Text* (Winter): 20–64.

Haren, Edward, and S. N. Townshend. 1887. *New Mexico: Some Practical and Authentic Information About Its Resources.* Chicago: Atchison, Topeka and Santa Fe Railroad.

Harmsen, Dorothy. 1978. *Harmsen's Western Americana: A Collection of One Hundred Western Paintings.* Denver: Harmsen Publishing.

Harrison, Michael. 1964. "First Mention in Print of the Hopi Snake Dance." *Masterkey* 38:150–51.

Hartley, Marsden. 1918a. "Aesthetic Sincerity." *Palacio* 5 (9 December): 332–33.

———. 1918b. "America as Landscape." *Palacio* 5 (21 December): 340–42.

———. 1918c. "Tribal Esthetics." *Dial* 65 (16 November): 399–401.

———. 1920. "Red Man Ceremonials: An American Plea for American Esthetics." *Art and Archaeology* 9 (January): 7–14.

———. 1921. "Dissertation on Modern Painting." *Palacio* 10 (1 March): 3–4.

———. 1922a. "The Scientific Esthetic of the Redman, I." *Art and Archaeology* 13 (March): 113–19.

———. 1922b. "The Scientific Esthetic of the Redman, II." *Art and Archaeology* 14 (September): 137–39.

Harvey, Byron, III. 1963. "The Fred Harvey Collection 1899–1963." *Plateau* 36 (2): 33–53.

———. 1981. *The Fred Harvey Company Collects Indian Art.* Phoenix: Heard Museum.

Harveycar Motor Cruises. 1928. "What do you know about the Forgotten Peoples of Pu-yé and Ci-cu-yé—of Pueblo Bonito and Penasco Blanco—of Aztec and Mesa Verde?" Full page ad. *National Geographic* 53 (5): n.p.

Harveycar Motor Cruises Off the Beaten Path in the Great Southwest. N.d. [Kansas City: Fred Harvey.]

Health Resorts of New Mexico. 1897. Topeka: Passenger Department, Santa Fe Route.

Heller, Adele, and Lois Rudnick, eds. 1991. *1915, the Cultural Moment: The New Politics, the New Woman, the New Psychology, the New Art and the New Theatre in America.* New Brunswick, N.J.: Rutgers University Press.

Henderson, Alice Corbin. 1920. *Red Earth, Poems of New Mexico.* Chicago: Ralph Fletcher Seymour.

———. 1923a. "The Dance-Rituals of the Pueblo Indians." *Theater Arts Magazine* 7 (April): 109–15.

———. 1923b. "A Plea for the Study of Indian Culture." *Palacio* 15 (September): 91–92.

———, ed. 1928. *The Turquoise Trail: An Anthology of New Mexico Poetry.* Boston: Houghton Mifflin.

Henderson, James David. 1969. *"Meals by Fred Harvey": A Phenomenon of the American West.* Fort Worth: Texas Christian University.

Herzog, Melanie. Forthcoming. "Aesthetics and Meanings: The Arts and Crafts Movement and the Revival of American Indian Basketry." In *Substance of Style: Perspectives on the American Arts and Crafts Movement.* Winterthur, Del.: Winterthur Museum.

Hickey, Ethel. 1922. "The Snake Dance of the Hopi Mesas." *Santa Fe Magazine* 17 (1): 45–48.

Higgins, C. A. 1892a. *Grand Cañon of the Colorado River.* Chicago: Passenger Department, Santa Fe Route.

———. 1892b. *The Land of Sunshine* Chicago: Henry O. Shepard Co.

———. 1900. *To California and Back.* Chicago: Passenger Department, Santa Fe Route.

Higham, John. 1965. "The Reorientation of American Culture in the 1890's." In *The Origins of Modern Consciousness,* edited by John Weiss, 25–48. Detroit: Wayne State University Press.

Hinsley, Curtis M. 1981. *The Smithsonian and the American Indian: Making a Moral Anthropology in Victorian America.* Washington, D.C.: Smithsonian Institution Press.

———. 1983. "Ethnographic Charisma and Scientific Routine: Cushing and Fewkes in the American Southwest, 1879–1893." In *Observers Observed: Essays on Ethnographic Fieldwork,* edited by George W. Stocking Jr., 53–69. Madison: University of Wisconsin Press.

———. 1989. "Zunis and Brahmins: Cultural Ambivalence in the Gilded Age." In *Romantic Motives: Essays on Anthropological Sensibility,* edited by George W. Stocking Jr., 169–205. Madison: University of Wisconsin Press.

———. 1991. "The World as Marketplace: Commodification of the Exotic at the World's Columbian Exposition, Chicago, 1893." In *Exhibiting Cultures: The Poetics and Politics of Museum Display,* edited by Ivan Karp and Steven D. Lavine, 344–65. Washington, D.C.: Smithsonian Institution Press.

———. Forthcoming. "From Pueblo to Parlor: The Anthropological Presentation and Consumption of Southwestern Indians in Victorian America." In *Images Across Boundaries: History, Use, and Ethics of Photographs of American Indians,* edited by Willow Roberts Powers. Albuquerque: University of New Mexico Press.

History of the Louisiana Purchase Exposition. 1905. St. Louis: Universal Exposition Publishing.

Holmes, W. H. 1890. "On the Evolution of Ornament: An American Lesson." *American Anthropologist* 3:137–46.

Hooper, Bruce. 1989. "Arizona Landmarks: Stereography of Natural Wonders in Arizona Territory, 1871–1930s." *Stereo World* 16 (5): 14–19.

Hough, Walter. 1900. *The Moki Snake Dance, a popular account of that unparalleled dramatic pagan ceremony of the Pueblo Indians of Tusayan, Arizona, with incidental mention of their life and customs.* N.p.: Santa Fe Route.

"How Fame Has Been Won for the Harvey Service by Devotion to a Business Principle." 1916. *Santa Fe Magazine* 10 (3): 31–47.

Hoxie, Frederick E. 1977. "Beyond Savagery: The Campaign to Assimilate the American Indians, 1880–1920." Ph.D. diss., Brandeis University.

———. 1984. *A Final Promise: The Campaign to Assimilate the Indians 1880–1920.* Lincoln: University of Nebraska Press.

Huckel, John F. [1913] 1934. *First Families of the Southwest.* Kansas City: Fred Harvey.

———. 1913. Letter to F. W. Hodge, 4 March. Hodge Collection. Southwest Museum Library, Los Angeles.

The Indian and Mexican Building. 1904. Albuquerque: Fred Harvey.

Jacknis, Ira. 1985. "Franz Boas and Exhibits: On the Limitations of the Museum Method of Anthropology." In *Objects and Others: Essays on Museums and Material Culture,* edited by George W. Stocking Jr., 75–111. Madison: University of Wisconsin Press.

James, George Wharton. 1900a. "The Hopi Snake Dance." *Outing* 36:302–10.

———. 1900b. "Types of Female Beauty among the Indians of the Southwest." *Overland Monthly* 35 (March): 195–209.

———. 1900c. "What I Saw at the Snake Dance." *Wide World* (January): 264–74.

———. 1901a. "Indian Basketry in House Decoration." *Chautauquan* 33:619–24.

———. 1901b. "Indian Pottery" *Outing* 34:154–61.

———. 1902a. *Indian Basketry.* New York: Henry Malkan.

———. 1902b. "Indian Blanketry." *Outing* 35:684–93.

———. 1902c. "Photographing Indian Babies." *Camera Craft* 6 (December): 58–62.

———. 1902d. "The Snake Dance of the Hopis." *Camera Craft* 6 (1): 1–10.

———. 1903a. "Palomas Apaches and Their Baskets." *Sunset* 11:146–53.

———. 1903b. "The Study of Indian Faces." *Camera Craft* 8 (December): 12–18.

———. 1908. *What the White Race May Learn from the Indian.* Chicago: Forbes.

———. 1914. *Indian Blankets and Their Makers.* Chicago: A. C. McClurg.

Judd, Neil M. 1951. "Nampeyo, an Additional Note." *Plateau* 24 (2): 92–93.

Jung, Carl. 1930. "Your Negroid and Indian Behavior." *Forum* (April): 193–99.

Kappeler, Susanne. 1986. *The Pornography of Representation.* Minneapolis: University of Minnesota Press.

Kavanagh, Thomas W. 1990. "A Brief Illustrated History of the Manikins, Statues, Lay-Figures, and Life-Groups Illustrating American Ethnology in the National Museum of Natural History." Unpublished paper.

Keller, Nell Clark. 1905. "The Moki Indian Snake-Dance—the Strangest Ceremony of Savage America." *Woman's Home Companion* 32 (March): n.p.

Kent, Kate P. 1976. "Pueblo and Navajo Weaving Traditions and the Western World." In *Ethnic and Tourist Arts: Cultural Expressions from the Fourth World,* edited by Nelson H. H. Graburn, 85–101. Berkeley and Los Angeles: University of California Press.

———. 1981. "Pueblo Weaving." *American Indian Art Magazine* 7 (1): 32–45.

Kramer, Barbara. 1988. "Nampeyo, Hopi House, and the Chicago Land Show." *American Indian Art Magazine* 14 (1): 46–53.

Kropp, Phoebe S. 1996. "'There Is a Little Sermon in That': Constructing the Native Southwest at the San Diego Panama-California Exposition of 1915." In *The Great Southwest of the Fred Harvey Company and the Santa Fe Railway,* edited by Marta Weigle and Barbara Babcock, 36–46. Phoenix: Heard Museum.

Lang, A. 1882. "The Art of Savages." *Magazine of Art* 5:246–51, 303–7.

Langlois, Karen S. 1988a. "Mary Austin and Houghton Mifflin Company: A Case Study in the Marketing of a Western Writer." *Western American Literature* 23 (Summer): 31–42.

———. 1988b. "Mary Austin and the New Theatre: The 1911 Production of *The Arrow Maker.*" *Theatre History Studies* 8:71–87.

Laut, Agnes C. 1905. "The Indian's Idea of Fine Arts." *Outing* 46 (June): 355–63.

Lawrence, D. H. 1924. "The Hopi Snake Dance." *Theatre Arts Monthly* 8:836–60.

Lears, T. J. Jackson. 1981. *No Place of Grace: Antimodernism and the Transformation of American Culture 1880–1920.* New York: Pantheon.

Levin, Gail. 1984a. "American Art." In *"Primitivism" in Twentieth-Century Art: Affinity of the Tribal and the Modern.* Vol. 2, edited by William Rubin, 453–73. New York: Museum of Modern Art.

———. 1984b. "'Primitivism' in American Art: Some Literary Parallels of the 1910s and 1920s." *Arts* (November): 101–5.

Long, Annie Bush. 1896. "First Woman to Witness the Oraibi Snake Dance." *San Francisco Examiner,* 4 October.

Longo, Donna A. 1980. "Photographing the Hopi." *Pacific Discovery* 33 (May–June): 11–19.

Lott, Eric. 1993. "White Like Me: Racial Cross-Dressing and the Construction of American Whiteness." In *Cultures of United States Imperialism,* edited by Amy Kaplan and Donald Pease, 474–95. Durham, N.C.: Duke University Press.

Lowell, Amy. 1955. "Songs of the Pueblo Indians." In *The Complete Poetical Works of Amy Lowell,* 588–89. Boston: Houghton Mifflin.

Lummis, Charles F. [1891] 1989. *Some Strange Corners of Our Country.* Reprint, with a foreword by Lawrence Clark Powell. Tucson: University of Arizona Press, 1989.

———. [1892] 1982. *A Tramp across the Continent.* Reprint, with an introduction by Robert E. Fleming. Lincoln: University of Nebraska Press.

———. [1893] 1952. *The Land of Poco Tiempo.* Reprint, with a foreword by Paul A. F. Walter. Albuquerque: University of New Mexico Press.

———. 1898. "Our First American Jewelers." *Land of Sunshine* 5:54–58.

———. 1899. "The Best Blanket in the World." *Land of Sunshine* 6:8–11.

———. 1900. "The First American Potters." *Land of Sunshine* 7:44–50.

———. 1905. "Catching Our Archaeology Alive." *Out West* 22:35–47.

———. 1925. *Mesa, Cañon and Pueblo.* New York: Century.

———. 1968. *Bullying the Moqui.* Edited by Robert Easton and Mackenzie Brown. Prescott, Ariz.: Prescott College Press.

Lyman, Christopher. 1982. *The Vanishing Race and Other Illusions: Photographs of Indians by Edward S. Curtis.* Washington, D.C.: Smithsonian Institution Press.

Lyon, Luke. 1988. "History of Prohibition of Photography of Southwestern

Indian Ceremonies." In *Reflections: Papers on Southwestern Culture History in Honor of Charles H. Lange,* edited by Anne V. Poore, 238–72. Santa Fe: Archaeological Society of New Mexico.

MacCannell, Dean. 1976. *The Tourist: A New Theory of the Leisure Class.* New York: Schocken Books.

———. 1984. "Reconstructed Ethnicity: Tourism and Cultural Identity in Third World Communities." *Annals of Tourism Research* 11:375–91.

McChesney, Lea S. 1994. "Producing 'Generations in Clay': Kinship, Markets, and Hopi Pottery." *Expedition* 36:5–13.

McGovern, Charles F. 1990. "Real People and the True Folk." *American Quarterly* 42:478–97.

McLuhan, T. C. 1985. *Dream Tracks: The Railroad and the American Indian 1890–1930.* New York: Harry N. Abrams.

McNitt, Frank. 1962. *The Indian Traders.* Norman: University of Oklahoma Press.

Marks, Laura U. 1992. "White People in the Native Camera: Subverting Anthropology." *Afterimage* 19 (May): 18–19.

Marriott, Alice. 1948. *Maria: The Potter of San Ildefonso.* Norman: University of Oklahoma.

Masayesva, Victor, Jr. 1984a. "Kwikwilyaqa: Hopi Photography." In *Hopi Photographers/Hopi Images. Sun Tracks* 8:10–12. Tucson: University of Arizona Press.

———. 1984b. *Itam Hakim, Hopiit.* Videocassette, 58 min. IS Productions, Hotevilla, Ariz.

———. 1990a. *Pott Starr.* Videocassette, 6 min. IS Productions, Hotevilla, Ariz.

———. 1990b. *Siskyavi: The Place of Chasms.* Videocassette, 28 min. IS Productions, Hotevilla, Ariz.

———. 1992. *Imagining Indians.* Film, 90 min. IS Productions, Hotevilla, Ariz.

Masayesva, Victor, Jr., and Erin Younger, eds. 1984. *Hopi Photographers/Hopi Images. Sun Tracks* 8. Tucson: University of Arizona Press.

Mason, Otis Tufton. 1899. *Woman's Share in Primitive Culture.* New York: D. Appleton.

———. 1901. "The Technic of Aboriginal American Basketry." *American Anthropologist* 3:559–78.

———. 1904. *Indian Basketry: Studies in a Textile Art without Machinery.* New York: Doubleday, Page.

Matteson, Sumner W. 1904. "The Snake Dancers." *Field and Stream* 9:331–39.

Matthews, Washington. 1896. "Songs of the Navajos." *Land of Sunshine* 5:197–201.

Matz, Duane Allen. 1988. "Images of Indians in Popular Culture Since 1865." Ph.D. diss., Illinois State University.

Maurer, Stephen G. 1986. "In the Heart of the Great Freedom: George Wharton James and the Desert Southwest." *Masterkey* 60:4–10.

Mauzy, Wayne. 1936. "The Tertio-Millennial Exposition." *Palacio* 37 (24–26): 185–200.

Mechling, Jay. 1980. "'Playing Indian' and the Search for Authenticity in Modern White America." *Prospects* 5:17–33.

Michaels, Walter Benn. 1990. "The Vanishing American." *American Literary History* 2:220–41.

Miller, Daniel. 1991. "Primitive Art and the Necessity of Primitivism to Art." In *The Myth of Primitivism: Perspectives on Art,* edited by Susan Hiller, 50–71. London: Routledge.

Miller, Michael. 1985. "New Mexico's Role in the Panama-California Exposition of 1915." *Palacio* 91 (2): 13–17.

Mindeleff, Cosmos. 1886. "An Indian Snake-Dance." *Science* 7:507–14.

Mitchell, J. A. 1893. "Types of People at the Fair." *Scribner's* 14 (18): 186–93.

Monroe, Harriet. 1917. "Editorial Comment, Aboriginal Poetry." *Poetry* 9 (February): 251–54.

Monsen, Frederick. 1907. "The Destruction of Our Indians: What Civilization Is Doing to Extinguish an Ancient and Highly Intelligent Race by Taking Away Its Arts, Industries and Religion." *Craftsman* 11:683–91.

———. N.d. *With a Kodak in the Land of the Navajo.* N.p.: Eastman Kodak.

Monthan, Guy, and Doris Monthan. 1977. "Dextra Quotskuyva Nampeyo." *American Indian Art Magazine* 2 (4): 58–63.

Moon, Karl. 1910. *Photographic Studies of American Indians.* Grand Canyon, Ariz.: Fred Harvey.

———. N.d. *Photographic Studies of American Indians.* Pasadena, Calif.

Moore, David L. 1994. "Rough Knowledge and Radical Understanding: The Postcolonial Critical Dance." Paper delivered at the American Studies Association annual meeting, Nashville.

Mullin, Molly H. 1993. "Consuming the American Southwest: Culture, Art, and Difference." Ph.D. diss., Duke University.

"Museum and School Share in San Diego's Triumph." 1914. *Palacio* 2 (2): 2.

Naranjo-Morse, Nora. 1992. *Mud Woman: Poems from the Clay. Sun Tracks* 20. Tucson: University of Arizona Press.

Nequatewa, Edmund. 1943. "Nampeyo, Famous Hopi Potter." *Plateau* 15 (3): 40–42.

———. 1980. "Dr. Fewkes and Masauwu." In *The South Corner of Time: Hopi, Navajo, Papago, Yaqui Tribal Literature*, 36–37. Tucson: University of Arizona Press.

New Mexico: Some Practical and Authentic Information About Its Resources: Issued for the Information of the Public by the Santa Fé Route. 1887. Chicago: Rand McNally.

New Mexico Vacation Guide. 1990. Albuquerque: New Mexico Tourism and Travel Division.

Oliver, Marion L. 1911. "The Snake Dance." *National Geographic* 22 (2): 107–37.

Oppenheim, James. 1923. "Artist and Artisan." *Freeman* 6 (7 March): 612–13.

Orvell, Miles. 1989. *The Real Thing: Imitation and Authenticity in American Culture, 1880–1940.* Chapel Hill: University of North Carolina Press.

Pach, Walter. 1920. "The Art of the American Indian." *Dial* 63 (January): 57–65.

Packard, Gar, and Maggy Packard. 1970. *Southwest 1880 with Ben Wittick Pioneer Photographer of Indian and Frontier Life.* Santa Fe, N.M.: Packard Publications.

Pardue, Diana F., and Kathryn Coe. 1989. "Earth Symbols: Nora, Roxanne." *Native Peoples* 2 (Winter): 42–47.

Paredes, Raymund A. 1977. "The Mexican Image in American Travel Literature, 1831–1869." *New Mexico Historical Review* 52:5–29.

Parezo, Nancy. 1986. "Now Is the Time to Collect." *Masterkey* 59 (4): 11–18.

Parker, Charles Franklin. 1941. *When the Smoki Dance.* Prescott, Ariz.: Smoki People.

Pearce, Roy Harvey. 1965. *Savagism and Civilization: A Study of the Indian and the American Mind.* Baltimore: Johns Hopkins University Press.

Pepper, George H. 1902. *The Making of a Navajo Blanket.* Reprinted from *Everybody's* magazine, New York.

Poling-Kempes, Lesley. 1989. *The Harvey Girls: Women Who Opened the West.* New York: Paragon House.

Pomeroy, Earl. 1957. *In Search of the Golden West: The Tourist in Western America.* Lincoln: University of Nebraska Press.

Porter, Joseph C. 1986. *Paper Medicine Man: John Gregory Bourke and His American West.* Norman: University of Oklahoma Press.

Post, Emily. 1916. *By Motor to the Golden Gate.* New York: D. Appleton.

Pratt, Mary Louise. 1992. *Imperial Eyes: Travel Writing and Transculturation.* London: Routledge.

Preziosi, Donald. 1989. *Rethinking Art History: Meditations on a Coy Science.* New Haven, Conn.: Yale University Press.

Price, Sally. 1989. *Primitive Art in Civilized Places.* Chicago: University of Chicago Press.

Proctor, Edna Dean. 1892. *The Song of the Ancient People.* Boston: Houghton Mifflin.

Prucha, Francis Paul. 1984. *The Great Father: The U.S. Government and the American Indian.* Lincoln: University of Nebraska Press.

Reisler, Mark. 1976. *By the Sweat of Their Brow: Mexican Immigrant Labor in the United States, 1900–1940.* Westport, Conn.: Greenwood Press.

"A Remarkable Indian Ceremony: Navajo Medicine Men Participate in Unique Housewarming with Rites Centuries Old." 1923. *Santa Fe Magazine* 17 (8): 17–22.

Riis, Jacob. [1890] 1971. *How the Other Half Lives: Studies among the Tenements of New York.* New York: Dover Publications.

Riley, Michael J. 1994. "Constituting the Southwest, Contesting the Southwest, Re-Inventing the Southwest." *Journal of the Southwest* 36 (Autumn): 221–41.

Roads to Yesterday Along the Indian-detour. [1926?] N.p.: Fred Harvey.

Roberts, Helen. 1927. "Indian Music from the Southwest." *Natural History* 27:257–65.

Rodee, Marian E. 1981. *Old Navajo Rugs: Their Development from 1900 to 1940.* Albuquerque: University of New Mexico Press.

Rodgers, Daniel T. 1974. *The Work Ethic in Industrial America 1850–1920.* Chicago: University of Chicago.

Rodríguez, Sylvia. 1987. "Land, Water, and Ethnic Identity in Taos." In *Land, Water and Culture: New Perspectives in Hispanic Land Grants,* edited by Charles L. Briggs and John R. Van Ness, 313–403. Albuquerque: University of New Mexico Press.

———. 1989. "Art, Tourism, and Race Relations in Taos: Toward a Sociology of the Art Colony." *Journal of Anthropological Research* 45 (Spring): 77–99.

———. 1990. "Ethnic Reconstruction in Contemporary Taos." *Journal of the Southwest* 32:541–55.

Rony, Fatimah Tobing. 1994–95. "Victor Masayesva, Jr., and the Politics of *Imagining Indians.*" *Film Quarterly* 48 (Winter): 20–33.

Roosevelt, Theodore. 1900. *The Strenuous Life: Essays and Addresses.* New York: Century.

———. 1913a. "The Hopi Snake Dance." *Outlook* 13:365–73.

———. 1913b. "A Layman's Views of an Art Exhibition." *Outlook* 13:718–20.

Rosaldo, Renato. 1989a. *Culture and Truth: The Remaking of Social Analysis.* Boston: Beacon Press.

———. 1989b. "Imperialist Nostalgia." *Representations* 26:107–22.

Rushforth, Scott, and Steadman Upham. 1992. *A Hopi Social History: Anthropological Perspectives on Sociocultural Persistence and Change.* Austin: University of Texas Press.

Rust, H. N. 1896. "The Moqui Snake Dance." *Land of Sunshine* 4 (2): 70–76.

Ryan, Dorothy B. 1982. *Picture Postcards in the United States 1893–1918.* New York: Clarkson N. Potter.

Rydell, Robert W. 1984. *All the World's a Fair: Visions of Empire at American International Expositions, 1876–1916.* Chicago: University of Chicago Press.

Said, Edward. 1975. *Beginnings: Intention and Method.* New York: Basic Books.

———. 1979. *Orientalism.* New York: Vintage.

———. 1989. "Representing the Colonized: Anthropology's Interlocutors." *Critical Inquiry* 15:205–25.

Salomon, Julian H. 1928. *The Book of Indian Crafts and Lore.* New York: Harper Brothers.

Sandburg, Carl. 1917. "Editorial Comment, Aboriginal Poetry." *Poetry* 9 (February): 254–55.

"Santa Fe Collects Oil Paintings." 1926. *Railway Age* 81:932.

The Santa Fe Tertio-Millennial Celebration and Exposition 1883. 1883. N.p.: Atchison, Topeka and Santa Fe Railroad.

Sapir, Edward. 1949. "Culture, Genuine and Spurious." In *Selected Writings of Edward Sapir in Language, Culture, and Personality,* edited by David G. Mandelbaum, 308–31. Berkeley and Los Angeles: University of California Press.

Sargent, Irene. 1904. "Indian Basketry: Its Structure and Decoration." *Craftsman* 7:321–34.

Scherer, Joanna Cohan. 1975. "You Can't Believe Your Eyes: Inaccuracies in Photographs of North American Indians." *Studies in the Anthropology of Visual Communication* 2 (Fall): 67–79.

Schultz, James Willard. 1908. "Why the Moquis Perform the Snake Dance." *Pacific Monthly* 20:161–66.

———. 1921. "The Case of the Hopi." *Sunset* 47 (October): 22–24.

Schweizer, Herman. 1905. Letter to William Randolph Hearst, 31 December. Fred Harvey Papers. Heard Museum Library, Phoenix.

———. 1906. Letter to William Randolph Hearst, 5 February. Fred Harvey Papers. The Heard Museum Library, Phoenix.

———. 1911a. Letter to William Randolph Hearst, 8 March. Fred Harvey Papers. Heard Museum Library, Phoenix.

———. 1911b. Letter to William Randolph Hearst, 12 May. Fred Harvey Papers. Heard Museum Library, Phoenix.

Seger, Karen, and Joseph Wilder. 1990. "Publishing the Southwest." *Journal of the Southwest* 32:377–80.

Seltzer, Mark. 1987. "Statistical Persons." *Diacritics* 17 (3): 82–98.

Shaffer, Marguerite S. 1994. "See America First: Tourism and National Identity, 1905–1930." Ph.D. diss., Harvard University.

Shannon, Christopher. 1992. "Conspicuous Criticism: Tradition, Autonomy, and Culture in American Social Thought, from Veblen to Mills." Ph.D. diss., Yale University.

Sheppard, Carl D. 1988. *Creator of the Santa Fe Style: Isaac Hamilton Rapp, Architect.* Albuquerque: University of New Mexico Press.

Shi, David. 1985. *The Simple Life: Plain Living and High Thinking in American Culture.* New York: Oxford University Press.

Shufeldt, R. W. 1895. "Beauty from an Indian's Point of View." *Cosmopolitan* 18 (March): 591–98.

"Sidelights on the Panama-California Exposition." 1915. *Santa Fe Magazine* 9 (4): 25–27.

Silko, Leslie Marmon. 1990. "Videomakers and Basketmakers." *Aperture* 119 (Summer): 72–73.

Simpson, William H. [1905?] *El Tovar: Grand Canyon of Arizona.* N.p.: Santa Fe Railway.

Sloan, John. 1924. "Pueblo Drama Dances." *Palacio* 16 (4): 59–60.

Slotkin, Richard. 1985. *The Fatal Environment: The Myth of the Frontier in the Age of Industrialization 1800–1890.* Middletown, Conn.: Wesleyan University Press.

Smith, Robert Elmer. 1926. "Hopi Indian Snake Dance." Visalia, Calif.: Great Western Music.

Sollors, Werner. 1986. *Beyond Ethnicity: Consent and Descent in American Culture.* New York: Oxford University Press.

Spence, Mary Lee. 1987. "Waitresses in the Trans-Mississippi West: 'Pretty Waiter Girls,' Harvey Girls and Union Maids." In *The Women's West,* edited by Susan Armitage and Elizabeth Jameson, 219–34. Norman: University of Oklahoma Press.

Spicer, Edward H. 1962. *Cycles of Conquest: The Impact of Spain, Mexico, and the United States on the Indians of the Southwest, 1533–1960.* Tucson: University of Arizona Press.

Starr, Frederick. 1893. "Anthropology at the World's Fair." *Popular Science Monthly* 43:610–21.

Steinman, Lisa M. 1987. *Made in America: Science, Technology, and American Modernist Poets.* New Haven, Conn.: Yale University Press.

Stephen, Alexander M. 1936. *Hopi Journal of Alexander M. Stephen,* edited by Elsie Clews Parsons. New York: Columbia University Press.

———. 1940. *Hopi Indians of Arizona.* Highland Park, Calif.: Southwest Museum.

Stewart, Susan. 1984. *On Longing: Narratives of the Miniature, the Gigantic, the Souvenir, the Collection.* Baltimore: Johns Hopkins University Press.

———. 1989. "Antipodal Expectations: Notes on the Formosan 'Ethnography' of George Psalmanazar." In *Romantic Motives: Essays on Anthropological Sensibility,* edited by George W. Stocking Jr., 44–73. Madison: University of Wisconsin Press.

Stineman, Esther Lanigan. 1989. *Mary Austin: Song of a Maverick.* New Haven, Conn.: Yale University Press.

Stocking, George W., Jr. 1968. *Race, Culture, and Evolution: Essays in the History of Anthropology.* New York: Free Press.

———. 1982. "The Santa Fe Style in American Anthropology: Regional Interest, Academic Initiative, and Philanthropic Policy in the First Two Decades of the Laboratory of Anthropology, Inc." *Journal of the History of the Behavioral Sciences* 18:3–19.

———. 1989. "The Ethnographic Sensibility of the 1920s and the Dualism of the Anthropological Tradition." In *Romantic Motives: Essays on Anthropological Sensibility,* edited by George W. Stocking Jr., 208–69. Madison: University of Wisconsin Press.

Sweet, Jill D. 1981. "Tewa Ceremonial Performances: the Effects of Tourism on an Ancient Pueblo Indian Dance and Musical Tradition." Ph.D. diss., University of New Mexico.

Talayesva, Don C. 1942. *Sun Chief: the Autobiography of a Hopi Indian,* edited by Leo W. Simmons. New Haven, Conn.: Yale University Press.

Taussig, Michael. 1993. *Mimesis and Alterity: A Particular History of the Senses.* New York: Routledge.

Thomas, Diane. 1978. *The Southwestern Indian Detours: The Story of the Fred Harvey–Santa Fe Railway Experiment in "Detourism."* Phoenix: Hunter Publishing.

Tinsley, Laura Rollins. 1904. *Practical and Artistic Basketry.* New York: A. S. Barnes.

Todorov, Tzvetan. 1984. *The Conquest of America: The Question of the Other.* New York: Harper and Row.

Torgovnick, Marianna. 1990. *Gone Primitive: Savage Intellects, Modern Lives.* Chicago: University of Chicago Press.

The Tourists. 1912. Directed by Mack Sennett. The Biograph Company. Paper print. Motion Picture, Broadcasting, and Recorded Sound Division, Library of Congress.

Townshend, R. B. 1926. *Last Memories of a Tenderfoot.* New York: Dodd, Mead.

Trachtenberg, Alan. 1982. *The Incorporation of America: Culture and Society in the Gilded Age.* New York: Hill and Wang.

Traugott, Joseph. 1983. *Nampeyo of Hano and Five Generations of Her Descendants.* Albuquerque: Adobe Gallery.

Trennert, Robert A. 1987. "Fairs, Expositions, and the Changing Image of Southwestern Indians, 1876–1904." *New Mexico Historical Review* 62:127–50.

Trimble, Stephen. 1987. "Brown Earth and Laughter: The Clay People of Nora Naranjo-Morse." *American Indian Art* 12 (Autumn): 58–65.

Truettner, William H. 1985. "Dressing the Part: Thomas Eakins's Portrait of Frank Hamilton Cushing." *American Art Journal* (Spring): 49–72.

———. 1986. "The Art of Pueblo Life." In *Art in New Mexico, 1900–1945: Paths to Taos and Santa Fe,* edited by Charles C. Eldredge, Julie Schimmel, and William Truettner, 59–99. Exhibition catalogue, National Museum of Art, Washington, D.C. New York: Abbeville Press.

Udall, Sharyn Rohlfsen. 1984. *Modernist Painting in New Mexico 1913–1935.* Albuquerque: University of New Mexico Press.

Vanderwood, Paul J., and Frank N. Samponaro. 1988. *Border Fury: A Picture Postcard Record of Mexico's Revolution and U.S. War Preparedness, 1910–1917.* Albuquerque: University of New Mexico Press.

Veblen, Thorstein. [1899] 1979. *The Theory of the Leisure Class.* New York: Penguin Books.

Viehmann, Martha L. 1994. "Writing across the Cultural Divide: Images of Indians in the Lives and Works of Native and European Americans, 1890–1935." Ph.D. diss., Yale University.

Voth, H. R. [1903] 1968. "The Oraibi Summer Snake Ceremony." In *Publications of the Field Columbian Museum Anthropological Series,* 262–358. New York: Kraus Reprint.

Wade, Edwin L. 1985. "The Ethnic Art Market in the American Southwest 1880–1980." In *Objects and Others: Essays on Museums and Material Culture,* edited by George W. Stocking Jr., 167–91. Madison: University of Wisconsin Press.

———. 1986. "Straddling the Cultural Fence: The Conflict for Ethnic Artists within Pueblo Societies." In *The Arts of the North American Indian: Native Traditions in Evolution,* edited by Edwin L. Wade, 243–54. New York: Hudson Hills Press.

Wallace, Susan E. 1888. *The Land of the Pueblos.* New York: John B. Alden.

"Walter Ufer." 1916. *Palacio* 3 (August): 75–81.

Walton, Eda Lou. 1924. "Navaho Verse Rhythms." *Poetry* 24 (April): 40–44.

Walton, Eda Lou, and T. T. Waterman. 1925. "American Indian Poetry." *American Anthropologist* 27 (January–March): 25–52.

Washburn, Dorothy K. 1984. "Dealers and Collectors of Indian Baskets at the Turn of the Century in California: Their Effect on the Ethnographic Sample." *Empirical Studies of the Arts* 2:51–74.

Webb, William, and Robert A. Weinstein. 1973. *Dwellers at the Source: Southwestern Indian Photographs of A. C. Vroman, 1895–1904.* New York: Grossman Publishers.

Weber, David J. 1979. "'Scarce More than Apes': Historical Roots of Anglo American Stereotypes of Mexicans in the Border Region." In *New Spain's Far Northern Frontier,* edited by David J. Weber, 295–307. Albuquerque: University of New Mexico Press.

Weigle, Marta. 1989a. "Finding the 'True America': Ethnic Tourism in New Mexico During the New Deal." *Folklife Annual* 88–89:58–73.

———. 1989b. "From Desert to Disney World: The Santa Fe Railway and the Fred Harvey Company Display the Indian Southwest." *Journal of Anthropological Research* 45:115–37.

———. 1990. "Southwest Lures: Innocents Detoured, Incensed Determined." *Journal of the Southwest* 32:499–540.

———. 1991. "Exposition and Mediation: Mary Colter, Erna Fergusson, and the Santa Fe/Harvey Popularization of the Native Southwest, 1902–1940." *Frontiers* 12:117–50.

Weigle, Marta, and Kyle Fiore. 1982. *Santa Fe and Taos: The Writers' Era, 1916–1941.* Santa Fe, N.M.: Ancient City Press.

"Weird Snake Dance of the Smoki People." 1923. *Santa Fe Magazine* 17 (9): 15–18.

Wells, Helen Pinion. 1976. "The Fred Harvey Fine Arts Collection." *American Indian Art* 1 (2): 32–34.

Wertheim, Arthur Frank. 1976. *The New York Little Renaissance: Iconoclasm, Modernism, and Nationalism in American Culture, 1908–1917.* New York: New York University Press.

Wheeler, Valerie. 1986. "Travelers' Tales: Observations on the Travel Book and Ethnography." *Anthropological Quarterly* 59 (2): 52–63.

Whiffen, Marcus, and Carla Breeze. 1984. *Pueblo Deco: The Art Deco Architecture of the Southwest.* Albuquerque: University of New Mexico Press.

Whiteley, Peter. 1988. *Deliberate Acts: Changing Hopi Culture through the Oraibi Split.* Tucson: University of Arizona Press.

———. 1993. "The End of Anthropology (at Hopi)?" *Journal of the Southwest* 35:125–57.

Williams, Raymond. 1958. *Culture and Society, 1780–1950*. London: Chatto and Windus.

Williamson, Judith. 1986. "Woman Is an Island: Femininity and Colonization." In *Studies in Entertainment: Critical Approaches to Mass Culture,* edited by Tania Modleski, 99–118. Bloomington: Indiana University Press.

Wilson, Olive. 1920. "The Survival of an Ancient Art." *Art and Archaeology* 9:24–29.

Wissler, Clark. 1915. "In the Home of the Hopi Indian." *American Museum Journal* 15:343–47.

Woloshuk, Nicholas. 1976. *E. Irving Couse 1866–1936*. Santa Fe, N.M.: Santa Fe Village Art Museum.

Younger, Erin. 1984. "Changing Images: A Century of Photography on the Hopi Reservation." In *Hopi Photographers/Hopi Images. Sun Tracks* 8:13–39. Tucson: University of Arizona Press.

Zilczer, Judith. 1977. "Primitivism and New York Dada." *Arts* (May): 140–42.

INDEX

Page numbers in italics indicate illustrations.